PRAISE FOR

Fully Alive

"This is a beautiful book about love, meaning, and triumph . . . I was lifted, edified, riveted." —Anne Lamott, author of *Small Victories*

"Wisdom surrounds us. We just sometimes look for it in the wrong places. Timothy Shriver, the chairman of the Special Olympics, has written a new book in which he finds wisdom, insight, purpose, and fun within people who are often overlooked and undervalued— people with intellectual disabilities."
—Scott Simon, NPR's *Morning Edition*

"Bursting with life energy. Profound and inspiring. A must-read."
—Deepak Chopra

"Timothy Shriver has written a lovely, honest, and inspiring book that draws on his own wisdom, life experiences, and pioneering work as a champion of the intellectually disabled to offer important lessons for all of us." —Michael Beschloss, author of *Presidential Courage*

TIMOTHY SHRIVER

Fully Alive

Timothy Shriver is an educator, a social activist, a film producer, and an entrepreneur. He has led Special Olympics, an organization that serves upwards of four million athletes in 170 countries, for more than a decade. Shriver is perhaps best known for cofounding—and currently chairing—the Collaborative for Academic, Social, and Emotional Learning (CASEL), the leading research organization in the United States in the field of social and emotional learning. He lives in Maryland with his wife. They have five children.

Fully Alive

Fully Alive

DISCOVERING WHAT
MATTERS MOST

TIMOTHY SHRIVER

Sarah Crichton Books
Farrar, Straus and Giroux
New York

Sarah Crichton Books
Farrar, Straus and Giroux
18 West 18th Street, New York 10011

Grateful acknowledgment is made for permission to reprint the following
previously published material:
Excerpt from "I Rise! A Tribute to Special Olympics" by Maya Angelou.
Reprinted by permission of The Helen Brann Agency, Inc.
Excerpts from "Postscript" from *Opened Ground: Selected Poems, 1966–1996*
by Seamus Heaney. Copyright © 1998 by Seamus Heaney.
Reprinted by permission of Farrar, Straus and Giroux, LLC.

The Library of Congress has cataloged the hardcover edition as follows:
Shriver, Timothy.
    Fully alive : discovering what matters most / Timothy Shriver.
        pages   cm
    ISBN 978-0-374-28091-8 (hardback) — ISBN 978-1-4299-4279-9 (e-book)
    1. Special Olympics.   2. Sports for people with mental disabilities.   I. Title.
GV722.5.S64 S57 2014
796.087'4—dc23

2014020245

Paperback ISBN: 978-0-374-53582-7

Designed by Jonathan D. Lippincott

Farrar, Straus and Giroux books may be purchased for educational, business, or
promotional use. For information on bulk purchases, please contact the Macmillan
Corporate and Premium Sales Department at 1-800-221-7945, extension 5442, or
write to specialmarkets@macmillan.com.

www.fsgbooks.com
www.twitter.com/fsgbooks • www.facebook.com/fsgbooks

1   3   5   7   9   10   8   6   4   2

Some names and identifying details have been changed to protect the
privacy of individuals.

To my families—the one my parents gave me, the one Linda and I created, and the thousands from New Haven to New Delhi who have welcomed me as one of their own. Family is a blessing anyone can give, and family is a gift that matters most.

The glory of God is a human being fully alive.

—Irenaeus

Contents

Fully Alive

Introduction:
A School of the Heart

The Yale Bowl was already eighty-one years old in 1995, but it looked one hundred seventy-five. Its crumbling concrete walls were overgrown with trees, its warped bench seats painted over dozens of times to withstand the cracking. It wasn't ready to handle seventy-five thousand cheering fans. It wasn't designed for a presidential visit, either, with the massive security requirements, extensive evacuation routes, and shielded spaces a president requires. Nor was the field big enough to hold seven thousand athletes with special needs, along with coaches and volunteers, or to accommodate a stage fit for a stadium show. Parking wasn't adequate, because entire lots had been taken over for other purposes—one for a helicopter landing pad for the president, others for makeshift soccer fields, and still others for bus staging.

But we chose the Yale Bowl for the Special Olympics World Games Opening Ceremony anyway. So on the evening of July 1, 1995, the president of the United States, Bill Clinton, and First Lady Hillary Rodham Clinton landed in an adjacent field on Marine 1 while athletes from one hundred fifty countries arrived by bus and paraded through the single entrance tunnel and seventy-five thousand spectators fought their way through neighborhood streets to sit on wooden bleachers and cheer the arrival of the biggest sporting event in the world. It was chaos.

As the athletes arrived at the Yale Bowl that night, each participant was given a disposable camera to record images of his or her triumphant moments. For most of them, the experience of parading into that stadium must have seemed surreal. Coming as they did from institutions and isolated classrooms and lonely corners of despair in villages and towns around the world, most of them would never have been applauded for anything before. They were society's outcasts, lost in the circle of life and rarely found. Over and over, in the countless languages they spoke, they each would have heard "retard," "defective," "sick," "delayed," and, maybe worst of all, "in-valid." Success experiences were nonexistent. Gentleness in the company of strangers was rare. Acceptance among peers was a distant dream. "I am never," one parent of a child with special needs wept, "able to be proud of my child."

But this was their night, a star-studded evening just for them. Sandra Bullock was part of the show. So were Bill Cosby, Jean-Claude Van Damme, and Louis Gossett, Jr. A thousand-voice choir assembled below almost two hundred international flags and welcomed the athletes as they paraded into the stadium. Native Americans on horseback charged around the perimeter in a ceremonial pageant of celebration. Aerial flybys of fighter jets boomed overhead in their honor. The greatest soccer player in the world, Pelé, walked with them and stood for a thousand pictures. Hootie & the Blowfish sang their number one hit "Only Wanna Be with You." The supermodel Kathy Ireland cheered. The hip-hop stars Naughty by Nature and Run-DMC made the stadium explode with energy.

One heroic Special Olympics athlete, Loretta Claiborne, was selected for a major role: to introduce the president to the massive crowd in the stadium and to the national television audience. The Secret Service had insisted the president address the crowd from the top of the stadium. Perimeter security at the Yale Bowl was porous, and the athletes had not been screened through metal detectors—there was no way the president was going to be allowed to walk down onto that field to mingle; no way he was going to stand onstage in the middle of that stadium, given the security unknowns. Instead, he was going to have to speak from one of the highest vantage points above the athletes and trust the television monitors to project his image on the jumbotron.

Midway through the opening ceremony, Loretta rose from her perch atop the Yale Bowl. "Ladies and gentlemen," she bellowed, her voice rising with an excitement bordering on glee, "the president of the United States, Bill Clintonnnnnn!" The crowd roared. For the first time in its thirty-year history, a president was in attendance at Special Olympics—smiling, waving, and applauding the athletes. The stadium may have been old, but in that moment, it was electric.

Down on the field, a professional photographer watched as a group of athletes clad in African dress raised their disposable cameras to take pictures of the president. But there was something peculiar about it. All of them, he realized—and there must've been a dozen— held their cameras backward, the lenses flush against their noses as they peered through the viewfinders. Clearly, he thought, they had never used cameras before. As Clinton's voice boomed across the stadium, the photographer burrowed through the crowd to get closer to the athletes, to help them avoid wasting all their film on blurry images of their own faces.

Not knowing whether they spoke English, he gestured to one of the athletes to lower his camera. "You're trying to get a picture of the president?" he asked. The athlete didn't reply—just looked at him, apparently unable to speak or to understand. "Yes, you're trying to get a picture of Clinton and he's way up there, but you have to turn the camera around. Let me show you." The photographer flipped the direction of the camera. "You see, you have to point the lens toward the president and then look through the viewfinder, and then you can get a good picture of him."

"Oh," said the athlete, in clear and conversational English. "Thank you, sir. But may I show you something? If you turn the camera around and hold your eye up to the viewfinder and look backward, it still works. It works like a telescope and you can see the president very clearly. So we're using these little cameras so we can get a good view of the president. But thank you for helping us."

The photographer was speechless. His mouth must have hung open as he looked into the eyes of that unnamed athlete. The athlete simply said that the camera works in reverse, that was all—"backward, it still works." But the photographer couldn't help feeling surprise and embarrassment: he'd had it all wrong. He'd assumed his own knowledge as a professional was superior, that a "disabled" man needed his help. But this man standing in front of him wasn't incompetent or stupid at all.

In that small moment amid the chaos of noise and humanity, it was as though the athlete changed before the photographer's eyes—or rather, as though the photographer's eyes changed as he looked at the athlete. It wasn't the athlete who was reframed; it was the photographer who donned a new lens. In a flash, he saw a different person—no longer "retarded" or hopeless. He saw someone else: a clever young man, a resourceful athlete, a kind person. The label disappeared, as did the traumatic if unconscious history of low expectations. He saw without assuming. Simply put, he saw from within.

There is a tension in this story that fascinates me and always will. Who was changed in this moment? Who was "disabled" and who was "gifted"? Who was treated to the experience of a lifetime and who did the treating? Who gave and who received?

In retrospect, the answer is as obvious as it is difficult to learn. Both the athlete and the photographer received, and both gave. Both had "disabilities," one from biology and the other from attitude. Both were gifted, one in cleverness and the other in kindness. Both were wounded by the assumptions of their pasts, and both were healed by a simple transforming revelation: you can see another view of the world if you turn your lens around. Keep your eyes open, and you will see both what is close and what may seem far away.

In the year 1112, Bernard of Clairvaux opened a new monastery in the French village of Claire Vallée. A reformer and a preacher, he was determined to inspire a new generation of men and women to see and act differently. He termed his monasteries "schools of the heart" and urged his followers to discover the presence of God in the here and now, where they could encounter it as "a love so great and so free." He became known as the "honey sweet teacher."

Although he lived almost a thousand years ago, Bernard confronted challenges that are not so different from our own. We live in a time when many have lost faith in God and, along with it, faith that anything is sacred or enduring. We live in a world that is changing faster than ever but at the same time is more rudderless than ever, too. We hunger for stability and safety, but we're surrounded by uncertainty. We place enormous value on lasting friendships and authenticity, in part because they're so hard to find. We wonder about ultimate things without knowing if our wondering is even worthwhile. "Consider your ways," the Jewish prophet Haggai wrote 2,500 years ago. "What do you really want? You sow much but bring in little; you eat but still hunger; you drink but still thirst; you clothe yourselves but can't get warm, and your wages run out through the holes in your pockets" (Haggai 1:5–7). Some elements of the human condition defy the particularities of a given period. Just as others did millennia before us, we live in a time of restlessness.

But like mystics in other religions, Bernard had a hopeful view of our searching. The search can be successful, he taught, but we'll be frustrated unless we focus on the right destination. Bernard called that destination a "love that is both great and free," and he tried his best to interest others in living for it. Some people—me included—use the common nickname for that love: "God." Others call it "peace" or "nirvana" or "unity" or "enlightenment." But whatever we call it, we know we want it. And if we want the kind of love that makes us want to get up in the morning and live; the kind that makes us feel held and cared for; the kind that leads us to believe in the exquisite beauty of one another and the goodness of life; the kind of love that has no conditions—then we have to direct our attention to it and not to the alternatives. *That* kind of love is what matters most, but how to find it isn't obvious.

Or is it? When teaching us how to search, almost all of the mystics agree on the path: we shouldn't waste our time trying to change ourselves or to meet the perfect mate or wander the world or learn some fancy skill. Just slow down and be awake to the present. "What you are looking for," Francis of Assisi said, "is what is looking." If we want to find that "something bigger," we don't have to go anywhere. To each of us, the poet Muhyiddin Ibn 'Arabi writes, the goal is "nearer to you than yourself."

Although it may seem counterintuitive, I believe that people with intellectual disabilities are brilliant teachers of that something bigger we're all looking for. They led me to the Special Olympics classroom of self-discovery, where my heart was caught off guard and blown open. It turned out to be a complete education with painful injustices, raucous field experiences, unexpected tenderness, and the breakthrough lesson that all life is beautiful. It was led by the most marginalized people in the world, who were well acquainted with suffering but also masters of healing. I met them in my backyard playing games, in institutions drenched in despair and injustice, in the eyes of mothers and fathers and brothers and sisters hungering for welcome, and in my own family. They taught me that we are all totally vulnerable and totally valuable at the same time. They modeled lessons in love and fulfillment that I didn't even know were possible. They changed everything.

Like all great educators, the athletes of Special Olympics taught me more about how to see than what to see. But isn't there just one way of seeing?

Not exactly. Over the years, I started to learn that there's another way of seeing: from the inside out. I couldn't learn the lessons the athletes of Special Olympics were trying to teach me until I learned to see the inside of things. Like most people, I tended to think that seeing required only a simple glance, but I was wrong. I needed to learn to see not just what was in front of my eyes but what was lurking silently beneath the surface of things, too. I needed to be able to use my mind to see the real stuff in the physical world but also to quiet all the distractions of my mind to see the equally real stuff of the heart that lay beneath them. I needed to practice seeing each and every little thing but also practice being open to the whole of the big things. I needed to understand how to see from within if I was going to learn anything worthwhile about finding the something bigger I was so eager to find.

The great Sufi mystic Rumi suggests that such a way of seeing creates a consciousness that enables us to see possibilities and realities that might otherwise be hidden:

> The intellect says: "The six directions are limits: there is no way out."
> Love says: "There is a way. I have traveled it thousands of times."

The athletes of Special Olympics taught me to trust Rumi's belief that there is a way of seeing the world given by love. I started out in a very different place, in encounters like the one between the photographer and the athlete on the field at the Yale Bowl. I arrived at those encounters with a misguided expectation that I would serve "them," but my expectations were turned inside out—and I began to see that the whole ethic of "serving the needy" could itself be an obstacle to opening my eyes. I discovered a new way of seeing individuals whom I thought of as "powerless" but who turned out to have a power I didn't even know existed. I found myself over and over again confused by the strength of people who seemed to be experiencing both pain and triumph at the same time. And, in my confusion, I felt yanked out of my narrow way of seeing and awakened to seeing from a space of soul and silence. Often just hanging out with the athletes was enough to crack me open to a power within them and within myself that I didn't know I was looking for. In short, I found my encounters with many of the people in this book to be windows into the eye of love, the "organ of perception" that Bernard wanted to cultivate in a school of the heart so that he could come close to the "love so great and so free" that he framed as the mind of God.

I found my way to the athletes of Special Olympics because the family I grew up in and the family that I made with my wife, Linda, and the God to whom I prayed all pointed me to them. I was restlessly looking for something that mattered. I didn't know that's what I was doing. I was looking and looking and looking and found myself staring right into the eyes of the most vulnerable and broken and powerless people on earth. I thought I had arrived at them in order to tell them what mattered, but of course, I had no idea what to say.

Instead, they were patient enough to wait for me to listen. And when I finally listened, they told me what to do with my "one wild and precious life": charge into the world with fearless enthusiasm, bearing the simple gift of myself and sharing it recklessly and gratefully and peacefully wherever and whenever I can.

ONE

Boat Races

When I was about five years old, I fell in love with my first game: "boat races." My mother and I played it on the little streams that ran through the woods at the edge of the vast field that stretched out behind our house. Those woods were a whole world to me. Looking out from my back door, all I could see was the field, and then the magical woods. On dark nights, beyond the vast expanse of the empty black field and the uneven, inky line of the woods rising above it, I could also see a row of four radio towers blinking red and white like silent sirens.

As a little boy, many nights I'd lie in bed and look out the window and watch those radio towers blinking their secret signals of warning. I knew they were located in the faraway city, but all I knew of the city was that my mother and father went to work there. Sometimes they came home with lots of friends, and sometimes they came home with beaten looks on their faces. Little children remember only moments of heaven or hell. One time when I was four, my mother came home to tell me my uncle had been murdered and I should run along and find something to do. But on other days, she would take me off alone, just the two of us, down through the field and into the woods to play our special game of boat races.

It was not an easy game. The "boats" were actually small sticks, and the race was actually a competition between my stick and my

mother's to see which could go down the stream fastest. So the first
challenge was to find a good stick—one that floated well and didn't
have any protrusions that would get stuck on a leaf or a rock. A
good boat was small enough to be quick but hefty enough to catch
the current.

Once we'd picked our boats, the second challenge was to throw
them into the stream at the count of three, hitting the water in
just the right place so they would catch the current and go. Then
came the breathless part: watching my boat wiggle and wash
its way down the stream toward an imaginary finish line, cheering like crazy, encouraging it on its journey toward (I hoped) victory. And then heaven's most often repeated exclamation: "Let's play
again!"

I loved the ritual of the game—the long walk down the field
holding my mother's hand, the passage from the open grass of the
cow pasture into the shade of the huge Maryland oaks, the crunchy
path across the leaves and twigs of the forest floor to the edge of the
stream, and the furious search for high-quality boats that I could race
against my resolute opponent, Mummy. We were all alone in those
woods, Mummy and me: quiet, beyond the reach of the hated phone,
beyond the city, the cars, and all those people asking Mrs. Shriver
what she wanted, when she wanted it, and where she wanted it. All I
had to do was pick up a stick and I had the power to make a boat
come to life. I could bring the only eyes and ears and heart and mind
in the world that I cared about—those of my mother—to focus on
my little boat as it navigated mighty rapids, skittered around treacherous leaves and pebbles and occasional whirlpools, and glided toward
a win.

They say a child can believe in anything—like Santa Claus with
his elves; like leprechauns with their rainbows and pots of gold; like
boats made out of sticks and their daring races against the hazards of
the elements; like a child being the center of his mother's life. In
those days of boat races, I believed. I believed in things I couldn't see
and in the secret power I had to change the world into a place of love
and mystery and eternity. It wasn't that I didn't know about the mon-
sters with grotesque faces and devastating strength that could attack.

I did, and from an early age. It's just that the magic of the game was powerful enough to defeat them.

Those are the kinds of things I believed as a child. It took a long time for me to find my way back to them, but I believe in them still.

TWO

Much Is Expected

My understanding of belief goes back to my grandmother Rose Fitzgerald Kennedy. She was a woman of warm elegance, impeccably punctual at family meals, fond of long walks (which we grandchildren were often invited to join), and full of witty stories. She went to mass every day and frequently alluded in conversation to her faith and to the teachings of the Catholic Church. She would sometimes speak of the role faith played in the public events of her life—visits with the Pope in Rome, gifts to the Archdiocese of Boston in support of Catholic causes, the political careers of her sons.

But she also had private lessons for her grandchildren. She was especially fond of paraphrasing Luke 12:48, the parable of the faithful servant: "Of those to whom much is given, much is expected." "Expected" was a word that had clear implications for her and for everyone in my family. Expectations were serious business, because, as I could easily discern from the large houses and plentiful possessions and ambitious people all around me, we had been given a lot. It was my job to figure out how to fulfill the expectation that I would give back.

Figuring it out, for me, took place in the midst of some rather extraordinary events. My family was immersed in politics—not just any politics, but the politics of the Democratic Party in the second half of the twentieth century. My grandfather became involved in the campaign of Franklin Roosevelt, but his role in that campaign, and his subsequent chairmanship of the fledgling Securities and Exchange Commission, was driven not so much by idealism as by pragmatic ambition. Joseph P. Kennedy was a conservative man in an administration many feared to be too leftist, hired because he spoke the language of Wall Street and could make SEC regulation palatable there. The business world had found Roosevelt's thundering inaugural words ominous:

> The money changers have fled from their high seats in the temple of our civilization. We may now restore that temple to the ancient truths. The measure of the restoration lies in the extent to which we apply social values more noble than mere monetary profit.

My grandfather's work, often as not, involved sending a more moderate and diplomatic version of this same message: "Don't worry, he didn't mean it *that* way." The SEC was about restoring public confidence in the free market, not about shutting it down.

My parents, however, learned the more idealistic version of New Deal politics. They not only supported FDR, but also *believed* in his message of courage and justice in the face of weakness and greed, and they raised my brothers and sister and me on it. Their Roosevelt was a man who'd proved that government could be a force for fairness in the economy. He was committed to the ideals of artists pursuing their creative passions, to public works, to the great economist John Maynard Keynes. He sided with the poor and against the rich; he envisioned a country where the elderly could be free of the destitution and stigma of old age. He believed, most of all, in action. His protruding jaw and his energy were as powerful as his legislation. I grew up with role models who were eager to forge ahead in the mold of Roosevelt: never fearing anything, least of all fear itself.

Most of the significant adult men in my life served in the armed forces during World War II. My father, Sargent Shriver, saw heavy combat in the Pacific theater and several times escaped with his life only by chance. One of my uncles, Joe Kennedy, Jr., was killed in a high-risk secret mission in the European theater. President Kennedy's much-heralded heroism in naval warfare was part of my childhood's daily conversational fare, and I wore PT-109 tie clips to every family event. Most of our friends and acquaintances had war stories, which they told more often than they probably realized. A longtime family employee who became a second father to me, Richard Ragsdale, often drove us children to important events, and while he drove he would recount the stories of the shrapnel wounds he'd suffered in the 1st Armored Division under Patton in North Africa. He liked to end his hellish tales by showing us a photo he'd taken upon his arrival in Milan as an intelligence officer: it was a black-and-white of Mussolini hanging upside down from a stanchion, executed in advance of the arrival of American troops.

With the New Deal and World War II as backdrops, my parents were married and started their family in Chicago, where my father had gone to work in the sprawling Merchandise Mart owned by my grandfather—perhaps the most lucrative investment of his storied business career. The wealth my grandfather had created was also a focus of the lessons we learned as children. Among the many gifts my parents gave to me and my siblings was their determination that the comfort and privilege of our childhood would not make us feel self-satisfied or entitled. My father reminded us relentlessly that the children of the rich "usually amount to a hill of crap," warning that such a fate was not an option for us. Both of my parents were vigilant in rooting out any traces of arrogance. One didn't have to go far in treating others with disdain or snobbery to hear a sharp, scowling adult crackdown: "Just who do you think you are, talking that way?" By a strange and muddled calculus, we learned of our privilege mostly in the context of denying it and, even more important, of repaying it.

There was also family grief—often the result of sudden, shockingly painful, enormously public events. In some ways, I was spared the full brunt of these unspeakable tragedies, since my own parents and siblings survived into my adult life. But in other ways, the large, extended, boisterous, and idealistic family system of which I was a small part was repeatedly crushed by violent losses. Through those losses, I learned one of the most problematic lessons of my childhood:

grief and other emotional traumas are not to be dwelt upon and in fact are barely to be acknowledged. We had one unspoken rule as children: deal with loss on your own, in whatever way you can. At the slightest sign of sadness, a stern reminder came down from above: "Get on to yourself! Everyone's happy in heaven, and besides, you could be much worse off than you are." Between the benefits of our wealth and the consolations of our faith, we had been given much, and in return we were expected not to show or feel or dwell in self-pity or pain. In the unlikely event that we questioned God's wisdom or wondered aloud why it mattered that children in Biafra were worse off than we were, it would only get worse. "That's enough!" End of story.

In the vacuum left by this emotional hush policy, religion became an outlet. Both of my parents were devout Roman Catholics, attending daily mass, reading extensively in religious ideas, and actively participating in the daily life of religious orders and institutions. For them, faith yielded enthusiasm and even fun, as they would lead debates about religion, poke fun at the eccentricities of this priest or that nun, and try to inculcate in us a sense of the relevance of religious doctrines. At the same time, in a kind of mystical sleight of hand, emotional issues were always converted to religious ones. We prayed the Rosary as a family on many occasions, and I remember hearing my mother dedicate the prayers again and again to the repose of her brothers' souls, intimating that our grief could be channeled through the beads and converted from pain to peace. Sometimes when we rode in the car with my father, he would take the opportunity to remind his captive audience that the Sermon on the Mount was "the greatest speech ever given—the greatest account of how to be happy ever given." Like my mother, he seemed convinced that emotional happiness could somehow emerge from devotion to Christian traditions and liturgical practices. When I once asked him about the insights of psychology, he was quick to remark that Freud and others might be helpful to some, but we had our faith, and it was far better than any therapist.

Therapists or no therapists, religion drew me in. Prayer was a practice where emotion was allowed and even nurtured. Church was the place where peace was sought as a personal experience in quiet and not just discussed as a political ideal. The Bible was a book about lost souls and escapes to freedom and suffering that was faced and heaven that was achieved. I watched my parents in church and saw my dad pull at his forehead in prayer and my mother look to statues of Mary and try to emulate her example of faith. I was an altar boy by the time I was seven, but I was also more than that: I was on a faith journey and already wondering, "Who is God and how can I find God's answer to my search for what matters most?"

But time in church, no matter how frequent, was still the exception. In the day-to-day, my family exuded restlessness. We were restless to fight poverty, restless to get elected, restless to win at sports, restless to help people with intellectual disabilities, restless to be charming, restless in a million ways. In part, this restless social energy found its healthiest outlet in competition, and competition in everything was the norm. My father would wake early in the morning and challenge everyone to see who was going to be the first one downstairs to breakfast, and the race was on. We would compare our performance on school report cards to see who was smartest, play touch football to see who was fastest, ride horses to see who was best, recount stories of parties to see who was the most charismatic, read the newspaper to see who had the highest poll ratings, work elections to see who could win political power, play water polo on weekends to see who could endure the most physical punishment. We were constantly on the lookout for chances to win and, equally important, for chances to guard against losing. Through it all, we would laugh at our failings and laugh at the world, just as we yearned to overcome both. The only lesson that rang as clear as those of high expectations, social justice, and religious fidelity in our family was the law of competition. Our self-definition and our individual value were measured on a scorecard. We were satisfied only if we were winning at something.

Ironically, this family system—so immersed in the world of politics, so restless in pursuit of power, so intensely focused on action—also kept returning us to the interests of life's most vulnerable. Just as we raced around our backyard and campaigned around the country and journeyed around the world, we were always doing so with an eye on the need to serve those who had neither wealth nor power nor influence. Somehow, this never seemed inconsistent to me and never created any conscious tension in my mind during my youth, but looking back, it was a bit of a roller coaster. We would travel abroad and meet a prime minister or a king and then, on the same day, visit an institution for people with intellectual disabilities or a Peace Corps project focused on sewage. My parents would hold parties for cabinet secretaries and movie stars, and the next day load up our station wagon to deliver canned goods and turkeys to a soup kitchen. At the dinner table, my mother would ask us to explain our position on the rising poll numbers of an incumbent United States senator and then explain what we had learned about how starvation could possibly persist in a world with so much wealth. It was all of a piece—politics, power, wealth, faith, competition, and the outrage of injustice. It was bound together by my grandmother's rule: you have been given much; you must serve others in exchange. "Serve, serve, serve," my father once said in a rousing speech. "It is the servants who will save us all."

In my immediate family, service was not primarily about electoral politics, and that was fine with me. Politics, after all, had produced the trauma of family deaths in the sixties, a frustrating string of public losses in the 1972, 1976, and 1980 presidential elections, and the humiliating lifelong experience of being a surrogate. Politics, despite its glittering reputation as an avenue for fame, camaraderie, and big ideas, seemed mostly an occasion for being asked, "Which one are you?" Campaigns could be exciting and the great ideas were compelling, but for me it was mostly a world of intense pressure, superficial rhetoric, mean-spirited confrontations, exhausting family separations, and experiences of personal insignificance. We laughed on campaigns, we went door to door with spirit, and we stood happily when our parents and uncles would recognize us in speeches, but elective politics was certainly not set up to make a child feel special. Quite the contrary: it made us feel small—in stature as children and in significance as young adults. For the most part, it sucked.

Another side of politics, however, did have an allure. It was politics

with a small "p"—engagement in political and social organizations
that existed to advance a public good. This was really the work of my
side of the family. My father came late to electoral politics. Despite
being the Democratic candidate for vice president of the United States
in 1972 and subsequently running in presidential primaries, he was
much more gifted—and happier—at the work of creating and championing social programs. Similarly, although my mother was often
referred to as a political animal, she was never herself a candidate for
public office. Rather, she chose to pursue her political ideals through
advocacy and social programs. And the programs both my parents
created were extraordinary.

These programs were also a part of my life, even though I was
just a child. When I was six years old, my father returned from one of
his many trips around the world with a special gift for the kids. We
each unwrapped beautiful navy-blue sweat suits, the jackets embroi-
dered on the right with our names and on the left with the logo of the
United States Peace Corps. Our "Peace Corps suits" would be worn
on Saturday after Saturday, when my father would convene his senior
staff at our house in suburban Maryland for all-day working sessions.
The Peace Corps was already the apple of the nation's political eye,
embodying the American values of exuberance, idealism, and tireless-
ness. And I could be a part of it every time I put on my suit and
showed it off to the grown-ups who were working in my living room.
There, politics was not about power or the defeat of opponents but
rather about important values and intimacy with my dad. I remember once, when I was about eight years old, hearing him call out to an
assembled team of colleagues in the backyard: "Look at Timothy run
in his Peace Corps suit! Look how fast he is!" The fight for social justice took place on a big stage, but it was also about family.

There were many more programmatic efforts like this in my
house—Head Start was conceived in that same living room, and in
one way or another so were the Legal Services Corporation, Upward
Bound, Job Corps, Community Action, and Foster Grandparents. I
couldn't have known, as a child, about all the injustice and challenges
that confronted these efforts to fight poverty, or about the real anger
and division they were trying to address in the tense and volatile cities

of the 1960s. What I did know was that these efforts were both important and fun—a rare combination that yielded a deep sense of satisfaction. And no work better captured that combination than the revolutionary experiment my mother conducted at that same house, Timberlawn, during the summers of my early childhood: Camp Shriver.

My mother is one of nine children, three of whom—Jack, Bobby, and Teddy—were known for their extraordinary political careers. My mother's sisters, while less recognizable to most, were also people of enormous energy and achievement. My aunt Jean founded an international arts program for people with disabilities and served as an ambassador. My aunt Patricia was an animated beauty who spent virtually her entire life volunteering for the causes that drove her siblings, and she lived at the center of New York's cultural life. But my aunt Rosemary, who died in 2005, was perhaps the *most* extraordinary of my mother's siblings.

Rosemary was born in 1918. I remember my mother often explaining Rosemary's challenges as resulting from a troubled delivery. "Rosemary lost oxygen during her birth, and we think that's what caused her difficulties. Loss of oxygen to the brain can do that—can cause problems for life." I never heard this explanation of Rosemary's condition corroborated, but whatever the cause, it became apparent soon after her birth that, in the jargon of the day, Rosemary was "mentally retarded."

As she reached school age, her disability made her unable to keep pace with her siblings. Her parents, like millions of other parents around the world whose children are different, struggled to find any support or help. Rosemary attended the same schools as her siblings until she was eleven. By then she had fallen so far behind that her parents sent her away to an experimental boarding school in Pennsylvania, which was designed for the education of the "feebleminded." Over the next twelve years, she would attend multiple schools, with brief intervals of living at home. None of her teachers seemed to know quite what to do with her; there was constant pressure on the family to do something to fix her.

My grandparents must have experienced the painful tension between wanting to fight for their child and wishing she would go away to be cared for elsewhere, out of sight, the weaknesses and embarrassing flaws hidden from view. At times, Rosemary must have felt desperately alone. At other times, she must have felt the warmth of the family who sheltered her, although her siblings undoubtedly struggled with how to make sense of the world from the point of view of their sister. They grew up loving someone whom others referred to as having something "wrong."

Finally, at the age of twenty-three, Rosemary Kennedy underwent experimental brain surgery—a lobotomy—in an effort to correct the emotional and cognitive vulnerabilities that appeared to be growing worse. It was a disaster. The procedure left her with only the most limited verbal and motor abilities. She would spend the remaining six decades of her life in the custody of nuns and caregivers in a Wisconsin institution. By most accounts, my grandfather never saw her again—ending what had been a lifetime of affection. For more than two decades, her mother and siblings visited her rarely. In most ways, she was simply gone.

By the time I arrived, however—almost twenty years after the lobotomy—Aunt Rosemary had become a frequent visitor to our home. She would stay for a few days or a week and spend her days shuffling cards, swimming, taking walks, or visiting sites in Washington. Only when I was older could I see the vexing predicament into which she thrust us. We were a family who lived as though winning and gaining influence were indispensable to our happiness. How then could we explain why Rosemary's life was of value, too?

In her own way, she may have had the most influence of any member of my family, because her message was by far the most radical: she was the only person I ever met who didn't need to *do* anything to prove that she mattered. In the midst of an enormously competitive family system, Rosemary Kennedy lived a full life to the age of eighty-six without ever giving a speech, writing a book, holding a job, or garnering the praise of the mighty. Despite failing to meet any of the expectations that were imposed on the rest of us, she belonged. She didn't have to do anything to earn that. Only in retrospect did I realize how, at some level, I envied her deeply. Her presence changed everything.

In any event, she was surely the catalyst for what took place in my backyard starting in the summer of 1962. There, my mother started a revolution and named it Camp Shriver. She was determined to prove to others a lesson Rosemary had proved to her years before, a lesson that remains shocking in its simplicity and shocking in its continuing and persistent disregard: people with intellectual disabilities are human beings, deserving of love, opportunity, and acceptance just as they are.

In the years before Camp Shriver, my mother had spent much of her professional energy touring facilities for people with intellectual disabilities, meeting with scholars and researchers, giving small grants to therapists and support agencies, and listening to parents and family members. That experience had led her to the point of fury and frustration, because the suffering of the people she met was so extreme, and so little was being done. Some combination of pain, outrage, and enthusiasm galvanized her to act. In 1962, she decided that the oppressed and forgotten children with intellectual disabilities who were grinding out their summers in the fetid institutions of Washington, DC, and suburban Maryland ought to be able to play games and have fun. And she further decided that since no one else seemed to care much, she would make it happen herself, in her backyard, with her children in tow. That's where I came in.

What I remember of Camp Shriver spans a child's emotional range: I went to the arts and crafts center at the camp, where along with other campers I built and painted my own wooden table and gave it to my father. I did the ropes course with other campers and walked the balance beams, hung from trees, and jumped through obstacles. I went with the other campers down to the riding ring and rode small ponies. And I wandered on summer afternoons through an array of games and activities that made my backyard into a virtual amusement park. My mother watched all this and noted shrewdly:

Should anyone be afraid of Wendell, a nine-year-old boy with the mental ability of a boy of four? He and Timothy, my own three-year-old son, did many things at our day camp at the same speed and proficiency and loved each other. Both picked up their clothes—with some prodding—after swimming;

both caught and threw a ball with the same ability, although Wendell kicked much better than Timothy. Both had the same table manners. Sometimes they would throw the food and would then have to go without dessert. Both ran about the same speed and rushed back and forth. Wendell and Timmy would hold hands and run down the hill together. Wendell would help Timmy climb up the hill when he was tired.

Camp Shriver was a bonanza of fun, complete with games, balls, swimming, and a friend named Wendell.

But it was also curious, in ways I can now see quite clearly. It must have occurred to me that it was anything but ordinary to have a hundred or so people with intellectual disabilities in one's backyard. Volunteers seemed to arrive at all hours of the day and evening, asking what to do. A vigorous, authoritarian former Olympic athlete, Sandy Eiler, was brought on to help manage the activities, but he, like others, had only the most limited sense of a plan. Prisoners on work release showed up regularly, tasked with some of the heavy labor involved in constructing games and moving equipment. Only occasionally did a camper's emotional outburst or unrestrained behavior concern me. At the center of it all was my mother—excited, charismatic, demanding, completely immersed, and always on edge. At the time, Camp Shriver certainly didn't seem to fall into the category of "revolutionary," but though few noticed it, the revolution was on. For my mother, it was activism wrapped up with sports, faith, and social justice—her way of attacking the pain and rejection that had marred Rosemary's life and hers. She was a camp director on a mission, and somewhere within her was Rosemary—a sister calling out for a chance.

During Camp Shriver, my child's eye took in scenes that have stayed with me for decades. I remember some summer mornings being alone in my bedroom, peering out the window as the campers would arrive and assemble for the raising of the American flag, listening for the trumpeter who would play the national anthem, and for the singing of "If You're Happy and You Know It." I watched as volunteers helped guide campers from the school buses to the flagpole, where they lined up in disorderly rows as the flag ascended the pole and the trumpet played its lonely ode to the nation. Then the clapping and singing began. "If you're happy and you know it, CLAP YOUR HANDS!"

I think I wondered many things as I watched the scene from my second-floor room. I was maybe four or five years old when I can first remember staring out my window as though it happened often; as though it happened yesterday. How do you become "happy" and how do you know it? What are "expectations" and whose should I meet? What matters most—becoming a senator or a president or playing outside with a child with intellectual disabilities in the pool? And who were these children with intellectual disabilities and why was it so important to help them be happy?

I think on some level I realized, even then, that my life was going to be about that scene. I was silent as I watched, my eyes fixed and wide, racing but motionless; my little mind searching the scene in front of me, pleading with it for clues for where I belonged.

All children have their share of moments in which time seems to stop and the full emotional and spiritual complexity of the world comes rushing through their eyes into their bones, there to stay for a lifetime. Flannery O'Connor once wrote that "anyone who has survived his childhood has enough information about life to last him the rest of his days," and in the daily experience of Camp Shriver, I could see the questions of my life. I wanted to recapture my mother's attention and escape to the woods and the wonderful delight of imaginary boats and speedy races and happy games. I wanted to figure out how to face the chaos and grief of our restless home while enjoying the excitement and lure of action and purpose that was right in front of my eyes. I wanted to explore the peculiar riddle of how we so often reject the very people and things that carry the secrets of belonging, and figure out what it would take to find my place. Later on, I wanted to learn how to pray, so that it would all make sense—how to kneel and grind out in silence my experience of the brokenness of the world, so that I could stand and defeat it in time and space.

Camp Shriver was a work of faith and fury made manifest in the most ordinary of tasks: we swam, we rode, we ran, we jumped. Some children came to our house, children whom most people thought of as worthless, and they got the chance to win at a few simple games. That was all. I played alongside them all those years, with only the faintest notion of the role they would later play in my life. Someday, I would realize how close those campers lived to the most important questions that I hungered to understand. And I would realize that they might just have shown me the most unlikely way to fulfill those great expectations my grandmother had instilled in me.

It would take me twenty years to come to understand that the biggest beneficiary of my attempt to make a difference for others would be me. And, even more remarkably, I would learn along the way that the most powerful role models in my search would not be the mighty and beautiful whom I had been raised to try to outdo, but instead the vulnerable and the forgotten on the edge of life whom I had been raised to help.

THREE

Pity or Purge

The route to belonging for people such as the children at Camp Shriver and my aunt Rosemary was not easy. In fact, it was brutal. The inability to do certain things turns out to be very dangerous and leads more often to rejection and humiliation than to belonging. I had no idea as a child how difficult it had been for them to live with the risk of being vulnerable—and no idea that I would need to learn to do the same.

The campers at Camp Shriver—those children and young adults with intellectual disabilities who got off the school buses every morning during the summers at my house—were part of a worldwide population of people with intellectual disabilities whose lives and histories were shrouded in secrecy. My memories inlcude being puzzled by their unusual qualities. Why did one girl make such loud and unintelligible noises? Why did one boy wear a helmet all around the fields? Why was it so hard to understand some campers when they tried to speak? What secret places did they come from and to what secret places were they going as they rumbled in and rumbled away in their big yellow buses in the afternoon? What I knew of their lives barely hinted at struggles of a magnitude I could not imagine. To me, they seemed playful and needy in some ways—happy and a little vulnerable. It would be years before I understood that their vulnerability resulted in most of them having to endure a living hell.

Though few know the history of people with intellectual disabilities, it stands out as one of the most sordid accounts of injustice in human experience. From place to place, century to century, people with intellectual disabilities have been dehumanized, marginalized, abused, rejected, and killed, their families left to despair alone, struggling with the specter of shame and ridicule.

Sadly, the deepest beliefs and values of the societies in which people with intellectual disabilities live have often been employed to justify their rejection. Start with the sacred texts of the Bible, for example, where the conundrum of disability emerges as a frequent topic. While I come from the Christian tradition and only know it personally, believers in other traditions have shared with me their own perspectives on the complexity—and sometimes confusion—that often comes from religious ideas.

Throughout the Bible, the writers try to understand what message God is sending in and through people with disabilities, and although no one knows for sure what the texts mean, many believers have interpreted the readings to suggest that disability is the result of punishment by God or evidence of sin. In sections of the Torah, when God gets angry and visits a long list of misfortunes on Israel—blindness, madness, and physical infirmity (for example, see Deuteronomy 28:15–68 and Zephaniah 1:17)—readers have sometimes seen a "strong negative association with disability as an unfortunate and undesirable state." In the Christian texts, the stories similarly have led believers to assume that disability was often evidence of sin or shame, as Jesus sometimes appears to "heal" those with disabilities of their sin and cast out "demons" from them, too. In one story, Jesus heals a "demon-possessed man who was blind and mute," and in another, he heals an apparently epileptic child by rebuking an "evil spirit." These and other texts have been thought to invite a kind of purging of people with disabilities—an exclusion of them from the midst of the community and an association of disability with suffering and an assumption that disability is undesirable or sinful.

But an alternate view emerges in these same books: disability sometimes appears to be a call to compassion, a reminder of God's demand that people show mercy and generosity, and even a means of understanding the mind of God. In the Torah, readers find a biblical commandment sometimes cited as the earliest effort to legislate protection of people with disabilities: "Thou shall not curse the deaf nor put a stumbling block before the blind nor make the blind to wander out of the path" (Leviticus 19:14). The prophet Isaiah extolls the virtues of those who offer care and healing to those with disabilities and labels them "repairers of the breach." Like his Jewish forbears, Jesus of Nazareth often willingly associates with the marginalized and invites them into the Kingdom. Outcasts become disciples, children are considered wise, and the "last" become "first." The blind man Bartimaeus has sometimes been a symbol of the pleas of people with disabilities. When Jesus comes near to him, the story goes, he cries out in a loud voice: "Jesus, son of David, have pity on me" (Mark 10:47). The crowds rebuke him for shouting, but he persists—an early and powerful example of self-advocacy. Finally Jesus hears him and announces that his faith is strong enough to cure him.

Other major religions repeat these same themes, albeit with different points of emphasis. The Qur'an, which Muslims believe to be the direct revelation of God, contains messages that many believers view as exhortations to include and accommodate people with disabilities: "There is no harm if the blind, the lame, the sick, or you yourselves, eat in your own houses" (Surah 24:61). Tellingly, in one Qur'an passage, God rebukes the prophet Muhammad for turning his back on a blind man who had interrupted a gathering in which he was speaking (Surah 80:1–10), appearing to reinforce the message that God wants people with disabilities to be treated with dignity and respect. However, as in the other Abrahamic faiths, Muslims have sometimes been confused by the ambiguous language of their sacred text. Surah 16:76 describes what appears to be a man who is mute and/or has an intellectual disability as "mute, lacks the ability to do anything, is totally dependent on his master . . . he cannot produce anything good." Although most interpretations argue that "mute" is here used metaphorically to indicate a person who strays from the path of God, some readers find that this verse makes it unclear what disability means. The Hadith—the sayings of the prophet Muhammad—is generally positive about people with disabilities, but nonetheless includes sayings such as "one should run away from the leper as one runs away from the lion."

The Hindu tradition has a comparable mixture of messages, sometimes calling for deferential treatment of people who are sick or who have disabilities, granting them full social inclusion, charitable treatment, and legal immunity. However, the law of karma can be interpreted to counter the call to pity and care with a purge message, linking intellectual and physical disability to misdeeds in a past life, implicitly devaluing or even blaming those with disabilities. Buddhism teaches that its Eightfold Path—Right View, Right Intention, Right Speech, Right Action, Right Livelihood, Right Effort, Right Mindfulness, and Right Concentration—is the way to the cessation of suffering. While many of these tenets emphasize interdependence and selfless kindness, Right Mindfulness and Right Concentration also place a premium on mental discipline and sustained mental control. Such capacities were sometimes seen to be beyond the reach of many with intellectual disabilities, leading some followers of this tradition to conclude that spiritual peace is not attainable.

There is of course more complexity in these religions—and in the many others not cited—than one can glean from just a cursory glance, but still, it is beyond doubt that religion has sometimes "been used to demean or diminish the full humanity of people with disabilities." One might be tempted to hope that among cultures that prize reason, the superstitious qualities of religion would yield to humanistic respect for dignity and individual rights, but history shows that secular and rationalistic societies have been just as hard on people with disabilities. The Greeks shaped their grand vision of politics, justice, and virtue—a vision that still shapes the modern world—without according any value to such people, arguing instead for the need to purge society of their presence. There are many accounts of ancient Greek and Roman societies using people with disabilities as ritual scapegoats and sometimes murdering them to appease the gods. Greeks practiced infanticide on newborns with disabilities, and Spartan law required it.

Plato offered a stark prescription for the treatment of those with disabilities: "This is the kind of medical provision you should legislate in your state. You should provide treatment for those of your citizens whose physical constitution is good. As for the others, it will be best to leave the unhealthy to die, and to put to death those whose psychological condition is incurably corrupt. That seems to be the best thing both for the individual sufferer and for society." Aristotle similarly advocated killing infants with disabilities: "Let there be a law that no deformed child shall live."

The dawn of the modern world, which we optimistically call "the Enlightenment," held out the promise of equality and freedom for all people regardless of birth or stature. Unfortunately, however, the opposite proved true for people with intellectual disabilities, whose value in society only decreased as reason became the highest expression of human value and science became the way to create human goods. The powerful words of the French philosopher René Descartes "I think, therefore I am" made rational self-determination the hallmark of modern life and, in so doing, helped validate a new and often more deadly form of dehumanization of those for whom reason was neither a strength nor a value.

If Descartes was the first to argue that reason was the most important human attribute, it was John Locke who made reason the bedrock of individual rights and political order. Locke, the celebrated philosopher whose writings helped set the stage for the American Revolution, articulated the rights of citizens in the new forms of government, freed from the tyranny of kings and religious authority figures. But he drew a hard line regarding people with intellectual disabilities. In Locke's view, being human meant being capable of abstract thought. Thus, people with intellectual disabilities were subhuman "idiots," incapable of morality and possessing no soul; as such, the state was not obligated to serve them, and practices such as infanticide were justified.

The ideas of European philosophers such as Locke and Descartes were carried to their logical ends in new social programs that made such dehumanization the foundation of policy and practice. These ideas found their way to the New World, where the first models of the twentieth-century institution emerged: "In 1752, with leadership from the physician Thomas Bond and Benjamin Franklin, the first

general hospital was established in the American colonies in Philadelphia. Care for persons with mental illness was a major motive in the
founding of this hospital." Although the hospital's founding petition
contains benevolent language, its treatments for those with mental
infirmities were anything but: dousing "alternately with warm and
cold" water; shaving and blistering the scalp; bloodletting to induce
loss of consciousness; purging the gastrointestinal tract; chaining to
walls in basement cells; using gyrating machines and tranquilizer
chairs. The first American mental asylum was built in 1773 in Virginia. A handful of other almshouses and asylums were scattered
throughout the colonies and Mexico at the time, boasting similar
methods of "treatment" and "care."

Thankfully, institutions such as these did not gain widespread
popularity until the mid-nineteenth century, at which time a social
activist named Dorothea Dix began traveling across the country to
inspect the living conditions and treatment of people with mental
illness and disability. She was motivated by having witnessed the
mistreatment of people with disabilities in her home state of Massachusetts. Her first report was published in 1843 and describes people con-
fined *"in cages, closets, cellars, stalls, pens! Chained, naked, beaten with rods,*
and *lashed* into obedience! . . . Irritation of body, produced by utter
filth and exposure, incited [one woman] to the horrid process of tear-
ing off her skin by inches." For the next thirty years, Dix would advocate the establishment of "caring" institutions where people with
disabilities and mental illnesses could be treated more humanely.

Her pleas would result in the construction of institutions across
the United States and Europe, following a "moral treatment" philosophy that discouraged the kinds of coercion, punishment, and abuse
she had described in her reports. But alas, it was a short-lived re-
prieve. By 1870 or so, economic woes were making it especially difficult to secure funding, and conditions in the institutions deteriorated
rapidly. In addition, almost as soon as they were constructed, institutions were flooded with inmates from overflowing prisons, and severe
overcrowding became the norm.

What then happened around the turn of the twentieth century
was unprecedented. The years from around 1890 to 1950 were some

of the darkest in all of Western history for people with mental illnesses or disabilities. Before then, "eugenics," or the study of how to improve the human race by selective breeding, had never been more than a shadowy pseudoscience. But during the late 1800s and early 1900s, it garnered an enormous amount of public attention and support. Intelligence, the eugenicists insisted, was a hereditary biological attribute; its opposite, feeblemindedness, was also hereditary and therefore a menace to the human gene pool, although a controllable one. A feverish race-deterioration scare took hold of the Anglo-Saxon world. Respectable scientists on both sides of the Atlantic spoke with impunity of the impending racial disaster. Many were convinced that if they did not enforce responsible breeding, the Anglo-Saxon race would undergo an irreversible and devastating intellectual decline.

Low intelligence was understood to go hand in hand with criminality, addiction, welfare dependence, sexual license, and indiscriminate breeding. In fact, few eugenicists acknowledged any difference between what was then termed mental "deficiency" and other types of deviation from proper middle-class behavior. The eugenicists recast original sin itself as a biological defect that could be rooted out of humanity through selective breeding. The influential American psychiatrist Henry Goddard insisted in 1919 that "the chief determiner of human conduct is a unitary mental process which we call intelligence." He and many others believed wholeheartedly that if you eliminated the unintelligent, you would thereby eliminate the sinners and criminals, and human society would evolve toward a utopia of bourgeois normalcy.

Great public energy followed the science in identifying the feebleminded to prevent them from procreating. In America (though not in Britain), legislators enacted compulsory sterilization laws with barely a murmur of protest from the public. Under these laws, more than sixty thousand "unfit" individuals were sterilized against their wills between 1907 and 1970. Eugenicists also pressed for involuntary institutionalization. "By legislative reform, we may segregate the worst types of the feeble-minded, the habitual criminal, and the hopeless pauper," wrote William Cecil Dampier Whetham, a British scientist and fellow of the Royal Society, and his wife in 1909, "and thus weed out of our race the contaminating strains of worthless blood." The Whethams then humbly expressed moral squeamishness at legislating anything harsher than involuntary confinement: "Beyond that point in this direction it would be unsafe to go, till we understand much more fully the principles of the science of inheritance."

A popular 1916 film, *The Black Stork*, featured a prominent eugenicist, Harry Haiselden, who played himself in the movie. Haiselden was a leading physician who sought to educate the country about the threat of people with disabilities. In the film, he persuades a mother to refuse lifesaving surgery for her newborn with disabilities and let the baby die by explaining that the infant's disabilities would result in a life of moral depravity and crime. In an act of heroic sacrifice and scientific triumph, the mother consents, and the film chronicles the baby's slow death.

The film provoked an outpouring of letters and articles, praising its depiction of the need to remove undesirable "parasites" from society. The head of the Department of Sociology at Columbia University wrote, "The idiotic child should mercifully be allowed to die," and a New York doctor further opined, "The day of the parasite, who eats his bread without earning it, will soon pass whether he be mentally or physically incompetent or not." In 1932, the popular movie *Freaks* depicted the lives of sideshow performers, many with physical and mental disabilities, carrying this disclaimer at the beginning: "Never again will such a story be filmed, as science and teratology [the study of physiological abnormalities] are rapidly eliminating such blunders of nature from the world."

In 1927, the Supreme Court joined the national discussion. In its decision in *Buck v. Bell*, the Court upheld compulsory sterilization of people with intellectual disabilities "for the protection and health of the state." The plaintiff in the case, a teenager named Carrie Buck, had been handed off to a foster family after her mother was forcibly institutionalized with a diagnosis of "Mental Deficiency, Familial: Moron." This foster family had Carrie herself institutionalized in 1924, after she gave birth to an illegitimate child at the age of seventeen. While a resident at the Virginia State Colony for Epileptics and Feeble Minded, the girl was sentenced to forced sterilization. In an eight-to-one decision, the court upheld the forced sterilization, accusing

Carrie, her mother, and her young daughter of promiscuity and feeble-mindedness. In his ruling, Chief Justice Oliver Wendell Holmes concluded, "It is better for all the world, if instead of waiting to execute degenerate offspring for crime, or to let them starve for their imbecility, society can prevent those who are manifestly unfit from continuing their kind . . . Three generations of imbeciles are enough." After the ruling, Carrie Buck was forcibly operated on and received a tubal ligation.

Years later, she was "paroled" from the Virginia State Colony for Epileptics and Feeble Minded and lived for decades employed as a domestic worker. She was known as an avid reader. Her lawyer in the case turned out to be a board member of the Virginia State Colony, who according to some reports was barely aware of the case even as it went to the Supreme Court. Carrie's daughter, Vivian (the third-generation "imbecile"), died of measles as a child—the year after she was listed on her school's honor roll. Later research showed that Carrie Buck had probably become pregnant as a result of rape by her foster mother's nephew, and was institutionalized mainly to preserve the family's reputation. She died in 1983.

A "blunder of nature," an "imbecile," a "parasite," "enough."

Perhaps the most painful wound of this history is the fact that it assumes the people affected by it had no inner lives, no capacity to feel the pain of humiliation, to understand the vicious ridicule, to fear the horrors of their treatment. But we know that they did—that they heard and felt and lived through it all. In one way or another, these human beings understood the fate awaiting them when they lined up to be imprisoned under the pretense of care; to be shuttled from place to place as if on a gurney to a morgue while still alive. "Blunders of nature," "imbeciles," "parasites," "enough." There can be no doubt that millions of children and adults heard these exact words used to describe them, that they saw the doctors coming and going with their tool kits of horrors, that they lived lives of terror and dread. The lockdowns, the abuse, the medical experiments, the electroshock therapies, the radioactive diets, the isolation rooms—all had victims who felt, feared, and suffered.

Decades later, the Brandeis sociologist of disability Irving Zola attempted to describe the extent to which he and others with disabilities had internalized the messages of the institutional model: "The very vocabulary we use to describe ourselves is borrowed from that society. We are de-formed, dis-eased, dis-abled, dis-ordered, ab-normal, and, most telling, in-valid." Imagine a parent receiving those labels for a child, and worse, imagine a child or adult hearing those terms applied to him- or herself. People with intellectual and other disabilities who endured these labels were full human beings—that must be restated over and over again—who endured the full brunt of cruelty and evil on a scale that remains barely acknowledged. Their dehumanization was unspeakable.

Not surprisingly, the treatment of people with intellectual disabilities reached its nadir during World War II, when the Nazi final solution targeted millions of Jews for elimination, but also systematically exterminated more than two hundred thousand people with intellectual disabilities and sterilized another four hundred thousand. The Nazi horrors fall into a category of evil all its own, but it is nonetheless a sobering and shameful reminder that one part of the Nazi genocide, the sterilization program, was based on a program started in California in 1909, where the state forcibly sterilized nearly ten thousand "unfit" people by the time of the war. Remarkably, at the Nuremberg trials the Nazis defended their actions by quoting Oliver Wendell Holmes's "three generations of imbeciles are enough" decision in *Buck v. Bell*.

How do we make sense of this sad history? It would be easy to point the finger at some distant belief system. But blaming the past both ignores the enduring complexity of the persistent stigma against people with disabilities and also prevents us from examining ourselves. However modern, rational, and inclusive we may perceive ourselves to be, it should come as no surprise that a group of people who bear the marks of social vulnerability and human frailty continue to remain easy targets for exclusion by the "normal" majority. Mainstream culture prizes reason and logic, and strength and beauty, but people with intellectual disabilities remind everyone of the limits of human reason and the inherent frailty of the human body. Our culture also values economic freedom and productivity, but people with intellectual disabilities remind everyone that such ideals are narrow measures of human value. And in a world in which we strive for independence and self-sufficiency, people with disabilities remind us that we are all dependent in some way. "Disabilities" are distractions from the way we prefer to see the world—as though weakness and dependence and mortality can be escaped by any of us.

The philosopher Arne Vetlesen has written that we all try to cope with five inescapable "givens" of human existence: vulnerability, dependence, mortality, loneliness, and frail relationships. These givens are all too visible in the lives of people with intellectual disabilities, and they in turn force us to confront frailties in ourselves. Too often, this confrontation takes the form of targeting people with intellectual disabilities for removal or elimination, as if by excluding them we can exclude the weaknesses within ourselves. At the heart of the history of people with disabilities lies the stubborn human predisposition to try to escape the painful givens of life.

But escape is not a strategy for feeling or living fully alive. In fact, it makes it impossible to do so. Only by facing fears and only by seeing beneath them to the center can any of us feel fully alive. Only by facing the "dis"-abilities that we think will hurt us and discovering that they cannot hurt us can we possibly distinguish pain from suffering and, by doing so, accept the inevitability of pain but reduce the internalization of suffering. None of us can see with the eye of love if we're afraid to see ourselves, including our own, often hidden disabilities. None of us can love others openly and generously if we're afraid to love weakness and vulnerability. None of us can find a place to belong if we're scared of the place we're headed. But if we pause long enough to face the fears and the givens, we have the chance to stop running away from them and accept them for what they are: the things that make us both strong and vulnerable, and thus the things that awaken us to the desire to trust others and to live for one another, too.

It was many years before I realized how deeply my own family had been imprinted by this history. The shame and vulnerability of intellectual disability was our family secret that even those of us within the family barely understood. Ultimately, it was a secret that could not be kept.

FOUR

Rosemary

How did my mother's family deal with the sister who was inescapably vulnerable? However one chooses to interpret the conundrum of "givens" that is disability (and life), it was into that world of confusion and vulnerability that my aunt Rosemary Kennedy was born in 1918—two years after infanticide had been depicted in *The Black Stork*, nine years before Oliver Wendell Holmes's *Buck v. Bell* decision, and in the midst of the ascendance of "scientific" treatments of deviance. She was born at the height of the eugenics craze, in the same year that the state of New York created a central database of all "mentally retarded persons, to monitor their breeding and take charge of their defective offspring." She was the third child and first daughter of my grandparents, Joseph and Rose Kennedy. Over the following fourteen years, my grandparents would go on to have another six children while my grandfather would amass a fortune in business. But in those same years, both he and my grandmother would also have an experience of powerlessness and isolation far from the glamour of politics or business. They would have to make sense of the pity and fear and shame and loneliness and love and struggle that every family of a child with a disability faces. They would have to make sense of Rosemary.

Like other parents the world over, my grandparents had few places to turn to find support for Rosemary. "She was slow in everything

and some things she seemed unable to learn how to do," my grandmother wrote in her memoir. "She could not keep up." When she went
off to elementary school, IQ testing for eugenic purposes—to keep
tabs on dangerous elements in the student population—was very
much in vogue. The IQ tests were later shown to be unreliable, but
at the time they had tremendous influence on a student's standing.
Soon the teachers reported the dreaded news to Rosemary's frustrated parents: her IQ was "low." Her mother echoed the frustration
of millions of others: "They all told me that she had a low IQ, but
when I said, 'What can I do to help her?' there didn't seem to be much
of an answer. There were no classes in the public schools. There didn't
seem to be any private schools, and I was really terribly frustrated and
heartbroken."

Heartbroken.

Was she heartbroken because of the embarrassment that Rosemary would bring to the family if she proved unable to perform at
the level of success expected from the other children? Or was she
heartbroken because she didn't think others would love or welcome
Rosemary due to her obvious differences? Maybe my grandmother
thought others would never value her or see her or love her. Maybe she
was heartbroken because she thought a child with differences would
never belong.

What may have hurt most of all was the advice she would receive
once the diagnosis became clear. Expert opinion at the time said that
people such as my grandmother should give up the child with a disability in order to not compromise their other children's development.
Scholars agreed: mothers of children with disabilities spent too much
time with their child with special needs and, as a result, neglected
the needs of their other children and their husbands. The best interests of the family would be served by convincing mothers that they
needed to turn over their "retarded" children to be cared for by "professionals." Perhaps that advice was what broke my grandmother's
heart.

In one of the most meaningful decisions of their lives, my grandparents resisted that advice and kept Rosemary at home throughout
her childhood. There she stayed to be raised like the other children,

sleeping in the same house, eating the same food, hosting the same guests, and playing the same games. "My parents always told us," my mother recalled, "remember, Rosemary is your sister and you always look out for your sister. Never leave her out!" Jean and Teddy included her in tennis. Joe and Jack brought her to the dances. Eunice and Pat and Bobby sailed with her and played touch football. Each of them was responsible for making sure she wasn't left behind.

And so they included her. Rosemary lived with the same sibling rivalries and games and laughter and expectations as the other children. Her presence forever imprinted them, just as she herself was forever imprinted by their lives and adventures. All eight Kennedy children grew up with a sister who was called "mentally retarded." All eight were little children and then school-age children and then teenagers with a sister called "mentally retarded" who they needed to understand and explain to their friends and integrate and hide. All eight were confused and conflicted about their sister—they had to be. She was accepted but sometimes rejected; a part of the family but sometimes apart. She was different, and all the children had to learn what to make of difference. Had Rosemary left for an institution and lived her life away from her brothers and sisters, they would never have known the meaning of difference in quite the same way.

In the early years, Rosemary attended the same schools as her brothers and sisters, but her performance never improved. My grandparents began to seek out help in the form of experts and services, but these were scant. Finally, in 1929, when she was eleven years old and her older brother Joe was sent off to boarding school at Choate, it seemed more normal for Rosemary, too, to begin to attend a residential program. So she left home at the same time as her older brother for an experimental boarding school in Pennsylvania: the Devereux School, designed for the education of the "feebleminded." The school's founder, Helena Devereux, had briefly studied under the prominent eugenicist Henry Goddard, but fortunately she did not share his enthusiasms.

Rosemary stayed for two years at Devereux, where she took courses that had been newly adapted to meet the needs of slow children: not only reading, arithmetic, spelling, and social studies but also arts and crafts, music, and drama. She came home once or twice a year and struggled with this first separation from her family. "Dear Mother, I miss you very much," she wrote in careful block letters on November 17, 1930. "Did you ask Miss Devereux if I could go home on Thanksgiving? You said you were going to do it. Please do." And to her sister Eunice, my mother, in April: "I miss you very much. Didn't we have fun together when I was home? I was so sorry I had to leave all of you . . . I feel very upset when I don't hear from Mother. Tell her that. Write me a long long letter and make it as long as you can, darling."

Despite Rosemary's loneliness, Devereux seemed to be helping. "She has developed enough mental control to attend to a task or piece of work long enough to really accomplish worthwhile results," a teacher wrote in June 1930. At age eleven, with patient and encouraging teachers, she was successfully doing schoolwork at more or less a fourth-grade level. She struggled with math and reading, especially vocabulary, but she did "exceptionally well in dramatics," noted the teacher, where she "takes the initiative." Rosemary was a fierce child, eager to do well, to please her family and teachers and make them proud. She was also persistently insecure about her ability to do so, which sometimes hindered her learning. The teacher's remarks on that subject are telling:

> Due to the fact that her reactions are as a rule quick, she jumps to conclusions and is therefore often inaccurate, but on the other hand, she has a real desire for her work and results to come up to a high standard. Since her work often falls short of her standards for accomplishment, we feel that this may partially account for her lack of confidence in her own abilities.

Rosemary completed two years of schooling at Devereux but went no further. She returned home to live with her family but was not enrolled in any school. There, at the cusp of her teenage years, she passed her time helping with housework and caring for her younger brothers and sisters. The family strove to give her as much of a sense of normalcy as possible. In fact, they tried to hide Rosemary's condition not only from the public but from their own close friends, and even from Rosemary herself. The public stigma of having a "feebleminded" child in the age of eugenics was certainly a consideration. There would have been people in their social circles who might have whispered about "bad blood" in the family had the fact become known. But they also believed that Rosemary would be happier if kept unaware of how different she was from her siblings. "Joe and I, knowing we wanted her to be brought up and treated in the most normal way possible . . . did not indicate either within the family (except as necessary, and then casually and indirectly) or outside that there was anything extraordinary about her," my grandmother wrote.

In principle, the idea of not treating her differently even within the family was a generous impulse: a "conspiracy of kindness," my grandmother called it. (She even went so far as to begin printing all her correspondence so Rosemary wouldn't know that her inability to master cursive writing wasn't "normal.") In practice, however, the strict code of silence led Rosemary to become confused and frustrated when she could not keep up. "She resented having someone always go with her to the station when she took the train to her school. Because, she said, other girls went to the station alone. Sometimes she would run away from the person accompanying her." Rosemary had been told she was just like the others, so she didn't understand why she was not allowed to do everything they were allowed to do—why she was constantly moved from school to school. Yet the family remained convinced that the disaster of disasters would be for her to understand that she had a disability, so they averted that at all costs. For countless reasons, they wanted to keep the secret.

After being homeschooled for two years following Devereux, Rosemary briefly attended a convent school in Providence, after which she was placed with a private tutor in Brookline, near Boston. She fared poorly there and began to become bad-tempered and to put on weight. Her tutor suggested consulting an endocrinologist about a new hormone-injection therapy. The family doctor concurred with this course of treatment: "I am hopeful that a systematic treatment with endocrines will do considerable good—in fact, I will make it even stronger and say that I am very, very hopeful that within a few years, as a result of these endocrine treatments, Rosemary will be 100% all right." There it was again: the hope that Rosemary might be fixed, that she might be "all right," if only the correct therapy could be found. It's the hope countless parents hold somewhere deep within: *Something or someone will make my child all right. Somehow, she will be fixed.*

The endocrine treatments did nothing to help Rosemary's learning difficulties, though they may have improved her mood for a time. The family moved Rosemary to yet another special school, this time in New York—where she could once again learn in a group setting and where the endocrine treatments could be administered more conveniently. It was the fall of 1936. Rosemary was eighteen and still achieving at the level of a fourth-grader. In effect, she had been repeating the fourth grade over and over for seven years, and she was responding with increasing frustration. My grandmother was still trying to protect Rosemary from full knowledge of the situation, even instructing her teachers to remove worksheets from the textbooks and then cut the tops off, "that she may not know what grade work it is." But after seven years this could not have fooled her entirely.

Her tutor in New York, Amanda Rohde, was a strict teacher who wasn't prepared to handle the fits of temper Rosemary displayed when frustrated. "After I have been able to change Rosemary's attitude toward her work, and consequently toward me, I feel that much can be done to improve her education," Rohde wrote to my grandmother. "Little by little she must be brought to face reality. It will be a long seige [*sic*], but it can be done for I think I shall have your cooperation." Rohde soldiered on for a year and a half attempting to make Rosemary "face reality," but then Mollie Hourigan, the director of the boarding school where Rosemary attended classes, notified the family that the girl simply could not continue there. Rosemary required constant supervision, and Miss Hourigan had found the responsibility too great.

Despite her continuing scholastic struggles, outside of school Rosemary remained an integral part of the family. Family letters and

photo albums show her sailing to Europe with my mother in the
summer of 1936. Together they saw the sights, attended parties, and
shopped in exclusive boutiques. Rosemary enjoyed herself immensely
and wrote cheerful letters to her family back in the States. On June 11,
on a postcard bearing pictures of the stately Hotel Richemond in
Geneva: "Dear Mother and Dad, We had a lovely time on the train to
Switzerland. The Train left at 815, and we had breakfast and lunch on
the train. We go sight seeing [sic] to-morrow." On July 6, on a postcard from Paris: "Dear Bobby, The Lafayette was glorious." On July 19,
from the Hotel Excelsior München: "Dear Pat, Jean, and Bobby
also Ted. We are now in Germany having a good time. Yesterday we
went to the largest Museum and saw ships of Natural History . . ."
Her disability was not obvious to strangers, especially when there was
a language barrier, so like her sisters she received her share of attention from young men. "The boys over here are not bad," she wrote to
Kathleen on July 15. "We saw some Swiss boys. A boy from the
Lafayette was going to take me out at the Contineal [sic]. He was 24
years old." Back at home, too, she was included in most if not all of
the family's activities. Away from the stress of school, she could be
charming, sweet, and playful, especially at Cape Cod, though she still
had outbursts of temper.

I remember my mother talking years later of sailing with Rosemary and racing sailboats with her, too. "Pull in the jib, Rosemary!"
my mother would command. Often there was no response until my
mother would repeat the order louder, more emphatically: "For
God's sake, Rosie, pull in the jib!" Then Rosemary would comply.
The sisters raced together, and my mother spoke of the races and the
games of Cape Cod often. It was at Cape Cod, in these activities, that
the anxiety of Rosemary's differences would sometimes yield to an
elusive intimacy, a place where caring for her yielded to being happy
with her. Although these races were serious business in a family
that prized winning, and although Rosemary was not as strong a
sailor as her other brothers and sisters, she was a part of the team.
The message from my grandparents was clear: Rosemary is your
sister. Include her. And by including her, let the heartbreak yield to
heart. My mother and her siblings were learning to care from the
heart.

But all the same, the vise grip of anxiety and fear was tightening all around them. At times my grandparents had followed the advice of the experts who said that Rosemary's life was a distraction, that she would never keep up, that she needed to be removed from her family. While some miracle cure might come along to make her "all right," she was, in the meantime, "retarded." They sought someplace where they could send her, but at the same time, they resisted. They kept her at home when she was between schools, seeking ever-better places for her to learn, insisting that her brothers and sisters include her, doing whatever they could to help her fit. My grandmother's word rings out across the decades: "heartbroken." Like so many other mothers, she fought back the despair with her faith and her perseverance—with the resolve to help her daughter, to be relentless in defending her against the threats around her, to do whatever was humanly possible to help her be successful and happy. But with Rosemary now entering young adulthood, there was no clear place for her to go outside the home, and her future seemed all the more confused. In her darker moods she was difficult, stubborn, and comfortable only in the easiest tasks. The emotional roller coaster her parents and siblings had been experiencing would only intensify.

In 1938, my grandfather was named ambassador to Great Britain, so his large and boisterous Irish family—Rosemary included— set sail for London. There, to everyone's surprise and great relief, Rosemary thrived. She was allowed to make her debut in London society, was presented before the king and queen at Buckingham Palace, and attended the most fashionable parties. It was a dazzling life; *she* felt dazzling and adored rather than slow and lonely, and she loved every minute of it. She began attending a school for Montessori teachers at the Convent of the Assumption in Kensington Square, where she flourished under the guidance of Mother Isabel. Taking care of very young children was a task in which Rosemary felt confident and capable. She read simple books to the children in her care, prepared their lunch, and helped monitor their recess, in addition to "many other occupations of a domestic kind which she is able to do <u>alone</u>." Mother Isabel wrote that Rosemary was "very well & obviously happy," and her father reported the same in his letters of the time, with a buoyant warmth and hopefulness that does not occur anywhere else in the family's correspondence about Rosemary. "It really makes me very happy to see the great improvement she has shown," he wrote to Rosemary's attendant, Miss Gibbs, in April 1940. "I can never thank you and Mother Isabel enough for all you have done."

Rosemary might have remained in England indefinitely had history not intervened. When World War II broke out, London was no longer a refuge. Joseph Kennedy had already sent most of his family back to the United States, but Rosemary was doing so well at the Montessori school, and she had suffered so many upheavals already in her life, that she was the only one of her siblings allowed to stay. With war encroaching, her school was evacuated to the countryside, where she continued her Montessori studies while enjoying her new place at the center of her father's attention—a place she had never occupied when her brothers and sisters were around.

As the intensity of the war increased, though, her father at last decided it was no longer safe for her to remain in Europe. Reluctantly, he sent her back to the United States with family friends in May 1940. The flight itself was harrowing, with inclement weather forcing an emergency landing in Bermuda. When Rosemary finally made it home, she found it was no longer the haven she remembered. Even her younger sister Kathleen had found her old home surprisingly shabby in comparison with the sparkling life of London and had difficulty adjusting. Rosemary, who had made her debut in London society right alongside Kathleen, was coming back to a considerably more limited and frustrating existence. Her siblings were growing up and beginning their lives out in the world, but nobody seemed to know where *she* belonged. The family, occupied with wartime concerns, had no time to search for elaborate solutions. She got a job as a summer camp counselor, but she was unable to cope with the work. Everyone hoped that the war would end and she would soon be able to return to London. Rosemary herself wrote to my grandfather on June 4: "I am sorry I did not talk to you on Sunday. But I felt a bit lonesome for you. But thanks for all the good-times in England. But I will be glad to get back to you when the war is over." And he wrote to a nun at Rosemary's school in England: "I appreciate more than I can say all that you and Mother Isabel have done. You won Rosemary's heart and she is tremendously fond of you both. I, too, pray for peace and hope that, with the end of the war, Rosemary may soon return to be with you."

In the meantime, my grandfather found a school for her in Washington, DC: St. Gertrude's School of Arts and Crafts. The nuns at St. Gertrude's did their best, but the school was a terrible fit for Rosemary, and compared with her situation in England it must have felt like a prison. The school normally took students only up to high school age, but she was already a woman in her twenties. She had no reasonable occupation there, no social life, and no companions her own age. The possibility of returning to Mother Isabel's became increasingly remote as the war dragged on. The glittering parties at Buckingham Palace had faded to a distant dream, and Rosemary did not fully understand why. Fierce and impatient when frustrated, she began to act out again. She repeatedly ran away from the school in the middle of the night. She was often angry and sometimes violent. "She was upset easily and unpredictably," wrote my grandmother in her memoir. "Some of these upsets became tantrums, or rages, during which she broke things or hit out at people. Since she was quite strong, her blows were hard. Also, there were convulsive episodes." The nuns at St. Gertrude's were frantic.

At the time, yet another new possibility for "fixing" Rosemary was gaining adherents: the lobotomy. Developed by the Portuguese psychiatrist António Egas Moniz in the 1930s, the procedure was popularized in the United States by the psychiatrist Walter Freeman and his colleague the neurosurgeon James Watts. Freeman and Watts advertised the lobotomy as a miracle cure for crippling mood disorders, especially severe anxiety and depression. Even during its heyday as a treatment for these conditions, though, it was never indicated for people with intellectual disabilities. My grandfather must have emphasized Rosemary's rages, tantrums, and rebellious wanderings when he consulted with Dr. Freeman. To the end of her life, my grandmother would maintain that this assessment was correct: "Manifestly there were other factors at work besides mental retardation. A neurological disturbance or disease of some sort seemingly had overtaken her, and it was becoming progressively worse." My grandfather, fatefully, chose

to listen to the advice of experts. He went ahead and scheduled a lobotomy for Rosemary—without telling my grandmother or any of
his other children.

The procedure itself was chilling. The surgeons drilled holes in
either side of a patient's skull, through which they inserted an instru-
ment shaped like a butter knife. They then swung the knife up and
down, severing the frontal lobe's connection to the rest of the brain.
A substantial part of deciding where to cut was guesswork. Patients
were kept mostly conscious during the operation, so the surgeons
could gauge how deeply to cut based on the patient's ability to answer
questions. When a patient's responses became disoriented and inco-
herent, they normally stopped cutting. Despite the enthusiastic attention the procedure had received in the press, their results had been
variable at best. Some patients' brains successfully rewired themselves
and they regained their coherence during the recovery period; others
had lasting deficits. Most of them suffered profound and permanent
personality changes. A later, more "advanced" form of the surgery would
involve accessing the brain tissue by inserting an ice pick through the
eye socket. Patients were also conscious during that version of the
procedure. Dr. Freeman's son remembers that the instruments his
father often used for the operation were stored in the family icebox.
Some forty thousand people would undergo a lobotomy in the United
States between 1936 and 1960, when the practice all but ended.
António Egas Moniz was awarded the Nobel Prize for Medicine in
1949 for pioneering the procedure.

My aunt Rosemary Kennedy underwent this operation in 1941 at
George Washington University Hospital in Washington, DC. Following the standard procedure, her surgeons—possibly Freeman and
Watts themselves—inserted their instruments into her brain while
she remained conscious. The outcome, in Rosemary's case, was devastating. If Rosemary's disabilities had indeed been the result of hy-
poxic brain injury during birth, then lobotomy, which fundamentally
consisted of more brain damage, could only compound the problem.
So it happened. After a few weeks, it became apparent that she had
been robbed of her speech and of significant cognitive capacity. She
became severely limited in her ability to process and recall infor-

mation. Her mobility was damaged. She lost her independence for the rest of her life.

Without warning or explanation, she disappeared from the lives of her brothers and sisters. She would never live at home again. My grandfather found a safe and comfortable Catholic institution in Wisconsin, St. Coletta's, where he placed his eldest daughter in long-term care. Stoic but shattered by the results of his decision, he would never visit her there or—as far as I can tell—ever see her again for the rest of his life. For years, her siblings did not even know what had happened to her. Members of her family were in the midst of such a flurry of activity at that time that they apparently never questioned one sister's absence until much later. The code of secrecy kicked in and Rosemary disappeared without a word from anyone. My grandmother found it almost unbearably painful to write about the ordeal even decades later: "Rosemary's was the first of the tragedies that were to befall us. In writing as I have, I have felt grief and pain hardly lessened despite the years."

I knew Rosemary only after her operation. She spoke only a few words—"baby," "Eunice," "something to eat," "Teddy." She smiled occasionally, walked tentatively, and could catch a soft foam ball. Her long-serving companion at the convent in Wisconsin, Sister Margaret Ann, loved being with her and told me that Rosemary's affection had changed her life. "I suppose I never felt worthy of anyone's love before," she said when we were together shortly after Rosemary died, "but Rosemary changed that. Some people tell me that she doesn't understand things, but I think she understands me. I loved her very much." Sister Margaret Ann's letters to my mother during Rosemary's life support the depth of their relationship. "Rosemary," she wrote, could be at times "very talkative" in her own way—"I love seeing her that way," Sister Margaret Ann wrote in 1988. One summer, they took a trip to a Norbertine abbey near Green Bay; "at one point even Rosemary said 'Ohooo, beautiful'" of the scenery. In 1997, she wrote: "Rosie is finding walking more difficult but she always still has that pleasing, lovely smile yet. Loves seeing people stop by to say 'hi.' Rosemary is a people person." When the small cottage where Rosemary had lived most of her life was being remodeled in 1999, Sister Ann wrote that she was perturbed and kept remarking: "What's going on here any-how?" She expressed opinions on her meals—"No diet food!"—and whether she might like to travel. But whether she had any inkling of how much her life had changed from what it might have been had a series of fateful decisions not been made in the 1940s, we will never know. She lived to the age of eighty-six and died peacefully at St. Coletta's in Wisconsin, where she had been cared for and loved for six decades.

The ultimate effect of Rosemary's life on those of her parents and siblings remains a mystery. As I reflect on the painful history of how society treated people with intellectual disabilities and their families, it seems that Rosemary's life was not unlike many others. She was born to a family who tried to raise her well. Her parents struggled to help her, to cure her, and to protect her in a society that had no place for people like her. Her siblings did the same. They had many moments of joy, happiness, and love. But despite their intentions and in part because of them, she suffered terribly.

Years after her childhood, when I was in my forties, I began to wonder more and more about the impact Rosemary had on her parents and siblings. By that time, hundreds of books had been written about my family, but almost no one had written about Rosemary or her role in their lives. Rarely was she treated as anything more than a sad footnote in an otherwise dynamic and controversial family epic. I wondered whether she'd played a more powerful role. Unlike almost any other group of historical figures in America, my mother's family had become distinguished by precisely that label: "family." Even after President Kennedy's singular success in politics and global leadership, he was often referred to as a "member" of the Kennedy "family." Rosemary was a member, too, but one who seemed to have played little or no part in the great achievements of the family. I wondered: Was that the whole story?

For my entire life, people have been coming up to me and my siblings and cousins to tell us what a unique brand of leadership the "Kennedy family" has brought to the world. I always couldn't help but wonder what distinguished my parents' generation from countless other charismatic leaders and passionate catalysts for change. Why had their brand of politics had such a profound impact on people around the world? What accounted for their ability to inspire so many people to join in campaigns for justice, equality, and human dignity? Was it some aspect of their personality? Was it their religion? Was it the era in which they were raised—an era dominated by massive struggles against economic depression, against fascism, against racism, against communism? Or was it something—or someone—else? What was their secret?

I knew that my mother had loved Rosemary, as any sister would. There could hardly be a doubt about siblings loving one another in my mother's family. There were nine of them, and, like most children from huge families, they raised and depended on one another. Children from large families learn one of life's important lessons early: you can count on your parents for only so much. For the rest, you'd better hope your brother or sister is around. So my mother was surely crushed to see her sister struggle so in childhood, crushed to see her own mother distraught and lonely as she endured the repeated rejection of her child.

My mother spoke rarely but with a controlled ferocity about her childhood with Rosemary. Even in her eighties, she still remembered the frustration. "When we were young, there was nothing for Rosie," she would mutter. "I can remember my mother picking up the phone and calling and calling—one person after another. She called schools, doctors, anyone she thought might help. And everyone told her there was nothing for Rosemary. Nothing." Her voice would trail off. "Nothing . . ."

The stories would spring up from time to time like the memories of war that soldiers hide as best they can, only to have them explode into consciousness with unforgiving vividness. "Sometimes, we would all be at dinner and Dad would ask us each questions about the events of the day and I would see Rosie sitting there knowing she wouldn't be able to answer like the rest of us. And . . ." Her voice would trail off again; her shoulders would drop; her head would shift almost imperceptibly from side to side in resignation. Rosie couldn't keep up, didn't fit in.

Pascal wrote that "the heart has its reasons that reason doesn't
know." I've often thought of my mother in the context of that expression. She had reasons—a kind of knowledge born not of information
or study but of the experience of loving Rosemary. Perhaps not surprisingly, my mother came to loathe "experts," disdain "analysts,"
avoid bureaucrats—all people who stake their claim to value on the
power of thought, the triumph of science, the routines of efficiency.
She trusted none of that, and for good reason: most of those "experts"
were part of the system that had devalued her sister. She trusted more
in the knowledge of the heart, in the love born of faith. Do you care?
Do you see the goodness that lies within? Will you trust the elusive intimacy that comes from learning to see another person—any person—
from the inside out, beneath the superficial distractions of labels
and assumptions? Rosemary's disability may have interfered with the
family culture of competing to be valued, but it opened that same family to the idea that value is not earned, only given and accepted.

Just once did I ask my mother and my uncle Ted directly about
Rosemary's influence. Only a few years before they died, the topic was
still rarely mentioned, even within the family, but if I were ever going to understand, I had to ask these two people who had grown up
with Rosemary about the effect she'd had on her parents and siblings
during their childhoods. As we sat at my parents' home in Maryland
for a typical Sunday-night dinner, I mustered the courage to broach
the subject. "Have either of you ever thought about Rosemary's role
in shaping you as people?" I asked. "Not in shaping your commitment to disability policy or programs, I mean, but in shaping your
emotional life and your identities. You have such a distinctive style
of leadership, such a remarkable concern for the vulnerable, for the
importance of service. Do you think it's possible that an important
source of all that might have been Rosemary?"

My uncle Ted gave me one of his long, pensive looks. As was often the case, I couldn't tell whether he was thinking that I had asked
a ridiculous question that he was going to ignore, or whether he was
deep in thought, or whether he was even paying attention. After what
seemed like an interminable pause, he finally spoke up. "I remember
when we were young in Palm Beach, we would go to big parties with

all the young people. And I remember one time I was at one of those parties during the daytime and it was outside—I can't remember if you were there, Eunie," he said with a laugh, looking at my mother. She shook her head at him and rolled her eyes playfully. "But Jack was there and of course Mother and Dad made sure that we took Rosemary with us. And I remember looking up at one point in the party, and I saw that Rosemary was off by herself, sitting at one end of the swimming pool. She was all alone."

There was a long silence. I didn't know if he was going to continue the story, but then he drew in a big breath and went on. "I saw Jack leave the people he was talking to and slip away from all of us and walk over to Rosemary. He just sat down with her—just the two of them at the other end of the pool together. I remember that just like it was yesterday, Jack and Rosemary sitting alone but together while the party went on." He said nothing more. The conversation shifted and was done.

I never asked either him or my mother about it again—where that party had taken place, or when. But I know that in the years that followed that party, loss would devastate my mother and uncle's family. In 1941, Rosemary had her surgery and then disappeared. Three years after that disaster, a lone black military car arrived at my grandparents' home and the officer asked to speak privately to my grandfather. Moments later, my grandfather emerged and announced to his children the news: "Your brother Joe is dead." He had been killed at the age of twenty-nine on a secret mission in World War II. Just a few months later, Jack narrowly escaped death in the Pacific. And in 1948, my mother's sister Kathleen Kennedy Hartington— herself already a widow whose husband had been killed in combat just three months after their wedding in 1944—died in a plane crash in France. In the span of seven short years, my mother's family was battered again and again by loss.

But twenty years after Rosemary's lobotomy, the same brother who had sat with her alone at the pool was sworn in as the thirty-fifth president of the United States. He, too, would be lost in the blink of an eye. But his call to serve the nation, his drive to heal the wounds of the forgotten around the world, his hunger for peace, and his resolute conviction that freedom was the destiny of every human being—all that still echoes today, and all that was embodied by his surviving brothers and sisters for decades longer. Not surprisingly, those values that stirred the world also fueled his administration's commitment to become the first in history to place intellectual disability on the public policy agenda.

I will never know the date or the location of the party Teddy remembered, but the moment I heard his story, I could tell it was a powerful clue. Whatever shame he and his siblings might have felt about Rosemary when they were growing up had found its counter in an empathy that took root deep in their souls, an empathy not learned in school or politics but triggered by countless moments when their sister was alone and the only response that made sense was to sit by her side. They were asked over and over again to look out for their sister, but in being asked to give, they had received something, too: hundreds of moments when they were alone with her, sitting with someone they loved, by the pool, legs dangling in the water together, saying nothing. At some level, they must have known how wonderful it was to be with her. At some level, they must have realized that in their sister Rosemary, they had received something far greater than they had ever been asked to give: a person whose love they didn't have to earn. With Rosemary, they needed only to give love in order to receive it back.

Today, I believe that Rosemary was a major source of the political genius that my uncles brought to public life, an energy that would change the course of a nation. "Ask not" wasn't borrowed from Roosevelt or Churchill or Lincoln or Jefferson. It did not spring solely from President Kennedy's service in the navy or the lessons he learned at Harvard. I will never be able to prove it, but I think it also sprang from the family and the faith that taught him to give himself to Rosemary and the unspoken happiness that he received from her in return. I believe it was from caring for her that they all gained the confidence to believe that they could ask others to give, knowing the joys of giving. I believe it was from playing with her that they learned the meaning of the faith in which they were raised—of being a part of something bigger and more mysterious than any book can teach.

I believe it was from feeling her frustration and loneliness that they felt the terrifying fear of being left out and from her that they learned to fight it. I believe it was from loving her that they learned to believe that peoples and nations could cross boundaries of fear and intolerance to join together in peace and friendship. I believe it was from her that they learned to believe that everyone has a gift. I believe it was from her that they learned to care from within.

That is a hunch, an intuition. What I know for sure, though, is that the unique combination of love and loyalty and anger and empathy that Rosemary inspired in her family would also give rise to a global movement. That movement would attempt to fulfill the high expectations that St. Luke demanded of believers and the promise of service that "ask not" had awakened in millions. It would attempt to satisfy the thirst for belonging that Rosemary had taught her family and to re-create the delight that they had experienced sailing the waters of Cape Cod with her.

The accomplishment of all this, however, would require one more step from my mother. It could happen only if the family secret was broken. And so it would have to be.

FIVE

The Greatest Effort

All families are alike in one way: they have secrets.

In 1941, Rosemary Kennedy became a family secret. After the war ended in 1945, her siblings began to pursue their various lives and careers while a peculiar silence enveloped her whereabouts. "We didn't know where she was," recalled her sister Jean Smith. "I was told that she had moved to the Midwest and had become a teacher—or maybe a teacher's assistant. That was the way things were going then. We all just kept moving."

And move they did. Twenty-nine-year-old John Kennedy, the war hero and Purple Heart recipient, returned from the Pacific theater and entered politics, running for Congress in the 11th district of Massachusetts in 1946. The campaign marshaled the full energy of both his parents and all his siblings, except Rosemary. His sisters Eunice, Pat, and Jean campaigned vigorously across the district, holding "teas" to introduce their brother to the voters. His mother, a "gold star mother," spoke over and over again of her son's heroism, using the political voice she'd honed from childhood as the daughter of the mayor of Boston. His brothers Bobby and Ted were close advisors. He won in 1946 and was reelected in '48 and '50. Then he ran for the Senate in 1952, against the establishment candidate Henry Cabot Lodge, who by all accounts should have prevailed due to his age, experience, and prestige. The upstart, however, surged to victory. John

Kennedy entered the Senate in 1953, full of potential and charm and the glow of a winner.

Meanwhile, my mother graduated from Stanford in 1943 and shortly thereafter headed to Washington, DC, where she moved into a Georgetown house to live with her congressman brother. The two were enormously close—peculiarly close, some would say. "Jack" was not only her brother but also her best friend. Years later, my aunt Jackie would often smile when talking about the two of them. "Your mother and Jack loved each other sooooo much," she said in her inimitable, lilting voice. "I mean, no one could separate them." My mother once challenged Jackie to a wrestling match in their brown-stone kitchen, throwing the unsuspecting girlfriend to the kitchen floor in a matter of seconds. To say that Jackie was surprised at being pinned to the ground by her boyfriend's sister would be an under-statement. "I never saw a brother and sister like those two, but I also never knew a woman like your mother," Jackie would say. "That was my first and last wrestling match. Thank goodness."

While he was in Congress, my mother started her career in the Department of Justice as part of a task force on juvenile delinquency. Her work was focused on getting programs in place to keep at-risk kids from falling through the cracks. She busied herself with the problem in what would become a lifelong pattern—working on it not just at the office but at home, too. She wrote to her father to ask for his help in placing adjudicated kids in jobs. She invited "delinquents" to her home to meet her brother, the congressman. Enthusiastic and idealistic, she wanted the young people who were struggling to see possibility, to have dinner, to become hopeful that with friendship and advice, they could live safe and productive lives. If it was possible to make the world a better place by sheer force of will, she was deter-mined to try.

But something else happened during those years that would soon take her away from Washington for almost a decade: she met my father, Sargent Shriver. In 1946, my dad was a Yale Law School graduate and, like John Kennedy, a recently returned navy combat veteran. My grandfather hired him to assist with managing an enor-mous new real estate investment, Chicago's Merchandise Mart. When it was built, the gargantuan art deco office building was the largest building in the world, spanning two city blocks, rising twenty-five stories, and boasting 4.2 million square feet of interior space. My dad always spoke of his pride at being hired by "Mr. Kennedy" for such a responsibility. He moved right away to Chicago, where he joined the management team that my grandfather was assembling to turn the distressed monstrosity into a profitable asset.

By all accounts, my father loved his new boss and the affection was returned. My dad was smart, handsome, bubbling over with earnest enthusiasm, and eager to be an impact player. He'd gone to college on a scholarship, played baseball for Yale, become the editor in chief of the *Yale Daily News*, graduated from the country's most prestigious law school, and been discharged as a lieutenant from the navy after serving in the submarine force and on the battleship USS *South Dakota*. He saw extensive combat at the Battles of Santa Cruz and Guadalcanal. Upon returning to civilian life, he'd been hired at *Newsweek* magazine as an assistant editor before he was spotted by my grandfather.

"Sarge," my grandfather had told him, "get yourself out to Chicago and find out what's going on."

"What exactly do you want me to do, Mr. Kennedy?" my father replied.

"Get into everything and give me a report on what it's going to take to make the place a success. Just get yourself out there and figure it out."

My dad moved to Chicago and loved it. And apparently, he impressed my grandfather enough to earn himself a new assignment. In 1947, my grandfather asked my father to move back to the East Coast, this time to Washington, DC.

"I'd like you to go to Washington, Sarge, to join my daughter Eunice in an important effort. She's working on juvenile delinquency and I'd like you to help her study the problem and find the right solutions."

My dad, ever the enthusiast for anything new and important, didn't pause. "Okay, Mr. Kennedy. If that's what you want me to do, I'll do it."

Within days of arriving at the Department of Justice to ass. Eunice Kennedy, my dad was immersed in the problems of disengaged teenagers and equally immersed in the challenge of courting his new boss. "I used to tell your mother that I would do anything she asked me to do, but only if she gave me a kiss." Whenever my father would relate his version of their first working relationship, my mother would roll her eyes and protest, "Sargent. Now, that's not true. Don't tell the children that." He continued undeterred. "One time, I refused to work until she gave me a kiss. She rejected me of course, so I chased her around her desk until finally she stopped and closed her eyes and stuck out her cheek and let me kiss her. And you know your mother: the next thing she did was say, 'Now for goodness' sakes, let's get back to work!' I just loved chasing her and was always hoping for action!"

Over the next six years, the two of them worked together, dated, and finally married in 1953 in a New York wedding to which my grandparents invited almost two thousand guests. My dad used to joke that he knew almost no one at his own wedding but had the time of his life. My mother remembered being introduced to hundreds of people whom she'd never met before and laughing all night long. They took their vows at the great altar of St. Patrick's Cathedral and danced for hours and hours at the Waldorf Astoria Hotel. They were surrounded by family on all sides—Kennedys, Fitzgeralds, and Shrivers. Only one close relative was missing from the gala: Rosemary.

When my parents returned from their honeymoon, they settled in Chicago and my dad returned to work at the Merchandise Mart, while my mother embarked on a new project my grandfather had asked her to lead: the Joseph P. Kennedy, Jr. Foundation. The foundation had been established in 1946 as a memorial for my mother's eldest brother, Joe, whose death had crushed his father and mother, a loss from which some suggest they never recovered. Decades later, my siblings and cousins and I would still hear the stories of Joe and how he had been the brother most likely to succeed. "Joe was so handsome," my mother would always remind us, "and he always did whatever Mother told him, so now why don't you be like Joe and do what I'm asking you to do?" My grandmother, too, would interrupt conversations over and over again to tell us how devout Joe had been: "You know, he would always come with me to mass, and on New Year's Eve one year, he left the biggest party in Palm Beach to go to serve mass at St. Edward's and then came back without any fuss later that same night. Jack and all the boys were so impressed by Joe, and that's why I always tell you children that the example of the oldest is so important. Joe set the example for Jack and the others." Her voice would often fade off as she described Joe and his larger-than-life gifts. But equally as often, a smile would creep onto her face when she'd remember his next brother. "Jack, of course, was always laughing and not as serious as Joe. You know, your grandfather always insisted that all the children be on time for meals, but if Jack was late, he'd just slip into the kitchen and smile at the cook and have a beautiful dinner in the back and never think a thing of it. Joe would never do that . . ."

In the wake of Joe's death in World War II, my grandparents created the Joseph P. Kennedy, Jr. Foundation without any clear focus for its work. Before long, it would become devoted to the problem of intellectual disability, but for all intents and purposes, it backed into its mission. My mother later recalled:

> In 1948, my father had given a few grants to Cardinal Cushing and Cardinal Spellman—the former to set up a hospital for cerebral palsy children, and the latter to set up some school for mentally retarded children and to name them after my brother, Joe, who had been killed in the war. He had no specific [purpose in mind] at the time, but my father was anxious to commemorate something to my brother Joe. He asked Sarge and myself to take steps to find out what the great needs in the youth fields were.

That request, to "find out what the great needs" were, came in 1958. By then, most of the foundation's work did center on intellectual disability, but my mother had been complaining behind the scenes that my grandfather was going about it all wrong. If the foundation was going to help people with intellectual disabilities, it shouldn't turn for advice to mental health professionals with no prior experience in the field. Psychiatrists knew about mental illness, not mental retardation. "You think you can do a better job getting the money to the programs that will make a difference?" said my grandfather. "Well, then do it."

So she and my father visited universities, special schools, and hospitals all around the country, met with the top researchers in the field, and came home with recommendations by the bushel. What they found in their travels was, in retrospect, predictable: hardly anyone had done any systematic research in the field of intellectual disability. Not even the basic financial problems involved in warehousing tens of thousands of people in institutions—the cost would be estimated at well over a billion dollars a year by 1970—had motivated scientists to study intellectual disability. The issue languished in a strange limbo between a medical problem and a social problem, with neither doctors nor social scientists doing much about it. My parents discovered that "there were literally [only] a handful of doctors interested in the field. Practically no medical schools. No foundations at all." Before 1960, "the federal presence in intellectual disability was . . . so modest that a grant of $1.25 million from the Kennedy Foundation in 1952 to establish a private school in Illinois exceeded the entire federal services budget for intellectual disability at the time." That, they felt strongly, was where the Kennedy Foundation could have a real and lasting impact.

My grandfather handed the reins of the foundation to my parents. From then on, when friends wrote him asking for money, he declined, making it clear that the foundation would henceforth be singular in its focus. Gone were the grants to causes of political allies, and to the Catholic Church's needs in greater Boston; gone, too, were the occasional gifts to schools. For the first time in more than a decade, my grandfather began to mention Rosemary in his correspondence. "The solution of Rosemary's problem," he wrote in 1958 to Sister Anastasia, a nun at St. Coletta's in Wisconsin where Rosemary still resided, "has been a major factor in the ability of all the Kennedys to go about their life's work." The secret of Rosemary had been well kept, but it must never have been far from the mind of the father who had raised her with such love and yet unintentionally sentenced her to such isolation. The Kennedy Foundation would become his way of fulfilling his devotion to her and, perhaps, of alleviating the pain he must have carried. In the first four years that my parents oversaw the direction of the foundation, it donated more than $17 million to a variety of universities, religious organizations, and caregivers who had only one thing in common: an interest in the treatment and care of people with intellectual disabilities.

During those same years, the other family business, politics, remained center stage. Senator John Kennedy was quietly preparing to seize opportunities for national office, and of course, his political career was the much more prominent Kennedy family work.

During his time in Congress, John Kennedy showed little interest in advocating for people with intellectual disabilities—perhaps to keep the family secret, or perhaps because it seemed so unlikely that the government would do anything to help such people. Elizabeth Boggs, a legendary advocate at the time, had hoped for more. A mathematician and chemist with a doctorate from Cambridge, she had begun advocating for people with disabilities after struggling to find any help for her own son who had severe disabilities, David. She'd heard about the sister the Kennedys never talked about and had assumed that the experience of growing up with Rosemary would make Senator John Kennedy a strong ally. But in 1957, as Boggs struggled to win attention for a neglected piece of legislation—it would have expanded support for special-ed teacher training—Senator Kennedy seemed uninterested. At one point in a subcommittee hearing on the topic, the senator left early and never returned or expressed support. Boggs had been hoping to capitalize on his private understanding of the need, but instead felt ignored.

The bill eventually did become law, but a decade later, Boggs recalled her disappointment:

> I have to say that this was an incident that was associated in my mind with some resentment because I felt that even if they [the Kennedys] did not wish to admit publicly that this was a problem in their family, the least that the Senator could have done would have been to attend to the [committee] business as any other sympathetic senator might have done . . .

I couldn't help feeling that he was leaving to others a task which he could have very well lent his support to at that time.

Would things change when John Kennedy was elected president in 1960 and his historic inaugural address challenged the nation to service? Boggs and other activists didn't see any reason to expect much help.

At the time of the election, Boggs's grassroots organization was called the National Association for Retarded Children—today it's the Arc. The group's members were mostly the parents of children with intellectual challenges. They had all experienced the same anguish Joe and Rose Kennedy had in the face of medical pressure to institutionalize their children; the same frustration at the lack of community resources; the same isolation and shame. They had banded together to stand up for themselves. *Our children can be helped*, they insisted. *They are not hopeless.* The secretary of the organization, Woodhull Hay, wrote that what these parents held in common was a commitment to challenge "the validity of the finality implicit in the words: 'Nothing can be done for your child.'" Over time the members of the Arc had gotten used to fighting tooth and nail for every legislative victory they gained. What they expected from a Kennedy administration was the same thing they had gotten from previous administrations: nothing. It was "a non-expectation," Boggs would later recall.

What Boggs didn't know, however, was that my mother's research and work in leading the Kennedy Foundation had rendered her increasingly frustrated and zealous, too. I can only imagine the anger in her face when she met doctors who were still recommending institutionalization, or her bottled outrage upon encountering hospitals whose protocols allowed for children born with intellectual disabilities to starve to death rather than receive care.

Years later, she described her research with words that barely contained her rage: "I have seen sights that will haunt me all my life. If I had not seen them myself, I would never have believed that such conditions could exist in modern America . . . adults and children . . . in barrack-like wards, their unwashed clothes and blankets in rags."

With the election of President Kennedy, he and his siblings had their chance to make a difference on the world stage, and Rosemary's influence would finally break through. She had been the teacher who'd first taught the lesson that everyone has a gift. She had been the person who'd first taught the lesson that value isn't determined by social or political or intellectual rank. In retrospect, I can see her influence in the president's campaign call to ask young people to serve the cause of peace around the world in what would become the Peace Corps. And I can see her influence in his inaugural address, when caring, serving, and peace moved to the center of his politics. And I am sure that my mother was imbued with that same influence as she, too, decided that the time had come to press for a breakthrough in the field of intellectual disability.

Within weeks of the inauguration, she began to work the levers of government. Whether out of respect or out of dread, the staff surrounding the president tended to give my mother what she needed, and the president knew her well enough to want to accommodate her agenda as well. Right at the outset, he asked one of his most politically effective advisors, Myer "Mike" Feldman, to be my mother's point of contact within the administration. Feldman was assigned to smooth over diplomatic wrinkles between her and other White House staff who sometimes chafed at her influence. He was also tasked with making sure things got done. No one had better access to the president, and no one had a more razor-sharp sense of how to deliver on Capitol Hill, than Feldman. He and my mother became a team.

My mother began by assessing the federal government's capacity to change the quality of life for people with intellectual disabilities. Various offices of the federal government had perceived themselves to be responsible for action in the field, but from my mother's point of view, none had done enough. The National Institutes of Health might have been expected to lead the charge, but the few projects they'd undertaken were housed in the National Institute of Mental Health and had almost no relevance to the needs of individuals and families. When the head of pediatrics at Johns Hopkins University, Dr. Robert Cooke, joined my mother to lobby the NIH for more attention to the needs of children, the organization's leader, Dr. James Shannon, pushed back with a memorable dust-off. Cooke had proposed the idea of a new center dedicated to research in child development; Shannon responded that there was no need for such an institute at NIH. After all, he smirked: "There aren't any major problems in children." Shannon's perspective, as shocking as it seems today, was probably the norm at the time. No agency of government was focused on child development, and certainly none focused on the challenges of development for atypical children.

Cooke joined my mother as a "scientific advisor" to the Kennedy Foundation, and together with my dad, they began to explore how to fight. Perhaps because there were so many complex social problems involved, my mother spurned efforts to focus on a single solution. The multifaceted problem needed a multifaceted response. The team searched for historical models and found one in the "Hoover Commission." Years earlier, in 1947, President Truman had appointed Herbert Hoover to chair a Commission on the Organization of the Executive Branch of the Government, a panel of experts whose mandate was to recommend administrative changes in the federal government of the United States. The Hoover Commission included distinguished leaders from Capitol Hill, from the executive branch, and from the business world. Among them was my grandfather Joseph P. Kennedy. Over the course of two years, the commission developed more than a hundred recommendations, the majority of which were adopted and put into action. On my grandfather's advice, my mother and Dr. Cooke held a meeting with former president Hoover, at which they explored whether the idea of a new commission focused on intellectual disability made sense. Hoover was encouraging enough, and my mother brought the idea to the president, who responded decisively. "Call Mike Feldman," he told his sister, "and let's get a meeting set for next week at the White House."

On October 11, 1961, President Kennedy officially announced the creation of the historic President's Panel on Mental Retardation. With his blessing, my parents, Dr. Cooke, and Feldman went to work behind the scenes, making key decisions—who would be on the panel, who would lead it, how long it would have to complete its report, which legislators could be counted on for support, and more. Leonard Mayo, a longtime advocate for children and a consensus builder by character, was selected to lead the panel. The first call he received was from Feldman. "Anything that is in the power of the U.S. Government to give you, you can have." He was joined by parent activists, medical leaders, and social scientists from across the nation. A week after the announcement, on October 17, the panel convened for its first meeting in the White House Fish Room. There was a lot of ceremony that first day. After just half a day of talks, they went out to the Rose Garden, where Leonard Mayo was asked to "summarize the morning's work" before television and radio crews. President Kennedy then addressed the members of the panel:

> This is a matter which I think should be brought out into the sunlight and given a full national commitment, and I want to express my thanks to all the members of this Panel who have been willing to serve, because I think that we can make easier the lives of many, many thousands of people and their families. It is high time that the country gives its time and attention to this.

Later, Mayo spoke briefly to the president in private, probing the source of his interest in the topic. "It's interesting to [the members of the panel]," he recalled saying to the president, "that whereas Mr. Eisenhower became very much interested in heart and cancer and did a lot for those areas, and of course before him President Franklin Roosevelt was deeply interested in polio, you apparently are thinking that mental retardation can be your contribution to the fields of education and health and social welfare." The president answered emphatically: "Exactly, exactly." Perhaps he had not shown interest in the topic while in the Senate, but with the power of the presidency, John Kennedy was searching for ways to bring the story "out into the sunlight." What was hidden was working its way to the surface.

In the weeks and months that followed, my mother was dogged. She called Mayo regularly and kept his nose "to the grindstone." She checked in with Feldman almost daily and pressed the members of the panel to work more quickly, more comprehensively, more ambitiously. Science, as Mayo later recalled, was practiced over months and years, and the panel's members were sometimes frustrated at being asked to pull it all together in days and weeks. The Hoover Commission had worked fast and delivered a report in twenty-four months. This President's Panel was going to have to do the same work but in half the time. The president himself told Mayo that he wanted recommendations in time for "the Congress when it meets at the beginning of '63." Mayo promised a finished job within a year and immediately set out to get the best recommendations that science, policy, and social services leaders could muster.

As the work moved forward, Mayo felt strongly about bringing in groups of experts from around the country to contribute their own experiences to the committee's efforts. He wanted everyone who'd been working tirelessly with so little support to feel that they'd been consulted and their opinions heard. He was able to convince my mother how important this was, and once she had agreed, she "went for it a hundred per cent." One day, a group of fifty people came to Washington to make reports to the committee. "Why not invite them to go and see the president, too?" thought my mother. So she marched the group of visitors over to the White House for a tour. When they reached the Green Room, she whispered to Mayo: "I'm going up and see if I can get the president to come down, and when he does, you must be prepared to introduce these fifty people." Off she went, and came back just a few moments later with John F. Kennedy, "bringing him literally by the arm."

At the very same time my mother was working the halls of power, she was also inaugurating Camp Shriver back at home in Rockville, Maryland. She was determined to use the power of the presidency to shift the nation's laws and attention, but she was also a mother, a coach, a teacher, a sportswoman. And, like every effective revolutionary, she was also an observer, an experimenter, a risk taker. In 1962, there was little consensus in the fields of science or public policy as to what, exactly, people with intellectual disabilities could *do*. Could they function in society outside of institutions? Could they form friendships, play sports, fall in love, hold jobs? No one knew for sure, because so few alternatives had been tested. One of Camp Shriver's primary purposes was to serve as a testing ground, an informal scientific exploration of whether kids with intellectual disabilities could play sports and games and, if so, whether they would benefit from doing so. My father reminisced in a 1999 interview:

> The marvelous thing is there never had been an effort made by anybody to bring a hundred mentally handicapped people to a country place and then experiment with them, using one person with normal intelligence to each mentally handicapped one . . . to see what they could do. What they *could* do, not what they could *not* do.
>
> And so I can remember very, very easily my wife in the swimming pool, standing up at the low end with children who were, let's say, six or eight, seeing whether they could be taught to swim . . . I can remember her putting them on little ponies and leading them around to see whether they could ride a pony. I can remember her helping getting the children to climb a tree, to see whether they would enjoy trying to climb a tree, and which ones would enjoy it and which ones wouldn't enjoy it.

Like many people in my mother's life, he, too, had been skeptical at first, but seeing these children in his backyard, meeting them, talking with them, seeing the joy the games brought them, and seeing how quickly some of them were learning to swim and race, he began to realize that a profound change in mind-set was under way. He was my mother's greatest cheerleader—eager to help, often in awe. "That woman right there," he would say in speeches and toasts, "is the greatest woman in the history of this country!" Never shy with superlatives, he nonetheless believed in her unconditionally. More than anything in his life, he wanted to make her happy.

The Camp Shriver revolution was, in some ways, a rediscovery. The camp revived the insights Edouard Séguin had discovered in his efforts to care for people with intellectual disabilities a century earlier. Séguin, a nineteenth-century French physician, pioneered the idea that children born with intellectual disabilities could be educated through physical movement and experiences. People could learn through exercising the body, he believed, even where analytic intelligence was limited. Séguin often clashed with the scientific establishment over these radical ideas, especially in France, but he pressed on. He knew the truth of what science now widely accepts when it comes to the effects of physical activity on the mind and the personality: the brain thrives on exercise, and physical activity supports the development of language and other mental capabilities. It's now common sense that physical activity supports a healthy heart, improved circulation, and good digestive function. Most studies suggest that it's also a powerful antidote to stress and anxiety. Today, these insights seem obvious, but Séguin had to learn them in the nineteenth century by observation, and he did so by caring for and observing people with disabilities. In 1962, people must have known that physical activity supported mental functioning, but the lessons were still fresh for the hundreds of counselors who arrived to help launch Camp Shriver.

When the counselors—most of them teenagers—arrived, they had no idea what to expect. Ann and Mary Hammerbacher were high school students who barely knew what intellectual disability meant. Most of the volunteers would have been raised to think that a "retarded" person might be dangerous or uncontrollable. Realistically, none would have thought that such children could amount to much. And few were prepared for how much fun they would have. One volunteer, Jim Turner, remembered, "My camper got off the bus on the first day and looked out over the huge expanse of fields and saw the cattle in a distant pasture and ran over to me screaming, 'The cows are gonna get me! The cows are gonna get me.' I tried to reassure him by saying, 'Don't worry. You see that big fence? The cows are on the other side of the fence and can't get to you.' But he was too clever for me. He answered, 'The cows jumped over the moon, they can sure jump over that fence!'"

But amid all the excitement of a summer camp, the counselors also learned, my mother wrote soon after,

> that mentally retarded children *can* be taught. They learned that the children they had been led to believe were "hopeless," "uneducable," could demonstrate astonishing capabilities in certain directions. There was 7-year-old Raymond, for

instance, who learned to post and canter on a horse in a week, far faster than most normal children could manage it. There was Veronica, with a 58 IQ, only a bit over half the normal IQ for her age, who could paint better than any of the counselors . . . They learned too, quite rapidly, what it has taken science centuries to understand—that there *is* a significant distinction between mental illness and mental retardation.

Over the next few years, Camp Shriver returned to our backyard each summer, shaping the attitudes and emotional lives of hundreds of young people with and without intellectual differences.

On the policy front, Mayo continued to lead the team of experts in their research and deliberations. Though not an "expert" herself, my mother, the "advisor," was deep into the action. "As far as I was concerned, [Eunice Shriver] was the chairman of my board," recalled Mayo. She was on the job at all times, it seemed, no matter how big or small the issue. When Mayo became concerned that the panel needed higher authorization for travel expenses to Russia and other countries he planned to visit at the president's request, the "advisor" stepped in to keep things moving: "I had a swim with the president last night," she told Mayo. "It's okay [for you to travel to Russia] . . . go right ahead." Her influence, Mayo recalled, made all the difference.

Years later, I asked her why she'd never wanted to be an official member, why she chose instead to remain an unofficial "consultant." Why, I often wondered, had she exercised her zeal and determination in such forceful ways and yet been reluctant to be named the leader? "I knew that this work had to be Jack's if it was to be successful," she said. "He was the president and I never for a minute doubted that he made all the difference. And I always wanted this to be taken seriously by the country and never wanted people to see me and think this was just about our family." She was looking for results, not credit, and her political judgment was as sharp as her determination. "The way to make things happen in Washington was for people to see this issue as important to Jack. It had to be an *important* issue, not a family issue."

I'm sure she was right in many ways. I'm sure she was right to think that the fight for rights and dignity should not be seen as one family's fight but rather as a nation's fight. And I guess she was right about another message: "I never wanted people to think that what President Kennedy was doing was about Rosemary. Then they would've dismissed it as being a personal matter. It wasn't. It was about the outrageous neglect. It was about the outrage. I wanted all those experts," she scoffed, "to face the injustice of it all and not write us off." That was surely the right decision politically, but the messaging never fooled me. Rosemary was the reason. As my grandfather had put it years earlier, Rosemary was crucial to the Kennedy family's life's work. And she was crucial to the fight to change the United States.

The work of the panel was not without tension. Professionals in the fields of medicine, psychiatry, and theoretical science had a history of working at cross-purposes, and now they were tasked with drawing up a unified set of recommendations. At the same time, parent activists had largely been ignored by the scientists, and their recommendations had to be harmonized with those of the "experts." Some of the researchers wanted to focus on treatment, others on prevention. Elizabeth Boggs represented the parent community and the Arc and pressed for community-based social services. Others were more concerned with special education and the training of teachers. Some thought the cause of research would be best served by joining forces with the National Institute of Mental Health. My mother was adamant that a separate institute was necessary: disability and illness were not the same thing. The field may have been small, but its leaders were strong-willed and determined. The debates were vigorous and divisive; the panel often struggled.

Perhaps more than anything, my mother wanted to make sure that the panel's report would be actionable—that it wouldn't sit on a shelf but instead would lead to substantive change. At one point in the summer of 1962, Mayo's team had completed a rough draft of a section of the report on vocational rehabilitation. My mother took the draft with her for a vacation in Hyannis Port with her family— including the president. During the weekend, Mayo's phone rang and it was my mother. "I just read the draft of the chapter on vocational rehabilitation to the president this morning," she informed him. Mayo was dismayed. The report wasn't ready for the president; it

hadn't even been approved by the full panel. But what came next was
worse than he could have imagined. "[The president] couldn't understand it," she reported.

Mayo was crushed, but responsive. "If the president can't understand it, there must be something wrong with us," he acknowledged.
She continued with more feedback from the commander in chief:
"[The president] said that on one page or a page and half, [Secretary
of Defense Robert S. McNamara] would state the problem, what
some key people thought about it, what he [McNamara] thought
about it, his suggested solution and how much it would cost . . .
Maybe you people can do a little better in saying what you mean in
a smaller space," my mother chided Mayo. Try to present your
ideas like McNamara, she counseled, so that people can understand them and act on them. Mayo concurred and later reflected,
"You know, I got a lesson in writing from the president. How high
can you go?"

By September 1962, the panel was nearing its self-imposed dead-
line for completion, and yet big gaps remained. Mayo flew to Turkey
for a medical conference. He hadn't been there long before he was
summoned to the phone in a hotel conference center in Istanbul. On
the other end of the line was my mother. She reported that the panel
was in an uproar. The biologists didn't think the social scientists'
findings had enough scientific rigor to merit inclusion in the final
report. The social scientists thought the biologists were out of touch
with the real world and didn't understand its urgent needs. My
mother hinted that it might be a good idea if Mayo cut his trip short,
though she didn't insist. "If you can't come now," she cautioned, "we'll
postpone our appointment with the president to give him the report."
Mayo felt a chill. He thought for a moment about the plenary session
at which he was scheduled to preside the next day. Then he had "one
of those flashes of intuition" and replied: "I think I'll come home
tomorrow." He canceled his presentation and flew back to the United
States the next day. Barely stopping to sleep, he reached Washington
just in time to broker an agreement.

The final days were consumed with haggling over the budget.
Representatives from the Bureau of the Budget bargained and coun-

terbargained, with Mike Feldman mediating. The "budget men" thought certain recommendations could be trimmed back. Mayo and my mother negotiated for two days straight. Finally, at 10:25 a.m. on October 16, the report was finalized. Somehow, despite all the wrangling and negotiating, the panel members were able to present a set of recommendations within less than a year. It was historic.

Just ten minutes after the panel completed its report, President Kennedy arrived to receive it. The president listened to the recommendations presented in summary form. He was engaged and curious, and asked pointed questions about where the nation should invest the strongest effort. "What have we learned from other countries? What really is the hope of prevention? Where should the greatest effort be put?" It was "a memorable morning," Mayo recalled. "I don't know any member of this panel who doesn't say that serving on that panel was the greatest experience in his life, both professionally and personally." They would realize how memorable it was only days later, when the president announced that the nation was under the threat of nuclear war with the Soviet Union over the placement of intercontinental ballistic missiles in Cuba. They were stunned to find out that President Kennedy had first learned of the threat just hours before he had arrived, casual and thoughtful, at the panel's presentation. "You can see what would have happened," Mayo recalled, "if I had put my return from Turkey off for another week. We never would have made it in the world."

The report stands even today as a landmark in public policy history. It speaks passionately of the "untold human anguish" that "blighted the future" for millions of families. It provides comprehensive recommendations covering prevention, treatment, social services, research, and education. "The Food and Drug Administration, the National Institutes of Health, and the pharmaceutical industry should develop and require the use of techniques for evaluating and assessing the effects of pharmaceuticals on the fetus, infants, and young children," read one recommendation. Today it's difficult to imagine a time when such a common sense precaution was not yet on anyone's radar. The report marked the first time in the history of the United States that a president would be called upon to include children with intellectual disabilities in the nation's schools, and to create a new system of support for adults with intellectual disabilities. And it was the first time that a president would welcome the challenge of providing support to families who, with help, could care for their children and avoid the scourge of institutionalization.

The report also lobbied for a new focus on women and pregnancy. The panel found that a skyrocketing percentage of women who gave birth in urban areas had no access to prenatal care during their pregnancies—in Baltimore, for example, 21.4 percent and rising. Their report warned:

> Many city hospitals now charge a daily fee and indigent women who are hospitalized during the prenatal period often sign out—against medical advice—because they cannot afford the daily rate. For these women and their babies this is a critical period; however, the management of their care is too often based on economics rather than medicine.

In response to the panel's recommendations, President Kennedy sent a "Special Message to the Congress on Mental Illness and Mental Retardation." He announced a "bold new approach." The following October, he signed the Maternal and Child Health and Mental Retardation Planning Amendments to the Social Security Act and then more legislation providing for research and community-based service centers around the country.

Among the most important changes was the creation of a new National Institute of Child Health and Human Development. It would be separate from the National Institute of Mental Health, as my mother and Dr. Cooke had wanted. It would focus broadly on the medical problems of women and children, issues that had been almost completely overlooked to that point. Over the next fifty years, the institute would sponsor pioneering research that would transform life for millions and garner more than a dozen Nobel Prizes. That research, had it been done earlier, might have saved the life of one child born in 1963: Patrick Bouvier Kennedy. He was born to the president and the first lady in 1963, five and a half weeks premature. He died just a few days later, from neonatal respiratory distress syndrome. No one had yet discovered the treatments for that condition. There "weren't any major problems in children."

It was the beginning of the end of the era of secrecy and shame. That same September, my mother decided—with the president's support—to write an article for *The Saturday Evening Post*, in which she admitted that all those family pictures that had won the nation's admiration were missing one person: Rosemary, her "mentally retarded" sister.

[Rosemary] was a beautiful child, resembling my mother in physical appearance. But early in life Rosemary was different. She was slower to crawl, slower to walk and speak than her two bright brothers. My mother was told she would catch up later, but she never did . . . Like diabetes, deafness, polio or any other misfortune, mental retardation can happen in any family. It has happened in the families of the poor and the rich, of governors, senators, Nobel prizewinners, doctors, lawyers, writers, men of genius, presidents of corporations—the President of the United States.

The family secret was broken at last. The news that the president of the United States had a sister with an intellectual disability helped discredit once and for all the myth of "bad blood" that had shamed so many American families into silence. Even the Hollywood portrayal of disability was changing. A mere half century after the chilling eugenic-infanticide film *The Black Stork*, movies such as *A Child Is Waiting, Light in the Piazza*, and the unforgettable exposé *Christmas in Purgatory* offered very different perspectives on intellectual disability.

In 1962, my mother sent the president a copy of a Kennedy Foundation brochure advertising new grant opportunities that pictured a new medal to be given by the foundation to leaders in the field. Her attention was not, however, drawn to the new grant monies. Her cover note read as follows:

Dear Jack,
    I thought you would be interested in seeing this. Everyone thinks the medallion looks like you at the age of six.
    Bunny hugs,
    Eunice

In the end, the changes for people with intellectual disabilities and their families launched by President Kennedy were among the most powerful and lasting legacies of his brief presidency. Their effect was not immediate, but the tipping point of change had been reached. Just three years later, in 1965, my uncle Robert, then a senator from New York, would make a historic visit to the Willowbrook State School in New York, where more than six thousand children with intellectual disabilities were housed in a facility built for four thousand. When he emerged from the prison-like grounds, he was visibly shaken and called it a "snake pit" that had to be shut down. That visit became a lasting testimony to the horrors of institutionalization in the United States. "Snake pit" could have referred to any number of institutions around the country, which even into the 1960s were sites for medical experimentation and animal-like filth and human degradation. The population of these institutions peaked in 1967, perhaps the clearest evidence that despite these first changes in public policy, the culture of the United States remained locked in the paradigm of denial and rejection through the decade.

But these first steps were nonetheless the necessary beginning and perhaps the most difficult steps of all. Where there are secrets, there is shame, and where there is shame, there is fear. For most, it is better to keep the secret than to risk the ridicule of exposure. The first step can seem too dangerous.

But in the life of a nation and in the life of a family, breaking the secret is the necessary first step to healing the shame. When the secret is broken, its power to create suffering is broken, too. Once Rosemary's identity was revealed, the healing could begin. And as it turned out, Rosemary hadn't been the problem at all. The problem had been the fear that her differences were too embarrassing to admit. It was made worse by the culture of fear and the attitudes of rejection that had grown so terrifying that whole nations had embraced them. But my grandmother's heartbreak came from fear, and it was only by ending the secret that the suffering could be ended, too.

Somehow, Rosemary broke through and surfaced in the 1960s. There, she finally became seen in her family and seen in her country as well. Once she was seen, the chance to heal both her family and her country was possible. It was a family that would need healing again and again. In the years that followed the *Saturday Evening Post* article, both Jack and Bobby died in flashes of terrifying violence. But the siblings who were left behind nonetheless persevered in inviting people all over the world to ease the age-old fear of vulnerability and discover in the simple gifts of play and sports a new vision of how to create belonging centered on the triumph of courage and the power of love.

SIX

Daybreak

We awaken on a low plane, on a plane of defeat—beneath the level
of possibility. Overpowered sometimes by a general climate of hope-
lessness. Promise even can be viewed as unattainable and into this
morass of misery a light shines—a light enters . . . Into the atmo-
sphere of gloom and despair, day breaks, light emerges, flooding the
grim meadow of misery with hope and promise. Light . . .

—Maya Angelou

Light is always breaking through from within us and all around
us, too. Once in a while, we have the mind and heart to welcome it.
And sometimes, more rarely, we experience the joy of welcoming
it together with others. That's what happened on the morning of
July 20, 1968. A whole new way of welcoming light was about to
emerge. A whole new way of learning how to win was about to emerge,
too. It could hardly have been expected.

On that summer morning in Chicago, a sports event was scheduled for Soldier Field, but there were lots of reasons to assume the
show would be more carnival than competition. The sun cast its early-
morning shadows across empty Soldier Field as it did on any other
summer's day. The weather was fine—hot, clear, and low in humid-
ity. The hot dog and cold beer concessions were not slated to open.

No vendors would hawk Chicago Bears pennants or tees. The mayor had ordered that an aboveground swimming pool be installed in the center of the stadium, which was a cumbersome job, but otherwise, it was almost a day off for the Soldier Field crew. Games were scheduled, but spectators were not. Athletes arrived from throughout the country, but their names were unknown to the public. Kevin O'Brien, Alice Katsoukis, and Michael Cusack, whose dad was a police officer, had all come from around Chicago to compete in the games. Others, like Marty Sheets from North Carolina, had traveled much longer distances. But would anyone cheer when they ran? Would anyone watch when they jumped?

Only a thousand people were expected to watch a few track and field competitions and some swim races in the makeshift pool. A municipal park might have seemed a more suitable venue than this massive hundred-thousand-seat stadium. Anne Burke, however, thought otherwise. Though only twenty-four years old, she had been given the job of heading what was being called the Chicago Special Olympics. She'd started work for the Chicago Park District three years earlier as the city's first-ever "special recreation" coordinator, charged with introducing sports and recreation to "retarded" children in Chicago. The Park District had never before been able to fund programming for children or adults with special needs; Burke's position was made possible by new grant money. William McFetridge, president of the Building Service Employees International Union and also of the Chicago Park District, had won the grant and sought out applicants. When Burke applied, she was a gym teacher. "There was no sport I didn't try—you name it—swimming, volleyball, baton twirling, tap dance. I loved them all." She'd had no experience with students who had disabilities—none. But she saw the new position and decided to take it on.

The source of the funding that created Burke's position? A $10,500 grant from the Kennedy Foundation. But in 1965, there was no road map for how to do what she'd been hired to do. How was she to identify participants, sign them up, train them, transport them? "No one told me what to do," recalled Burke. "I had never even seen a kid with intellectual disabilities before I got the job, so I just did what I already knew how to do, which was to find kids and try to teach them sports." She was too young to know that she was a pioneer and too naïve to know that she was likely to fail. She found out quickly, though, that it wasn't going to be easy. "I met all these parents who were afraid for me to take their kids to the park. It was so surprising and frustrating, but the frustration just emboldened me." She went door to door—literally—introducing herself to parents whom she'd discovered through word of mouth. She tried to convince them of the simplicity of her offer to teach their kids to play sports and have fun. She told them of her background as a teacher. She showed them the games she was going to play. And then she discovered the source of most of the resistance: "My kid will be made fun of if you take him out to the park," one parent told her pointedly. "I don't want to take that chance."

"Really," Burke reflected, "most of the parents were embarrassed. They had these kids and no one knew about them. They didn't want their neighbors to see and talk. It was terrible."

And it wasn't just the parents. "There were barriers everywhere," Burke recalled, especially barriers created by those who should have known better. The head of one of Chicago's most respected philanthropies, Tribune Charities, derided Burke's effort to get "retarded" kids out into the open. "Who do you think you are," he scoffed at Burke, "putting these kids on display like that!" Even her colleagues within the parks department dismissed her work as futile—an impression underscored by the fact that Burke's own department didn't even pay her; her position had to be funded by an outside source. "So many people thought what I was doing was fruitless work and, even worse, mistaken. 'How could you subject those kids to being ridiculed? How could you mislead them into thinking they can do these things when clearly they can't?'" But Burke persisted, and the program she was running began to grow, little by little. And she had the support of her boss, William McFetridge, and he in turn had the support of Chicago's all-powerful mayor, Richard J. Daley. Burke plowed on.

In 1967, she got her first real break. "I decided to put on a show, but I didn't really think anyone would come to see sports, so I put on a version of *Mary Poppins!*" She assembled almost a hundred people with special needs and somehow coached them into roles in the musical. She had kids as young as five and adults as old as forty. They prepared for months, and when they were finally ready, Burke invited McFetridge and other city leaders, including Dan Shannon, an accountant and former All-American football standout at Notre Dame who was vice president of the Park District and a major power broker in Chicago. Burke was somehow unafraid of the potential disaster that a show starring almost a hundred children and adults with special needs might become. Some of the "performers" had never been to school and had no idea of how to behave in a group. None had ever acted in a play. Several had disabilities that limited speech. Memorization was out of the question for most. Funding for costumes and transportation and staging was zip. The chance of a successful performance wasn't much better.

Despite all that, Burke persevered and the Chicago Park District presented an unusual and unprecedented production of *Mary Poppins*. The actors acted. The singers sang. The plot unfolded with children and magic and imaginary worlds brought to life. One can almost picture it even now—the young children in need of a nanny, the windborne Mary arriving with her bag of potions and dreams, the carousel horses coming to life, the happy uncle floating in the air, held aloft by his laughter, a world of possibility and happiness conjured up by Burke's hundred outcasts. McFetridge watched and "could not control himself," Burke recalled. Shannon, the hardened union leader, watched, too. "Shannon ran everything in Chicago, and he was so moved. He barely said anything."

"How many people are like this in Chicago?" McFetridge asked.

"I don't know," Burke responded.

Shannon made a simple offer: "I'll do anything you ever want. Anything for these people. Just ask me."

Burke couldn't believe it. "Here was this big, strong, gruff, and powerful man, and he was practically in tears when he watched the show. I just thought to myself, 'Wow. We should do more of this!'"

It was a breaking through—for the performers, for Burke, and for McFetridge and Shannon, too. And it was just a glimpse of what was to follow.

When Burke tried to figure out what to do to follow up the

success of *Mary Poppins*, she had no knowledge of the efforts taking place in Washington. As early as 1962, my mother had been working with Dr. William H. Freeberg, a professor at Southern Illinois University who'd been running the Little Grassy Lake residential home and day camp. Freeberg was a pioneer in the area of physical activity and recreation for people with intellectual disabilities, and together, the two of them had convened meetings of recreation directors to explore what might be effective for children with these disabilities. They'd also convinced the United States Jaycees to develop day camps and exercise programs, and the Kennedy Foundation had funded more than a dozen camps around the country. My mother had pushed research, too, providing funding for Dr. G. Lawrence Rarick, a professor at the University of Wisconsin and coauthor of the 1960 monograph *Motor Characteristics of the Mentally Retarded*, to create physical fitness tests for children with intellectual disabilities. And she'd hired a new advisor to the foundation, a Canadian researcher of physical fitness for children with intellectual disabilities, Frank Hayden, whose work had confirmed that physical activity would help children develop not only physical skills but also emotional, social, and even intellectual skills.

When Burke was casting about for her next project, I'm sure my parents were emboldened by people such as Hayden and Freeburg and Rarick to think that something more than just another camp or another research project might be possible. It was 1967. The political and cultural climate was fertile for change.

By then, my father had taken over the leadership of President Johnson's historic War on Poverty. Between 1965 and 1968, my father and his team launched an array of initiatives that is almost impossible to believe today. Their work included the creation of Legal Services, the first-ever federally funded legal program giving poor Americans access to lawyers for civil cases; Community Action, the first-ever federally supported effort to empower communities with large concentrations of low-income people to organize themselves; and Job Corps, the first-ever federally funded jobs training program to equip low-income Americans to become job ready.

Though my father was the face of these federal programs, perhaps his most lasting effort was the unlikely result of a collaboration with my mother: Head Start, the nation's first preschool program for low-income children, launched in the summer of 1965 with more than five hundred thousand children entering centers nationwide. It was, by any estimation, among the most ambitious and popular of President Johnson's domestic programs, but few people knew at the time what had led to its creation.

My mother had been in the midst of her search for scholars and practitioners interested in recreation for children with intellectual disabilities. In the course of that search, she discovered Dr. Susan Gray at Vanderbilt University's Peabody College. Dr. Gray was doing research on the developmental growth of young children with intellectual disabilities who came from economically and socially marginalized communities. She was taking what was a revolutionary approach at the time—focusing on the learning of children as young as three years old, and even visiting their parents at home, encouraging the parents to learn as well. What Gray found surprised her: with play and nurturing stimulation, very young children with intellectual disabilities could make dramatic progress in their use of language and in their cognitive skills. In 1964, my mother announced: "Sarge, I'm going to Nashville to meet Dr. Gray. What she's discovering with children who have disabilities might make a difference for all children. She's terrific and you should come with me to meet her." Reluctantly, my father agreed to fly to Nashville with my mother, and they visited Dr. Gray's office at Vanderbilt together.

"Sarge and I went to visit Susan Gray," my mother wrote years later. "We watched her with deprived youngsters and their families raising their intelligence and motivation. Sarge said (I can remember it like it was yesterday), 'If Susan Gray can do this in Nashville, this should be done throughout the country' and that was the germ, the initiation of Head Start." Within months of the visit, Head Start was born: a national commitment to marshal the power of early childhood education and family support to improve the chances of the nation's most vulnerable children to escape poverty.

If my parents were immersed in the politics of the 1960s, they were also immersed in the Catholic life of that same period. And there, too, they must have felt exhilarated by the possibilities of change. In those same years—the early 1960s—the Catholic Church underwent perhaps its most significant change since the Protestant Reformation of the sixteenth century. The unlikely leader of the change was a soft-spoken and cheery Italian cardinal, Angelo Roncalli, who became Pope John XXIII in 1958 at the quiet old age of seventy-seven. Just months after his election, "good Pope John" shook the Christian world by convening a surprise ecumenical council, Vatican II. In his opening address to the council leaders, he left behind the Catholic worldview that had been dominated by an unbending condemnation of the modern world and an insular defense of Catholic supremacy and authority. In its place, he announced that "a new enthusiasm, a new joy and serenity of mind" should guide the encounter between the Church and the secular world. He called on the Church to prefer "the balm of mercy to the arm of severity." He saw the future as guided by the vital importance of "personal dignity and true self-realization." He could have been quoting my parents' favorite theologian, the Jesuit paleontologist Pierre Teilhard de Chardin, when he predicted that "the human family is on the threshold of a new era." Fifty years after the council, the archbishop of Canterbury, Rowan Williams, reflected that with Vatican II it was "at last possible to be properly human." The council brought a flood of possibilities to Catholics the world over.

The Second Vatican Council is often remembered as an event that changed the language of the Catholic mass from Latin to the language of the local community and, further, as an event that changed the roles of priests and nuns. But it could just as easily be remembered for the way in which it inspired ordinary Catholics such as my parents to believe that the role of religion was not simply to offer a system of beliefs that had to be followed, but instead to inspire a new way of seeing the world: as the place of encounter with the divine in all its many forms. The Church signaled a new priority for the work of social justice. And it offered a new view of prayer as the discovery of the divine in all things—what the young German Jesuit Karl Rahner called the "mystical way in everyday life."

My mother kept Teilhard's books all over the house, pulling them out at random times and reading a chapter or two for an infusion of emotional energy. Her copy of *Building the Earth* includes scores of underlined sections and dog-eared pages. At one point in the introduction to that volume, Teilhard's centuries-old family motto is mentioned: "Fiery their vigor and celestial their origin." My mother penciled in the margin: "quote!"

My father read voraciously of Teilhard, too, and even included his books in the curriculum for new Peace Corps volunteers. He quoted Teilhard in political speeches, often referring to him simply as "the philosopher." Together with other religious pioneers, Teilhard promised a new theological anthropology based on the idea that divine experience was available and immediate for all people. My father dove into these new thinkers and loved trying to transpose their ideas into the political arena, where he could create innovative ways to achieve their vision of a more just and peaceful world for all.

The Vatican council was a vindication of both my parents' ideas of what it meant to be Catholic, of the ideas they'd learned from Teilhard and from movements such as Dorothy Day's Catholic Worker houses in New York, which embraced radical poverty and solidarity with the poorest of the poor. It reinforced the urgency of the work of social change in the secular world and supported the idea that, in the words of Rowan Williams, "it is faith itself that shapes the work of humanizing [the world]." One of the council's most dramatic decrees articulated a universality that resonates even today. Its first sentence stunned the Catholic world: "The joys and the hopes, the griefs and the anxieties of the men of this age, especially those who are poor or in any way afflicted, are the joys and hopes, the griefs and anxieties of the followers of Christ. Indeed, nothing genuinely human fails to raise an echo in their hearts."

There is no doubt that faith animated my parents' almost frenzied approach to their work. And none of their social change campaigns drew as much from their faith and their spiritual worldview as their efforts to change the world for—and with—people with intellectual disabilities. They believed in the ethos of Vatican II and Pope John's interest in the unconditional dignity of all life, and they wanted to make that dignity the standard of society for all people, no exceptions.

Years later my father wrote a prayer that captured the spirit of his worldview:

> Almighty God, we thank you, we thank you . . . for giving us a chance to work on behalf of the 170,000,000 human beings on earth with Intellectual Disabilities. For helping us to understand why you have created them! Because they teach us to love one another; because they teach us to respect all of your creatures of every race, every religion, every nation, of all ages; because they teach us that we are all—every one of us—dependent on you and on one another. Help us, Lord, to respect and love all of your creatures and all of your creation. Help us, Lord, because we are your servants! Amen.

Back in Chicago, Anne Burke knew about none of this—the research, the meetings, the faith, the zeal, the possibility of breakthrough change. What she did know was that she wanted to continue her work and expand it in whatever way possible. She'd felt the frustration of obstacles, but she'd also tasted the power of change in Dan Shannon's few words and in her boss William McFetridge's emotional connection. And she found a great opportunity to take her work to the next level in an announcement that came to McFetridge in 1967: the Kennedy Foundation announced to all its grantees and collaborators that it was seeking to expand its investment in physical activity and sports for children and adults with intellectual disabilities. Specifically, it requested proposals from any of its several collaborators to hold a national athletic competition for people with intellectual disabilities.

Burke kicked into action. On behalf of the Chicago Park District and the Recreation and Outdoor Education program at Southern Illinois University, she submitted a proposal for a one-day sporting event called the "National Olympics for the Retarded." The National Olympics would be hosted by the Chicago Park District, and Burke herself would lead the effort. The application was submitted with the strong endorsement of Mayor Daley.

I know Chicago was not the only city considered for the launch of the athletic competitions. There were other cities in which start-up programs such as Burke's were growing and universities where programs such as Freeburg's were attracting attention. Did Mayor Daley's prominence and influence figure into the decision to select Chicago? Did Anne Burke's dynamic personality make the difference? Did Chicago's position as a major American city help make the case that it could be influential in inspiring others to follow its example in future years? I don't know. "I was guided by the spiritual aspect," Burke remembered. Perhaps that's what won the day. In any event, Burke and McFetridge won the competition and received a grant to get started. They immediately began the planning process. They would have a lot to do.

My mother made a few changes to the proposal, among which was changing the name to "Special Olympics," in order to avoid the stigma of the label "retarded." She further spelled out the training and recruitment elements of the games, which the Kennedy Foundation would oversee. Even with the grant, funding was tight for an event of this size, and volunteers would be needed by the dozens. Burke went to Tom Maher, head of an association of United Airlines flight attendants called the Clipped Wings, and asked him to provide volunteers. He said yes. She went to Joe Pecoraro, head of the pools division of the parks department, and asked for help with swimming. He not only said yes but also reached out to his personal friend the legendary Johnny Weissmuller, and asked him to come and help attract media attention. Weissmuller said yes. She asked Mayor Daley to locate the event at Soldier Field and to provide the necessary security and staff; he agreed. From the Kennedy Foundation, Frank Hayden offered his services designing the training materials to send out to athletes who would be invited, while Herb Kramer, a public relations specialist at the foundation, offered to call his contacts at the Travelers insurance company to ask for donated umbrellas in the event of rain. Freeburg planned the onsite training stations; the La Salle Hotel was chosen to host the visiting athletes; Burke pitched Chicago media. The difficulty of pulling off the games was lessened by the good will of so many who responded. One of the volunteers thanked Burke for inviting her to help and, she recalls, said, "These are beautiful kids. They've had nothing up till now. We're going to give them the best!"

Then, just two months before the games were to take place, all of a sudden trouble struck. Burke received a letter from Avery Brundage, a prominent Chicagoan, the owner of the La Salle Hotel, and (more important) the president of the International Olympic Committee. Brundage had gotten word that people with intellectual disabilities were going to be staying in his hotel, but that wasn't what caught his attention. What caught his attention were the invitations and the public relations materials announcing an event in Chicago that violated the trademark he controlled: the word "Olympics." His message was simple: you cannot use the word. Cease and desist. Brundage made it clear that he would use any legal means necessary to ensure that "Olympics" would appear nowhere at the event to be held in Soldier Field.

Burke opened the letter and realized that it meant the certain cancellation of the games. Everything had already been printed. All the plans were finalized and all the press releases sent out. There was no way to change the name. The only option was to start over—at best, postpone the event, and at worst, cancel it and hope for new momentum in another year. She burst into tears, collected her thoughts, and then burst into tears again. Then she decided to go straight to the mayor to let him know of the impending humiliation. "I went to see Daley right away. I couldn't stop crying over the whole thing. I walked right into his office—that's how important Special Olympics had become to him. I could just walk right in to see the mayor. And I told him, 'Mr. Brundage wrote this letter and there's nothing we can do. We should've thought of this before. I don't know what Mrs. Shriver will think, but we have to cancel.'"

Daley looked at the letter and bellowed out to his secretary, "Get me Avery Brundage on the phone."

Burke sat silently in the office while Daley waited. Neither said a word. Seconds passed that seemed like minutes. The phone buzzed: "Avery Brundage on the line, Mr. Mayor."

"Avery. How are you? Fine, fine. Yes. Of course. Now, Avery, you're not serious about this letter you've sent us, are you? You can't be serious, Avery. Oh, is that so?

"Well, if that's what you're saying, I have some news for you, too. I want you to know I've walked through your La Salle Hotel, Avery, and there are fire code violations everywhere. Fire code violations *all* over the La Salle Hotel. I'm afraid you know what that means."

There was a long pause as Daley listened to Brundage. Then the slightest smile crept onto Daley's face.

"You understand? Thank you, Avery. That's very helpful. Goodbye."

Burke watched, incredulous. Daley hung up the phone and looked at her.

"You go along. You'll have no more problems from Brundage. I'll tell Eunice. The Olympics people think 'Special Olympics' is a fine name."

So on they went. A brochure for the event boasted, "The thrill of a lifetime awaits retarded children who come to Chicago this summer." They would be entertained by such world-famous guests as the astronaut James Lovell and the Olympic champions Jesse Owens, Barbara Ann Scott, and Bob Mathias. They would be welcomed by the mayor himself and stay in an "Olympic village" at the La Salle Hotel. They would have their meals at specially prepared "training tables." When not competing, they would be invited to tour the city, attend sports clinics, and celebrate at a mixer.

The contestants were given an expansive message: sports can make a difference in your life and the life of your country. "The need for a special athletic competition for the retarded is well established," one brochure declared. "The value of exercise and games for the retarded cannot be overemphasized," said another. "A series of failures in various endeavors causes the retarded child to look at himself as a failure. His first real success may come in athletics. Here is an area where he can succeed and start building a positive self-image, gaining confidence and self-mastery as well as physical development." The planners clearly envisioned a connection between physical activity and quality of life. In a letter of welcome, my mother addressed "all those interested in creating a better life for the mentally retarded" with her hope that "this national Olympics will stimulate hundreds of communities throughout the United States." Mayor Daley's letter brought wishes "of happiness and pride" to the athletes and their families. The president of the Chicago Park District, William Mc-Fetridge, offered a vision worthy of high ideals: "Our ultimate goal is to provide happiness for all children."

But why Soldier Field? Why not a local park or a large high school that would have had ample facilities for an event of this size? The organizers had to know that the stadium would be all but empty, and that its cavernous structure would make even a respectable crowd of five hundred or a thousand look insignificant. They had to know that the "athletes" would be more than thrilled to compete in a high school stadium with even a small number of people cheering. They had to notice the mismatch between Soldier Field's majestic Roman colonnade that rose high above the field as a monument to athletic greatness, and the hodgepodge of athletic endeavor that would take place on the field below.

They did, in fact, realize all this, but they also realized that their dream was much bigger than the event they were organizing. "We wanted to send a message that we had a big idea and we wanted to be in a place that was a draw," said Burke. What, one might wonder, made Anne Burke and Eunice Shriver and Dick Daley and William McFetridge think that their "Special Olympics" for people with intellectual disabilities would be a "draw"? It could only have been a draw in their dreams. But their dreams were just the stuff from which the Chicago Special Olympics were to be made.

The athletes arrived in Chicago the day before the games and stayed overnight at Avery Brundage's La Salle Hotel. In what would become a Special Olympics tradition, each athlete was evaluated for skill and ability before he or she arrived, so that they could be placed in competition with others of like ability. Everyone would have a chance to compete, and each athlete would compete only against others of similar skill. There would be no "finals" and no "eliminations." Every race would be a "finals" unto itself. In this regard, the Special Olympics were going to be completely unlike the "real" Olympics. Every winner of every race would be awarded a medal. The message was clear: Everyone will have a chance to win. Disability will play no role in limiting an athlete's chance to claim Olympic greatness.

Among the athletes who arrived in Chicago was Marty Sheets, a fifteen-year-old high school student from Greensboro, North Carolina, who had Down syndrome. Marty had been born to Dave and Iris Sheets on March 31, 1953, at a time when there were almost no services or support for him or his family. He had two older sisters, Nancy and Jamie. "It wasn't easy," Iris Sheets remembers, still fighting back tears more than fifty years later. "We had difficulty getting him in school, since they didn't have a place for him. There were no events for him. We moved him to five or six different schools because they didn't have teachers or rooms or programs. When he got to junior high, they called him 'educable' and we actually thought that was good. It was the best we'd gotten from anyone till that time." Not surprisingly, Marty had also faced the inevitable humiliation from his peers. "One day, two little girls were making fun of him," his father recalled, "and then another time, a big boy pulled a knife on him. We complained to the school and we fought as hard as we could." Not much changed. Marty responded in a way his parents couldn't: "Mom," he said, "words won't hurt me. Will they, Mom?" Iris couldn't answer. "Sometimes," she reflected, "I think it was easier for him than it was for me."

Marty had, however, participated in one program specially designed for him: a summer camp for special needs children run by the Greensboro Recreation Department under a grant from the Joseph P. Kennedy, Jr. Foundation. "Marty did well in that camp," his dad bragged. "Marty loved swimming and he was pretty good at it." He went to Boone, North Carolina, where he slept away from home for the first time and enjoyed an array of activities and social experiences not unlike those enjoyed by any kid attending a summer camp. His parents were delighted: "Lem Cox headed it up and he was the athletic director of the Greensboro Public Schools. But we trusted him for another reason: we knew him from our church. Marty was well cared for there."

Marty had never been to a place where he didn't know the people. He'd never been on an airplane. He'd never competed in any sport, at any level. "He'd never," Dave Sheets noted calmly, "been cheered or anything like that." So when the games in Chicago were scheduled, and the Greensboro Parks and Rec Department chose Marty as one of their five athletes to send, his parents were reluctant. "We were concerned about it, oh, yes. I mean, how could we not be? Marty was so young. But we were thrilled, too—happy, you could say."

A young teacher, Frank Starling, was chosen to train Greensboro's athletes and accompany them to Chicago. "I was outright scared," he remembers. "I'd never traveled with these kinds of people, and I didn't know what they might do or anything. I was just a PE teacher, and here I was going all the way to Chicago with five kids. I thought I might be crazy to do this, but then I just said, well, what the heck. I'll give it a try." Dave Sheets got over his anxiety, too. On July 18, Starling and Marty Sheets and Marty's fellow competitors boarded a plane bound for Chicago, Illinois, to participate in the first Special Olympics.

On July 20, 1968, at 7:15 a.m., buses lined up outside the La Salle Hotel to carry the athletes to Soldier Field. There was a press conference scheduled for 9:00 a.m., and the Opening Ceremony would commence at 10:30. The immense stadium was largely empty, as expected, but athletes and volunteers streamed in—volunteers from the Jaycees, Caritas, the Saturday Afternoon Club, Clipped Wings, the Chicago Park District, and the Chicago Kennedy Campaign Workers. Gary Irwin, a local gymnast, was there. He'd signed up to serve as the trampoline teacher. There were members of the Chicago Blackhawks and Toronto Maple Leafs, as well as the entire Notre Dame football team, on hand to help with sports clinics. For entertainment, there were, among others, musicians from the Great Lakes Naval Station, St. Rita High School, the Chicago Fire Department's clown band, and Connecticut's Mansfield Training School.

One of the most recognizable athletes in the world was at Soldier Field that morning, too: the Olympic decathlete Rafer Johnson. Johnson had traveled his own journey of change to get to Chicago: his childhood had been spent in a segregated town in Texas, where he'd grown up on the other side of the color line. "I went to an all-black school, I rode on the back of the bus, I sat in the colored section of the movie theater, I went to a bathroom marked 'colored' and I drank from a water fountain marked 'colored' too." But at the age of nine, he and his family moved to California, to a town where they were the only people of color. There was no segregation. The shift was profound.

"California turned my world upside down." Almost miraculously, Johnson felt no discrimination in his new home. "I went to a mixed school and saw all these people treating me like I was one of them and I thought to myself, 'I never knew any of this could even exist.'" He was a leader in his high school. He was elected president of his class and went on to attend UCLA, where for the first time he decided to try track and field. He competed in his first decathlon as a freshman in 1954, and just months later broke the world record. It was his fourth competition. By 1958, he was *Sports Illustrated*'s Sportsman of the Year. Two years later, he won an Olympic gold medal in Rome after a dramatic finish against his biggest competitor, Yang Chuan-kwang of Taiwan, who had been a classmate at UCLA.

After his gold medal, Johnson retired from sports and became a film star, a sports announcer, and a global celebrity. "But somewhere in my soul," he said, "all the opposition to people of color, all the sense of amazement I had when I realized that there was a world that I didn't know existed . . . it had an impact on me. I came from one society to another. I saw the world change right in front of my eyes. So I knew it could happen."

He was invited by President Kennedy to participate in the 1961 inaugural celebration, and there he met the president's sister Eunice— and his brother Bobby, who mesmerized Johnson. "I just loved Bobby. He was the most amazing man I'd ever met."

For years after meeting Robert Kennedy, Johnson was on call to him, traveling with him, visiting him and his family, joining his mission to change the politics of the nation. And then, just five weeks before the first Special Olympics, Rafer was with Bobby Kennedy when he lost his life in Los Angeles. Along with the NFL great Roosevelt Grier, Rafer Johnson tackled the murderer and seized his weapon. Johnson held on to the gun that killed my uncle until the police came to take it. The experience devastated him. "I got lost. I went home and built a seven-foot-high wall around my house. I didn't come out. I couldn't come out. I didn't have anything to live for."

Bobby Kennedy had spoken not just to Rafer Johnson's politics but to his heart. And with Bobby's death, Rafer's heart was broken. He couldn't imagine a future that mattered or a reason to live the one he had. There were millions like him in the United States in 1968, one of the stormiest years in our nation's history. Dr. Martin Luther King, Jr., was murdered in April, the war in Southeast Asia dragged on, and people were disgusted by their political institutions and leaders at home. The center was unraveling. And Rafer, enclosed in his house and behind his wall, couldn't imagine a way forward.

But he did answer the phone one day to hear an invitation he would have been embarrassed to refuse: "Will you come to Chicago?" my mother asked. Amazingly, despite the horrific situation surrounding her brother's death, she had decided to proceed with the games. Years later, when a close friend of mine died, she gave me the advice that must've animated her decision: "Just keep going. There's no point in sitting around. That's what my dad always told me. 'Just keep going.'"

Rafer didn't really know what it was about, but after more than a month holed up in his house, he decided he would force himself to try. "I had no expectations. I had only just enough energy to say 'yes' and show up."

On the morning of July 20, a group assembled for the 9:00 a.m. press conference. It had been planned at the last minute because my mother wanted to go public with long-range plans for the still-nascent Special Olympics organization. "I wish to announce a national Special Olympics training program for all mentally retarded children everywhere," she told the reporters.

Anne Burke wasn't there. On the way to the stadium, my mother had asked Burke a favor. "Could you go to Sears and pick me up a bathing suit, so I can get in the pool with the swimmers?"

"Of course, I was shocked," said Burke. "I mean, she was the sister of the late president of the United States, and she'd flown in from Washington, DC, to give the opening speech, and she was hosting the mayor and all that. But she wanted a bathing suit! So I got her a suit."

Eventually the moment arrived and the games began. Following the ancient Olympic tradition, athletes paraded into the stadium as an announcer introduced each group according to the institution or state from which they'd come. The bands played marching tunes and flourishes. Seventeen-year-old Philip Weber carried the Olympic torch and lit the forty-foot-high cauldron. The fire was called the John F. Kennedy Flame of Hope. McFetridge gave a speech; other city officials did as well. And, from a microphone just above the field level, my mother gave her first Opening Ceremony speech.

She challenged listeners to imagine a future Special Olympics program that would grow from the thousand athletes assembled on Soldier Field that day to include more than 1,500,000 athletes "who should be competing in games like this all over America." She compared the special athletes with Roman gladiators who fought life-or-death battles against predatory lions. She imagined those gladiators going into their battles, facing the real likelihood of death. She imagined that they might have had a sacred oath: "Let me win. But if I cannot win, let me be brave in the attempt." She challenged the athletes of the first Special Olympics to compete with this oath just as if they, too, were facing life or death. And she finished simply with the words "Let us begin the Olympics."

"Let me win. But if I cannot win, let me be brave in the attempt." She told me years later that she wrote those words in her hotel that morning, or perhaps on the way to the stadium. Her longtime public relations assistant, Herb Kramer, told me that he had drafted them for her earlier that day. One thing is certain: they were spoken from her core. They were aspirational words, but they were also gut-wrenching ones that framed the challenge starkly: for each individual on that field, there was a real danger that the predatory lions of life would defeat them. In the face of this adversity, there was but one calling: be brave. Even if they might not mount the winner's stand of life, they could be brave. Bravery was its own reward. And when it came to bravery, these athletes could not be outdone. They had no disability when it came to bravery.

With the end of the speeches and declarations, the athletes were led to their respective contests—some to the pool, some to the high jump, some to the starting line of the 50-yard or 300-yard dash. And there, on the field and in the largely empty stands of Soldier Field, the spirit of Special Olympics was born.

As luck would have it, Marty Sheets fell ill that morning and had to stay behind in his hotel room, but his coach, Frank Starling, wandered around the infield in disbelief. "It's not easy to run a multisport track meet, especially with almost a thousand athletes. But there were volunteers everywhere and everything had been planned perfectly, and I just couldn't believe the whole scene. These athletes were treated like world-class competitors, and so was I."

Rafer Johnson went from station to station—from the pool, to the high jump, to the starting line of the 50-yard and 300-yard dashes—caught between tears and wide-eyed amazement. "Everywhere you turned, you saw an experience no one had ever seen before. No one had seen these people. No one had ever seen their exhilaration. It was so simple, but it was so amazing." He could almost feel his life change: "I looked at the athletes, and I knew what it was like for them. I knew how it felt when someone slapped me on the back for the first time. The athletes had these smiles that I will never be able to describe. And when I went to congratulate them, I got a bear hug instead of a handshake." Not a man given to excessive emotion, Rafer put it simply: "Something came from inside me. I just wanted to say over and over again: *thank you.*"

There were many races that day, but one in particular stood out from the rest. It has been described so many times since then that it has become like an ancient tale from an oral tradition—told and retold with ever new versions and ever different characters. It enjoys periodic bursts of popularity on the Internet when it is rediscovered and "liked" many thousands of times. From what I have been told, this is what happened.

At the start of the 300-yard dash, a group of about seven athletes was led to the starting line. Like all the other athletes at the games, they'd been placed in a heat against others of similar ability. Their race would be once around the track. First-, second-, and third-place finishers would win gold, silver, and bronze medals respectively.

Those who finished lower than third would receive participation ribbons. Like every other race during the games, this one was a "finals" of sorts. There was no elimination round, no second race for finalists, no additional rung up the ladder for the racers to climb. This was their one and only race.

Their names have been lost over time, but by all accounts, the runners were evenly matched. They sprinted the first hundred or so yards, mostly keeping pace with one another. As they took the outside turn, one runner started to pull away and grabbed the lead. They continued down the back stretch bunched together but with a clear leader. Volunteers who were assembled around the perimeter of the track cheered them as they came to the final turn. They were close enough to hear and see one another; close enough to push one another to dig deeper for that little bit of extra energy; close enough to know that the final hundred yards would determine the winner.

And down that final hundred yards they came, the leader now commanding his position, flanked by the other six runners, who were trailing but not giving up. It was all adrenaline now. The finish line was in sight; the cheering grew louder; their energy was fading and surging at the same time.

And then the runner in second place leaned too far forward and fell hard into the track. He let out a painful grunt followed by a sprawling fall, legs overhead, tumbling into the hard surface of the track. And then, the runner in first, by now just a few yards short of the winning finish, stopped. It was his friend who had fallen. He turned around as the other runners sped by him and raced backward to his friend, who was lying on the track. He bent over and lifted the fallen runner, who stood, limped a step, and then put his arm over his friend's shoulder. The two of them walked together toward the finish line and crossed it arm in arm in last place.

I can hear the hush and the cheers of that moment. I can see the wonder of the volunteers, the officials, the onlookers. And I hear a mystic's riddle, as simple as it is impossible to answer: Who won that race?

To this day, no one remembers who was given the gold medal for the race, but everyone knows that on that track the two athletes who crossed the line last offered a new vision of what it means to win. And it wasn't just those two, either. All over Soldier Field, children of scorn and lonely teenagers tried their best and won. People who had so little to give gave the one thing they had: their hearts. And those around them were given a chance to unleash their spirits, too, by cheering them on, by watching their bravery come to life, by meeting their smiles with eyes opened to loveliness. On that day, winning had nothing to do with beating anyone and everything to do with playing like no one is judging even though everyone is watching. Sports had never seen anything like it. No one had.

"Those at the edge of any system and those excluded from any system," writes the spiritual master Richard Rohr, "ironically and invariably hold the secret for the conversion and wholeness of that very group." On July 20, 1968, for the first time in history, people with intellectual disabilities were celebrated as great individuals by others who discovered their gifts in the joy of sports. Gifts! The idea of Olympic triumph, of winning, of bravery, of being gifted—none of these qualities had ever been conferred on these human beings. But on the first day, there was something in their persistence, something in their emotional tenderness, in their uninhibited openness to others that burst to life and awakened those who could see to a different way of defining what it means to win. They won from within. For those who had eyes to see, it was an awakening.

The Chicago Special Olympics was a classroom of the heart. The whole unstated purpose was everywhere in plain sight: each competitor was celebrated as being more beautiful and valuable than anyone dared imagine. No one had anticipated this.

Before leaving the stadium, Mayor Richard Daley turned to my mother and said, "Eunice, the world will never be the same." He couldn't have imagined how true time would prove his words to be. Later that night, even though he had not been able to play in the arena that day, Marty Sheets willed himself out of bed and went to the banquet celebrating the games. For whatever reason, my mother tracked him down. She was speaking from the podium with a spotlight on her when she stepped off the stage and into the crowd. She worked her way through the dozens of tables where athletes, celebrities, coaches, and dignitaries sat and found Marty, and with the spotlight still shining, asked him to stand.

"I understand you trained to come to the games but you got sick," she said in front of a thousand people. Marty was stunned to be standing with all eyes on him. He didn't say a word. His coach fidgeted. "Well, Marty, for your guts and for your effort, I want you to have a gold medal, too. Here you go. Marty Sheets is the winner of the Special Olympics gold medal for bravery."

She could have spoken those words to herself. She could have been giving that medal to her own sister or to millions of others around the world awaiting their chance. Soon enough, she would be able to do both.

SEVEN

As Simple as Possible

What you are looking for is what is looking.

—attributed to Saint Francis

In 1968, there was no way I could learn how to win from within or, for that matter, understand how to live fully alive, either. Special Olympics was ready to teach, but I wasn't ready to learn. After all, I hadn't learned that it was possible to see from within, so how could I have seen or learned the secrets of the heart that were all over Soldier Field? It took me another fifteen years to begin to get it.

But a few years after the games, one change did capture my attention: Rosemary became a frequent visitor at our home for the first time. With Special Olympics a public success and with an ambitious vision for growing it, my mother must have felt empowered to welcome her own sister more openly into our lives. So Rosemary began arriving regularly at our home with a dedicated nun traveling with her and a guest room all prepared for her visit. She would stay for a week or two, and she became a part of our family routines. In warm weather, she would swim with us after school. Even if the air had a chill, my mother would insist that Rosemary get into the pool: "Come on, Rosie. Get your fanny in the pool!" During colder days, she would take walks around the fields or rides into town. She would sit with us at dinner and listen to the rousing conversations. Years later, my mother would deliver her most remembered speech at the Opening Ceremony of the 1987 Special Olympics Summer Games at Notre Dame University, when she ferociously asserted, "The years of segregation and separation are over!" In our home, the years of segregation and separation ended with the arrival of Rosemary.

At the same time, my mother emerged as an increasingly public figure as her "games" started to break through into the national consciousness. From a sports point of view, the founding genius of Special Olympics was its embrace of "divisioning," a process by which every competitor, regardless of ability level, is placed in a competitive heat and given a realistic chance to win a medal. Divisioning made it possible for every athlete to have a chance to experience the joy of victory, thus forever banishing the idea that sports could reward only the elite few who triumphed over all. But the practice also brought another, equally powerful concept to the public at large, and it was this: everyone can succeed if they marshal the bravery to try. The organization was sharpening its most powerful message: winning isn't about *being* the best—it's about *doing* your best.

The power of this new venture in the world of sports was not lost on the media and marketing leaders of the world. In 1973, the leading sports show in the world, ABC's *Wide World of Sports*, featured the first-ever nationally televised segment on Special Olympics alongside the usual sampling of elite sports competitions from around the world. The fabled producer of the show, Roone Arledge, made the unilateral decision to devote a fifteen-minute segment to the games being held that year at UCLA, hosted by Frank Gifford. Even though the games were relatively small, they were already attracting the attention of such corporate brand powerhouses as Coca-Cola, which outfitted volunteers and sent hundreds of volunteers from their own workforce to local events.

Back home, all of us crowded around the television on Saturday afternoon to watch the show. When it was over, my mother rushed to call Arledge to lavish him with gratitude for his gutsy move in devoting airtime to people with intellectual disabilities. Gifford remembers Arledge's reaction: "He loved it, not only because it was the right thing to do but also because he won the ratings for the time slot. Roone was a genius and he could see that Special Olympics was great television."

The movement continued to build. All over the United States, local clubs and church groups and civic organizations signed up to run their own versions of Special Olympics games. Soon, every state in the nation had its own Special Olympics organization, each committed to following the official Special Olympics training and competition protocols, each certified by Special Olympics International. In 1975, the president of the United States, Gerald Ford, added to the growing momentum by agreeing to be the honorary chair of the first-ever Special Olympics Gala. With Barbra Streisand performing at the Kennedy Center, the movement that had begun in my parents' backyard had suddenly become downright glamorous.

Little did the president know that moments before he arrived at the Kennedy Center, my mother was in a total panic. She'd shown up in a dress that didn't fit. In one of her most lovable and spontaneous problem-solving moments, she ducked into the ladies' room to try to fix it but gave up, and in desperation cornered another woman and asked for her dress.

Imagine the shock of that woman. Black-tie gala. Kennedy Center. President of the United States. She enters the ladies' room only to find the hostess, Eunice Kennedy Shriver . . .

"You want me to give you my dress?"

"Yes. I need it right away. The president is waiting and I can't wear this one."

The unknown woman obliged.

My mother enjoyed every minute of telling the story later—even if she was a little embarrassed that she never found the woman to return her dress.

For all the emerging fame and glitz of Special Olympics, I had yet to see any of it as a pathway to satisfying my own hunger to figure out how to fit into the world. As it turned out, that was the first and most difficult lesson for me to learn. Like most teenagers, I was preoccupied with what others thought of me, and like most teenagers, I was completely focused on trying to impress my peers and shield them from my insecurities. You can't see from the heart if you're constantly afraid of being judged by others. Fear obstructs your vision. You look for belonging in all the wrong places. And it's even worse when you internalize the judgment and obstruct your view of yourself. You see something much less than your true self, so your true self never has a chance to see.

The person who tried the hardest to get me to stop judging myself, and to stop being afraid of others, was someone I met just a few months after high school: Linda Potter. Just before I set off for college, I fell in love with Linda, who was the most beautiful girl I'd ever seen and also the happiest and most generous soul I'd ever met. Her smile rocked my world. She was the first person to love me for who I was and not what I could do. When I was with her, all I felt was happy. I couldn't believe it.

But Linda and I had terrible timing—she was graduating from college while I was just starting. She was entering the workforce in New York and had signed up for a job at a foundation dedicated to fighting apartheid in South Africa, while I was entering the social scene of dormitories in New Haven, Connecticut. We started dating and Linda would show up at the occasional rugby party, a beautiful young professional woman from New York City. My friends would swoon while she would beg to leave. I'd show up at professional functions in New York City with scholars and political activists and young bankers, and her friends would look puzzled at the peculiar and immature boyfriend Linda had in tow. And I'd beg to leave. Our long-distance love affair was a challenge in every way, except that each of us was crazy about the other.

Miraculously, Linda and I survived my four years in college, and then, just as I entered the workforce, Linda set off for law school in Tennessee. Her attention turned to learning the law and volunteering at the local legal aid clinic and bonding with her new "little sister" from Nashville. Meanwhile, my attention turned to the issue that had most captivated me during my college years: serving high-risk teenagers in New Haven's poor and struggling neighborhoods. While still an undergraduate, I'd volunteered as a big brother to a ten-year-old child from New Haven's Hill neighborhood, and then entered the teacher certification program so that I could teach at New Haven's Lee High School. I taught U.S. history classes, tutored students in English and math, and tutored in summer Upward Bound programs for college-bound students, and I loved every minute of it. The kids were tough and gentle, eager and disaffected, restless and discouraged all at once. They were raw and magnetic. If I was searching for what matters most, I could tell they were, too.

When I graduated, I decided that the best way for me to meet the world's expectations was by applying myself to elevating the expectations of hundreds of teenagers in New Haven's toughest neighborhoods. I thought I had a lot to teach them about how to fix injustice and perform and rise. As it turned out, I had much more to learn about how to listen and empower and see. I wouldn't be able to do anything for them until I learned.

My first full-time job was as a teacher-counselor in the University of Connecticut's Upward Bound program, working for a brilliant educator named Bob Brown. Bob was a master at understanding that all learning is a relationship. He could get his students to do almost anything. The kids were so alluring—complicated but also so funny; difficult to reach but also so eager to connect; angry but also so tender. I latched on to Bob to help me navigate my role in changing their lives.

Bob proved a wise mentor. At the time, he was everything I wasn't. Bob was tough and smooth and effective; I was coarse and confrontational and ineffective. Bob only had to give a kid a look, and everything would change. I would lecture and whine and nothing would change. Seeing my frustration, he took me aside one evening after dinner in the dorm.

"The problem isn't what you say, Tim," he said. "It's how you say it."

My dignity was wounded. "I'm just trying to let these kids know that they have to follow the rules here, or their chances of being successful will collapse," I protested.

Bob must've had to hold back a sigh. "You're giving them good advice, Tim. You don't have to change the message. But you might want to say it differently, that's all."

"You mean, don't be so tough on them?"

"No, not at all. You could even be tougher. It's just that your tone of voice makes it sound like you're talking down to the kids. You have to remember, they're only a couple of years younger than you. Besides, you haven't experienced their world, and they know it."

I wondered what exactly he was getting at. One night, I had a particularly rough run-in with several students in the dorm. I'd caught them sneaking out of their rooms and followed them downstairs.

"Ernel!" I called. "What's going on? Who else is in that bathroom? You guys know you're not supposed to be down here."

Ernel rolled his eyes. "Don't worry about it, man. We're going."

"Who else is there? Turn on the light. I'm going to need all you guys to come see me in Iris's office tomorrow morning."

"Chill out, man," said Tony. "We're not going nowhere. We're just going to our rooms, so why don't you leave us alone and mind your own damn business?"

"Don't lie to me, Tony," I shot back. "You weren't going to your rooms. You were going out. You're violating the rules and I need to report you."

"Shriver, why are you such an asshole?" Eugene chimed in. "Just leave us alone and let us go, and nobody won't know nothing and it will all be cool. Stop being such a jerk, man."

"I'm not a jerk, I'm just trying to enforce—wait a minute!" The kids had started going up the staircase, refusing to acknowledge me anymore. "Okay, you guys," I called after them. "I have to do what I'm going to do. You'd better . . ."

The door to the third-floor hallway slammed shut and they were gone.

I was trying hard, but I was tiresome. I didn't understand that I needed to learn how to understand the kids before I tried to direct the kids. That would take time.

For four years, I tried as best I could to be successful. My students were facing the toughest of circumstances, growing up in the middle of the crack epidemic in Hartford and New Haven, two of the most violent cities in the nation. Their neighborhoods were poor, and jobs

for their parents were scarce and low-paying. The rates of absentee-
ism, dropouts, and discipline problems in the schools were atrocious.
As much as I saw them as young people with potential, I also saw
them as kids who needed support and help in order to make it—in
effect, kids who needed me. I stayed late after school, visited housing
projects in the evenings, and gave everything I had to trying to solve
their problems.

But in retrospect, I can see that I was also attracted to them because so many of them were searchers, seeking something or someone
or someplace to belong, and though I couldn't have said so, I was, too.
Lenice Falk was a tender fifteen-year-old who tested well but could
never quite focus on her work. I worked with her, hour upon hour, for
months until one day she told me that she was pregnant and needed
to take a break and drop out of school. Darrell Mickey was a talented
basketball player, a hard worker, and a smart kid, but he didn't want to
give himself to the promise of college. Over and over again, I found
myself with students who were searching—often in tragically unhealthy ways—for something bigger. And I was ill equipped to help
them find what they were looking for. To be honest, I was mostly a
failure at helping them because I didn't yet understand that I needed
them to help me.

After working with hundreds of high school students in Upward
Bound, I began to realize that I was missing something. I turned to
experts for help and found my way to Dr. Donald Cohen, the director
of the renowned Yale Child Study Center, who was making news
around the world with his work on post-traumatic stress disorder and
theories of mind that were central to understanding autism. He was
also training child psychiatrists and suggested that I bring one of my
students to the center to explore the challenge of how to engage them
in learning. With two dozen psychiatry students looking on, Dr. Cohen interviewed the student, and afterward, met with me to discuss
his perspective. "There are enormous challenges facing your students,
Tim. So few of them have been given the tools to understand their
inner lives. They are surrounded by so much chaos, so much conflict.
They need tremendous support to make sense of what they're feeling."

"Inner lives?" I had never heard the term. What in the world was
an "inner life"?

I turned to Dr. James Comer, another internationally prominent expert on child development at the Child Study Center. Comer is an African-American medical doctor who grew up in a large family that today we'd call poor. But he rose through the education system with continual success and, after completing his psychiatry training, decided to devote his life to reforming urban schools, in which he saw children of color failing in massive numbers. "Schools are not set up to understand the developmental needs of these children," he explained to me. "They need a new focus on how to use the techniques of the mental health world to help students attach to teachers and develop optimally, while teachers need to understand how to interpret behavior and promote positive outcomes."

I was mesmerized by the clarity (and stature, too) of men such as Dr. Cohen and Dr. Comer—by how well they reasoned and how crisply they argued their points of view. They were pointing me toward a game-changing insight: Learning is not a mechanical process for distributing knowledge into machines called children in an assembly line of parts. Instead, learning is a relationship within which people cultivate meaning and attachment. Without a relationship of shared meaning and value, there is no learning. But with a strong relationship, learning is the endlessly exciting process of pursuing the questions and dreams that animate teacher and student alike. The science of child development was filled with insights about how to help teachers understand student behavior, shape student motivation, and cultivate student and family commitment to learning.

But for me, there was still something missing. I left my encounters with these brilliant scholars only to find the puzzles and mysteries of my students all the more frustrating. I looked into the eyes of Stephanie Linker—a bright, young, hardworking student who was careful about every risk in the neighborhood, never venturing into drugs or sex. Stephanie did everything right and got top grades. But she carried her head down, never quite looking me in the eye, a part of her always absent from the conversation, distracted, occupied with other worries. She was getting good grades but not getting inspired. Her lips would tighten when I'd encourage her to be even more relentless so she could go to an even better college. "Sure, Tim," she'd say. "I'll go meet Mr. Granite for extra help. But I don't really need a better college."

The promise of college clearly did not resonate with her. "What does she think she *does* need?" I wondered. I searched for words, language, definitions. Was there something more than success in school that I needed to talk to the kids about? If so, what was it? Did I need to teach them how to be critics of societal injustice while at the same time teaching them how to play by society's rules? Did I need to bring in more African-American role models and mentors? I took my students on visits to businesses and colleges. We saw submarines being built at Electric Boat in Groton, Connecticut. We visited the big corporations to see how business works. We went to Bryant College in Rhode Island, Emerson College in Boston, Trinity in Hartford, Sacred Heart in Bridgeport, and dozens more. Did I need to take them even more places, so they could see for themselves what they might not have been able to imagine—that real social benefits and economically stable ways of life were accessible?

I did need to do all those things. And yet, there was still something missing. Dr. Cohen's words about the "inner life" nagged at me, but I still didn't know how to interpret them. I had a vague idea that my students had a deeper hunger that neither money nor education could fill, but I didn't know how to address it. What were their deepest longings? What were their dreams? And what were mine?

In retrospect, I think what fascinated me most was that for better or for worse, most of the students I taught in those years had come to believe that it was fruitless to try to belong in the mainstream world I represented. They'd given up on the system because they perceived it to have given up on them. They not only thought the system was rejecting them, but they felt it, too. Everywhere they went, they saw stares and rejection. In the media, they saw negative characterizations. In the world of their parents, they saw low-wage jobs and exhaustion and barriers. They felt judged, negatively, unfairly, and even cruelly. And when you feel unfairly judged and marginalized, you don't feel seen or understood. They rejected the world that was rejecting them, and a part of me wanted to as well. Part of me was just as confused as they were. For better or worse, I didn't have the guts to walk away. But they did.

What I missed was that they'd learned to see a *different* world than

I saw. When you decide that the way things are in the "real" world is somehow wrong, you're forced to find a different way to see. You don't just reject *what* you see but learn *how* to see differently, too, and that's exactly what I needed to learn. Most of the students I taught in those years had concluded that an economic "promised land" was more of a charade than a real option for them, so most of my exhortations to compete and achieve fell on deaf ears. They had long since lost interest in grades and colleges, because those things seemed to be unreal. So they'd developed an eye for what was real—at least to them. And what was real was the feeling of belonging. They seemed to care much more about finding people who cared than about finding anything else. The thing that mattered most was feeling seen and understood. Despite all the pain and disappointment in their lives, and also because of it, my students had learned how to see from the heart, because nothing else made much sense. Some say there are only two pathways to the heart of God—love and suffering. For my students, suffering was often it.

I was jealous of that authenticity, but, more than that, confused. My students dealt with their anger and hunger by expressing it with raw indifference to the consequences. I wondered what I would have been like if I'd been able to tell my high school teacher who humiliated me so many times to go to hell. I wondered what I would have been like if I'd been raised in the Baptist churches that dominated the neighborhoods where I worked and been able to stand up in front of a church full of people and plead with God for a miracle instead of standing, sitting, and kneeling in the orderly Catholic Church fashion. I wondered what I would've been like if I'd wandered the streets at night like a blues singer composing chords for a bass guitar, as one of my students did. And I wondered how to listen to those kids in a way that would convince them that I cared about them and not just their grades. And if I did that, would I still be recommending math and English homework as a way to find purpose, or would I instead be teaching them to first find their purpose elsewhere? Everywhere I looked, I saw an elaborate construction of walls that separated the world I had grown up in from the world in which I was now living. And what surprised me more than anything was that I felt more at home in that new world.

Then Linda graduated from law school and called with a bomb: "I think it's time we see other people."

Linda and I had known each other for over a decade, since 1973. I'd had a crush on her since the first time I saw her, when I was only eleven. Now, however, her life was moving in a different direction. We'd decided to see other people several times before—often because of me and sometimes because of her. But this time, it sounded final. It was time for her to get on with her life. "I've made up my mind," she said. Relationship over.

I was heartbroken, but it was the best thing that could have happened to me, because it forced me to myself. I had nowhere else to go. My search for new eyes entered a solitary phase. Linda was gone. My parents and siblings were back in Maryland, but psychologically they were worlds away. I thought night and day about poverty and how to help kids survive on the smallest amount of money. I thought about racism and all the subtle ways it appeared: in television sitcoms, in stares in public spaces, in history textbooks, on the front pages of newspapers that chronicled the lives of political and business and entertainment leaders—almost all white. There were precious few people of color in those roles, but I had never noticed that until I tried to understand my students and the way they saw and felt. All of a sudden, my world seemed oblivious, blind. I wasn't the solution. I was the problem.

Four weeks later, I moved out of the apartment I shared with two friends and into the rectory of St. Martin de Porres Church on Dixwell Avenue in the heart of the housing projects and community centers and Baptist churches and street life of the African-American community in New Haven. I was five blocks from Hillhouse High School, across the street from the Elks Club, and a block away from the fire station, whose ambulance was busy almost every night. I wanted to be close to that community, because I somehow knew that the community was close to the answers I was trying to find. And what better place than in a church rectory, so I could focus on my religious practices? Maybe, I thought, only God has the answers to the restless searching in my heart. Maybe praying more or reading the Bible more or talking to priests and nuns more would unlock the secret I was trying to name. Jose Salazar, the pastor, rented me the spare room above the church, and Bertha Corley, the woman who kept the church running, welcomed me in. I was living in a church.

During this time, my dad arranged for my family to spend Christmas vacation in Rome and meet the new Pope, John Paul II. So off we went. I had been impressed with the Pope's dramatic story of growing up in communist Poland, an athlete, an actor, an agent of political change. He was drawing crowds in the millions as he left the confines of the Vatican and journeyed around the globe, but I was on edge as we headed to Europe to meet him. I was still focused on the scene in New Haven. A trip to Rome for a private audience with the Pope only reinforced the distance between my world and that of my students. I resented being confronted with the reality of the gap and the fact that privilege was inextricably a part of me. Flying to Rome and arriving at the Vatican with Swiss Guards in elaborate costumes all around me was just another reminder.

We were escorted to a small holding room and asked to wait. My father had a dozen or more rosaries, which he'd brought for the Pope to bless. There were few chairs, and it became obvious that our meeting was going to be brief—most likely just a passing handshake and quick greeting. Suddenly the door opened and an official came through and told us to line up: the Holy Father was coming. Seconds later the Pope bounded through the door, dressed in simple but radiant white, with a big smile and arm outstretched. He greeted my father and mother, then shook hands with each of us. We assembled for a picture in near silence.

Then my father stepped forward and asked a question that surprised me in its sincere and spontaneous expression of faith: "Holy Father, we believe that you are the vicar of Christ, so I'd like to ask your guidance. What should we do with our lives?"

John Paul gave my dad a wry grin. "You are doing good things. You should continue doing what you're doing," he replied.

My father wanted something more than that. "But what else should we do, Holy Father? What can we do for you?"

I couldn't tell whether the Pope was pleased or annoyed by my father's persistence.

"Continue doing what you're doing," he repeated, "and pray as much as you can."

Then, surprising even myself, I blurted out a question of my own: "But how should we pray, your holiness?"

The Holy Father looked over at me, curious to see who had spoken. He smiled slightly and answered in the strong Polish accent I will never forget: "As simple as possible."

Seconds later, one of his assistants intervened and told us that the Pope had to go. He blessed the rosaries, shook hands again, and headed for the door.

"How should we pray?"

"As simple as possible."

The words stunned me. The rest of the trip was full of churches and museums and adventures and laughs, but the four words of the Pope were by far the most memorable. I returned to New Haven thinking, " 'As simple as possible.' Those are words worth trying to understand."

But how? I loved the prayer group at St. Martin's that convened on Thursday nights. There were about ten of us in the group, and we met in the church basement, a one-room hall with ceiling-level half windows looking out onto the street and the Elks Club bar. From week to week, we shared prayers, studied prayers, and listened to the prayers of one another. It felt like a twelve-step program, not for substance addicts, but instead for refugees of the anxious and fearsome world around us. We sat on metal folding chairs arranged in a circle. We read, shared, and held hands with our eyes closed to call upon a higher power, which we named "the Lord." All my restless struggling and searching must have been more obvious to others than I thought, because after a few weeks, our leader, Elaine Fitzpatrick, gave me some advice. "Have you ever given centering prayer a try?" she asked. "I think you would enjoy it. There's a book you might like—*Centering Prayer*, by Basil Pennington." Something in the way I was searching must've made it clear that I was searching for something deeper. I took the book and began to read it. Without realizing it, I was diving into a whole new world.

Pennington was a Cistercian monk, which meant he was part of one of the most austere religious orders in the Christian tradition.

The Cistercians are known for their strict observance of the ancient rule of Saint Benedict and for their emphasis on simplicity, silence, prayer, and manual labor. Needless to say, Cistercians are not the type of people you meet every day at the grocery store or at the pub. They were, and are, apart. I knew nothing of them.

Pennington's book opened with a quote from St. Paul's letter to the Ephesians that I had heard before, but never *really* heard. "Out of his infinite glory, may God give you the power through his Spirit for your hidden self to grow strong." This time, I did listen, and I was embarrassed to realize I had not the faintest clue what my "hidden self" was.

The book went on to describe a way of being that would turn my world upside down. Pennington taught that prayer wasn't about asking for things or telling God what I wanted to have happen or about apologizing for not being good enough. Prayer was about listening, emptying myself, and being silent. Faith wasn't about a powerful God in the sky who could alter the course of the physical universe but was rather about an experience of inner gratitude for all that is seen and not seen. Prayer was about pausing the inner noise of thoughts and feelings and words and drawing yourself toward nothingness. Most dramatically for me, religion wasn't about judging others or fixing others or conforming my will to an abstract set of principles that were arbitrary and hard to explain. Instead, religion was the pathway to experiencing my soul as a part of me that was already joined to the divine.

The lesson was as simple as it was radical: within each of us, Pennington explained, lay a shrine of ultimate holiness that was empty of all material things but full of love. St. John of the Cross taught the lesson in what seemed outrageous terms: "The soul is somehow God." As I read his words, I couldn't help but stop in shock. "My soul is somehow God?" I thought. Yes, the book offered, and centering prayer was a means to reach and give life to my soul, a means for allowing my soul to find rest in itself and in its source.

As I read, I came to understand that centering prayer relied on insights from the Jewish psalms and prophets, from the Buddhist sutras, from Sufi mystics, from the ritual prayers of Hinduism, as well as from the largely forgotten teachings of the early desert mothers and fathers of Eastern Christianity. Centering prayer was as old as religion itself. Spiritual practices focused on simplicity and union with the divine have existed in most of the world's great religious traditions. But those practices had been all too often forgotten over the course of time, in favor of things that are easier for the reasoning mind to latch on to: dogma, organization, activism. In centering prayer, the goal of prayer is not to fix the world, or the church, or even oneself. The goal is to be at peace with the world and at peace with oneself.

I began to feel as if I had been missing the whole point of religion, and similarly that Pennington might be offering me a path for better understanding the gulf that was separating me from my students, too. Pennington broke it down into a simple framework that was accessible to someone like me, who had never really reflected on my own inner life and, worse, who had been unconsciously afraid of what a little soul-searching might reveal. In my world, therapy was for the weak, help was to be given by the strong, and knowledge and values were my ego's tools for exercising my need to make a difference. I'd made religion into duty.

Centering was different. To be strong was to be silent. Being silent required patience and vulnerability, two qualities I didn't have but all of a sudden wanted to acquire. Knowledge and attention were distractions. They were most often the work of my false self, acting out. Help was what we all needed in order to slow our lives down and find the still space within. To make a difference in someone else's life, I had to start with knowing the difference between my false self and my true self. And I had to have some idea of what my true self was searching for.

For years, I had been frustrated with my inability to change my students, yet also drawn by the mysterious intensity of their search for meaning. I had been stuck between wanting them to conform to a more stable way of life and wanting to imitate their nonconformity and their passion and fearlessness. Chapter five of Pennington's book ended with a story that helped clarify the situation for me.

Among the Syrian Jews there is a series of stories about a very lovable old fellow by the name of Mullernestredon. One day this good man was seen busily searching in the village square, around the trees, under the carts, behind the trash cans. A sympathetic friend approached and asked if he had lost something. "Yes, my key," he answered. The friend joined in the search. After several fruitless and frustrating hours, the friend began to interrogate the old man: "Are you sure you lost your key here in the square? Where did you last see it?" "On the table in my house," was the reply. "Then, why in the name of the heavens are you looking for it out here?" "Because there is more light out here."

"Is that me?" I wondered. Was I searching for a way to meet "expectations" by searching for a solution to poverty, searching for the key to improving education, but looking for both "out there" in the light of ideas and programs and experts? There was more "light" in the world of action and social change and fixing, I thought. And there was no light in my inner life and no light that would let me see the inner lives of my students. But what if the lost key of my purpose and its fulfillment was in some other place—in a darker space, where I'd lost it? What if I had missed the most important lesson of meeting expectations and helping others—that it had to start in silence, doing absolutely nothing?

Maybe my problem wasn't just that I couldn't find answers; maybe the problem was that I wasn't looking in the right place. Pennington continued:

> Like Mullernestredon, we often look for God in our thoughts and imaginings, our feelings and affections, because they seem to us more lightsome. But that is not where God is ultimately to be found. God is to be found in the depths of our being, at the center, at the ground of our being, perceived by the searching light of faith or the knowing embrace of love. All the feelings, thoughts, and images that float around in our prayer do not really put us in touch with him. These are "out in the square." He is within. And there we are so one with him that we are communion, union, prayer.

I don't remember where I was when I read the first few chapters of this book, but I remember exactly where I was when I read these pages. I was sitting in the Church of St. Martin de Porres at night by myself, with only the altar spot lighting on.

The church is small and rectangular, with a single center aisle dividing about a dozen pews. The altar is simple and the side statues— one of Mary, the other of Joseph—are also simple carved brown wood. Dominating the small church is a work that covers the entire front wall behind the altar: a floor-to-ceiling fresco of two scenes from the life of the indigent monk Martin de Porres—Martin of the Poor.

Martin was a man of mixed African and European descent, scorned because of his mixed race and consigned to cleaning toilets at a Dominican monastery in Lima, Peru. Legend tells us that this simple man did not fight the treatment he received but welcomed the lowest duties in the monastery without bitterness. His humility was in itself a form of holiness. But he is remembered today for his frequent forays outside the monastery walls to bring whatever small amounts of food or medicine he could to Lima's teeming masses of indigent and often starving street dwellers. We have nothing that he ever wrote or said to count him among the great saints. We have only the stories of his generosity and personal poverty.

Centuries after his death, I sat alone in a New Haven church at night, paperback book in hand, the story of Mullernestredon in my mind, silence all around me except for the sirens of the street outside my window. I stared at the frescoes. In the scene to the right of the altar, Martin towered from floor to ceiling, clad in simple monastic garb. His eyes were cast down as he handed morsels of food to the poor folk of Lima, who lunged desperately toward him. In the scene on the left, Martin cradled a dying man in his arms, while below him others lay in want and squalor. "What am I seeing here?" I wondered. I turned back to the book. Pennington wrote:

There is another story told of a rabbi—Rabbi Zuscha. On his deathbed he was asked what he thought the Kingdom of God would be like.

The old Rabbi thought for a long time; then he replied: "I don't really know. But one thing I do know: When I get there, I am not going to be asked, 'Why weren't you Moses?'

or 'Why weren't you David?' I am going to be asked, 'Why weren't you Zuscha?'"

This is what Centering Prayer aims at: being who we really are.

At that moment, I felt Rabbi Zuscha rise out of that book and, as far as I was concerned, he took a seat right next to me in that dark church. He was as real as the wooden pew I was sitting on. Without saying a word, the two of us looked up at the Dominican saint, and I understood as never before that Martin de Porres was a saint for only one reason: he'd become Martin, the Martin God made him to be, the Martin God loved, the Martin God cherished. He was a saint because he'd filled his unique purpose and no one else's. Now, in effect, Rabbi Zuscha turned to me as if to give me a preview of what I, too, would be asked someday, a question I had never considered: "Why aren't you being Tim?"

I had no idea how to answer it. I had worked hard to become like the scholars at Yale. And I'd tried hard to become like my father the poverty warrior and like my mother the relentless fighter. I'd tried to be like my friend Bob Brown, who was beloved by thousands of young people. And I'd tried to be like my uncle Jack, the gigantically famous hero of millions around the globe—and my mother's hero, too. But I'd missed the point where it all came together—my political zeal, my educational insights, my love interests, my religious longing. God was not "out there," waiting for me to perform some act of brilliance or fame, but was rather within. God's presence wasn't to be sought in grand designs but in profound simplicity. The faith that had so animated my search had been missing the critical piece: God's satisfaction with me, which I had no need to earn. I sat in that dark church and for the first time in my life, I felt the ultimate presence of God sitting with me. But she wasn't a moving statue or a voice talking from the clouds. The ultimate was the restless longing within my own spirit, the same longing that had urged Martin to be Martin de Porres and feed the hungry, that had urged the Cistercians to know themselves by seeking God in the center of all things, that had brought me to that moment in that church to offer me a different way.

My mind continued to scramble to understand what was going on. If I could follow Rabbi Zuscha's lesson, I thought, and believe that it was worth being who I was created to be, what might happen? It sounds simple in retrospect, but "Be the unique person you were created to be" was a goal I had never imagined. I had no idea what it meant to be me. But I felt tears well up in my eyes as I sat with Rabbi Zuscha and with St. Martin and realized that I'd never really thought this "me" was a person worth being. And I realized in that dim light that all those struggles with my students were really just a struggle with myself. If I wanted to be of any help to those teenagers, I would first have to practice recognizing the unique beauty of each one of them. And I would have to start by recognizing mine, as well.

That was the first step in learning how to see from within, how to see with the eye of love. And although I was just a beginner, I started to see differently almost right away. Right away, religion had a new goal: to find God at the depth of my being. It was a goal that I needed to reach with my heart, not my head. Teaching had a new goal: not to "fix" anyone but to see my students from the inside out and to love each one so each would love the life they were meant to lead. And I had a new career goal, too: to follow the rabbi's deathbed admonition and learn to understand how the world could have so much suffering and yet be so filled with love, too.

My first stop was to try to figure out my relationship with the love of my life, Linda Potter. My challenge was to figure out how to tell her and everyone else what I had discovered.

EIGHT

Being in Love

Being Tim.

That sounded great, but it also sounded weird. I wasn't about to call my friends and announce to them that I'd found the secret of life and it was "being Tim." I was afraid that "seeing from within" sounded silly in the real world of thought and power and struggle. I worried that centering might just be an escape from reality. As it rumbled around in my mind, I worried that it might be just a nice-sounding way of deluding myself. I wasn't about to admit to anyone that I had been so confused about myself or my work that I'd been reduced to sitting alone in a Catholic church and doing some time travel with a dead Syrian rabbi and a dead Peruvian monk.

If you want to know what I felt like, try looking in the bathroom mirror some morning and saying to yourself: "I really want to be me today. I don't want to be inauthentic, fake, or superficial. I want to be me because being me is enough." If you're like me, this can feel really good to say *as long as no one is listening*! But by the time you leave the bathroom, if you're like me, you will have forgotten about it altogether. Within moments, you're getting dressed and getting ready for the tasks ahead of you that day: work, family, money, health, fun, friends, whatever. If they require you to act confident when you're not, you do it. If they require you to pretend to be someone you're not or do things you don't really want to do, then so be it. That's the attitude I had, at any rate. Being myself sounded amazing, even liberating, but I didn't know how to turn it into an option for the real world. I was excited by the idea that I could fulfill all those high expectations of my childhood simply by being myself. But I was clueless about how to turn my true self into a skill for me or a message for anyone else.

In retrospect, I can see that throughout most of my work in New Haven, I had been trying to prove that *I* mattered, not just that I could do work that mattered. I think people in their twenties often confuse the two, and for many the confusion is lifelong. It's hard to believe in yourself when you're trying to prove yourself. In my family, we mixed up believing in one another with proving ourselves to one another all the time. Doing well and achieving great things seemed to result in more attention, more affection, more love. And the formula seemed clear and reasonable: if you want to be someone who counts, do something that counts. My cousin Patrick Kennedy served in the U.S. Congress for sixteen years. But, as he once noted, "I didn't run to get a seat in Congress. I ran because I wanted to get a seat at the family dinner table."

Therein lay another problem. If you wanted to win attention in my family, you knew the goalposts were painfully high. The primary goal against which everyone was measured was becoming president of the United States. I didn't need to be a math major to realize that given the fact that I had twenty-seven cousins, we weren't all going to make it. I wasn't as funny as the charismatic people in my family, and they were hilarious. I wasn't as smart as the successful people in my family, and they were brilliant. I wasn't as good-looking as the entertaining people in my family, and they were so good-looking they'd splashed themselves into history books and magazines by the thousands. In my worldview, self-doubt was justified. It was obvious to me that I was never going to live up to those high expectations.

So how could I possibly become self-aware? When I tried centering prayer and sitting in silence, I mostly fidgeted and wanted it to end. When I read poetry that captured the emotion of self-awareness, I mostly worried that it was just a distraction. When I went to church, I mostly worried that I was in a private club that had little relevance to the real world. Most people are at least a little like me:

they want the benefits of self-emptying and detachment, but they have a hard time paying the price of working through the discomfort to get there. As much as I wanted to believe that finding my "inner self" was the solution, my head kept telling me to face the real world and get to work.

And then, another breakthrough. Linda wrote and then called me and then swept me off my feet by telling me that she wanted to come back into my life. Linda had spent the fall during her first year after law school running the issues research team for Al Gore's first Senate campaign. During those six or so months, she'd written me several times, and the message was always the same: "I love you. I hope someday we'll get back together." I always read the letters quickly and put them away. I wanted to believe them but wasn't strong enough to trust them. I was living in a rectory and trying to move on from our relationship. She was dating other guys and I was dating the idea of priesthood. I just put the letters away and tried to ignore them. I would only reread them several times a week.

When she called to say she wanted to come visit me in New Haven, I had my defenses ready. "Why come?"

"Because I want to see you and talk to you."

"We can talk on the phone."

"Did you get my last letter? I want to come tell you that I love you."

"I got your letters, but we have to move on. You're on your way to other things and so am I."

"Can I just come see you?"

"I don't think it's a good idea."

"I do."

"I don't."

"I do."

"I don't."

"How about I just come up for the day? What about next week? Wednesday?"

"Wednesday? I'll be around, but I don't think it's a good idea."

"Okay. I'll come Wednesday. We can have dinner."

"I don't know."

"Great, see you Wednesday."

Yes!

And so we fell in love again—not that we'd ever fallen out—and we started over. She finished with the Gore campaign and left Nashville to move to Washington, DC, for a job at a major international law firm. I finished my fellowship at the Yale Child Study Center and decided to go to graduate school to study spirituality and education—in Washington, too. I'd learned a huge amount about child development and become enamored of James Comer's idea that schools needed to be retooled around the social, emotional, cognitive, and spiritual needs and developmental abilities of children. As I packed my bags in the rectory of St. Martin de Porres Church in New Haven, I set off for a year of graduate school with the hope of finding professors who could help me understand both the developmental needs of children and the longing of their spirits, too. I wanted to learn about the "lure of the transcendent," but I also wanted to learn about the science of child development so I could make the search for ultimate meaning and value into inspirational teaching and learning. And I wanted to do both with Linda.

In September 1985, I arrived on the campus of the Catholic University of America to begin a master's degree in religion and education with a focus on spirituality. It was an unlikely destination, because I didn't really want what I thought a "Catholic" university would teach: a lot of dogma and papal proclamations. On the other hand, it was in Washington, where I wanted to be, and it had the combination of disciplines I wanted to learn. So I showed up in September for my first class: an introduction to spirituality.

Much to my surprise, it was scheduled to be taught by a visiting professor from Georgia State—a public university that was hardly known as a bastion of Catholic piety. Dr. James Robertson Price III was young, intense, and Episcopalian, no less. He had recently completed a Ph.D. at the University of Chicago with a concentration on a saint from the Eastern Church, Symeon the New Theologian, who was utterly unfamiliar to me. His special interest was the teachings of the mystics. But he was also trained in philosophy. He'd mastered the work of the Canadian philosopher Bernard Lonergan and his massive study of human understanding. Price was just as interested in how to think as he was in how to pray. That was a combination I was desperate to find.

Professor Price was twenty minutes late to our first class and entered our small seminar room on an upper floor of a gray gothic building out of breath. "I forgot the syllabus," were his first words, "but I will give you a quick overview of what we're going to do this semester. This is a science course, and you are the lab. Our experiment will be about the interiority of religion. We will explore the work of the mystics, and we will learn a method for applying those lessons to everyday life. Both are essential to an understanding of spirituality. The head and the spirit are never separate. Head and heart always operate together. In this class, you'll learn how."

In the weeks and months that followed, we read Buddhist teachers on the science and practice of non-attachment, and we learned that non-attachment is another way of removing anxiety and fear from your mind so you can see clearly. We read the unknown medieval author of *The Cloud of Unknowing* on the practice of interior silence and self-emptying consciousness, and we learned that self-emptying is a way of creating the openness to be able to see your own unity with the universe and thus to see clearly the unity of all creation. We read the German mystic Meister Eckhart on understanding that within each of us, there is "a spirit that alone is free," and we learned that spiritual freedom liberates the mind to see without judging and thus to see clearly. We read Julian of Norwich on the power of love to make a world where "all will be well," and we saw in her the practice of the kind of peace that reveals love in all things. And we read the Hindu guru Ramana Maharshi on the power of non-dual consciousness to sustain a way of seeing unity always.

On top of the lessons of the great spiritual masters, we also read the philosophy of religion to make sure that we could not only experience the eye of love and the presence of God, but also learn how the search for God was actually operating in all of our action and thinking. Price taught Aristotle and Aquinas and introduced Lonergan's "method" for applying them to the moral and political and religious issues of our time. I had always been afraid that the whole religious undertaking rested on a quirky and indefensible image of God as a magical being with a white beard, whose existence was unsubstantiated by anything other than fantasy. As it turned out, the opposite is true.

Price taught that there is ample evidence of the existence of God, but the evidence doesn't necessarily come from the clouds or the Bible or some other revelation. It comes from within each of us, from an honest examination of our own consciousness. Despite the enormous variations in human experience, Lonergan argued, we all have one thing in common: we are all conscious. Consciousness begins with pure experience without any interpretation. It's awareness without any object. It isn't being aware of "this" or "that" but rather pure awareness itself. If you can be aware of your own awareness and aware of the questions that draw you from awareness to action, you begin to experience consciousness itself, and you begin to see that it is infinite possibility and infinite desire with no beginning and no end.

Lonergan called the source and destination of consciousness God. In our day-to-day search for knowledge and meaning and belonging, we invariably find ourselves seeking what we can't get: perfect happiness, harmony, justice, beauty, the "peace that passes all understanding." In one way or another, everything we do is a form of searching for the unconditional truth we call God. Turning inward allows us to see this wellspring of energy and to see ourselves searching for it, too. The best way to reach for the presence of God is to peel back the layers of our thinking and feeling and see that God is in all of it. Whenever we have thoughts of any kind, we are also thinking about the one perfect thought: God. And regardless of how many millions of different ways we answer the question of God, whether we be theists or atheists or agnostics, our asking and searching and wondering and hoping are enough to show us that it is our nature to want to belong to the one thing that is beyond all things: God.

That was class with Professor Price. It was amazing. It taught me that searching for the inner eye of my heart was the way to understand all my thoughts and actions, not just religious ones, and that the eye of the heart was within others, too. It taught me that my longing to believe in the God of unconditional love was the most reasonable way of seeing the world, despite all its apparent flaws and pains. As I listened and studied, I could feel my students back in New Haven with me, too—frustrated but searching in their own smart ways for what matters most.

But unconditional love is not a theoretical experience. Weeks after my first course with Dr. Price, I pulled a sapphire ring I had bought in New Haven out of my pocket and asked the most loving human being I had ever met, Linda Potter, to marry me. We had been together off and on for eight years, but even before we had started dating, I had fallen in love with her at first sight when I was only eleven years old and we played tennis together. Her eyes were happier and more curious and more gentle than any I'd ever seen. She was flirtatious, too—just enough. All I can really remember is the sight of her on the court, smiling, laughing, asking me for advice on how to hit a forehand. I was transfixed.

But getting married is not the same as being crazy about someone. Linda and I came from different backgrounds and different cultures. Her family had roots in the Mayflower and old New York; mine in the famine ships of the nineteenth century and upstart Boston. Hers was private and circumspect and Episcopalian; the Potters were *nice*. They were restrained in the outward expression of emotion, but they cultivated strong relationships. My Irish Catholicism, on the other hand, was extroverted, communal, but not gentle. It was political in the broadest sense—striving, assertive, proud, hungry for social justice—but it steamrolled delicate feelings in the exuberance of its activity. It could trample people on its way to championing a cause.

Linda's parents had their children baptized, took them to church on Sunday, and introduced them to the ideas and rituals of religion. But her dad believed faith to be a personal pursuit, so he never forced the children to do anything religious. Linda's mom was generous and compassionate, but not religious in any traditional way. In her experience, religion was all too often a vehicle for exclusion, judgment, and bias, and she wanted no part of that. Linda grew up under her mother's wing, never taking an adversarial stance against faith but never embracing it, either.

Then along came me. As much as we loved each other, we had a ton of differences that needed reconciling and letting go. We approached the big questions from opposite directions. I was all about figuring out the God question and trying to get it right. She was try-

ing to figure it out, too, but her focus was on being inclusive. I wanted
to go to church; she wanted to help people. I wanted to read theology;
she wanted to read beautiful novels. I wanted to practice centering
prayer and analyze spiritual ideas; she wanted to talk and make sense
and connect emotionally. When I used words that were drawn from
the Bible, she heard Catholic superiority. When I brought up what I
thought were beautiful parables from the gospels or poetry from the
prophets, she heard proselytizing and dogmatic arrogance. When she
focused on core values like kindness and fairness, I heard relativism.
When I wanted to say a "Hail Mary," as I had done all my life, she
wanted to take a break.

Our struggle came to a head one evening as we began the "Pre-
Cana" process, a series of meetings required for marriage in the
Catholic tradition. Pre-Cana is the post–Vatican II Church's way of
preparing couples for the serious and lifelong commitment of marriage. All couples are required to pursue a short course of reflection
and preparation. We decided to do ours with a wonderful Franciscan
monk, who was also a marriage counselor of sorts.

We rang the bell to the dark Franciscan monastery that sits on
the hill overlooking Catholic University. In time we heard the shuffle
of footsteps. Father John Appledorn, OFM, came out to welcome us.
He was wearing his long brown Capuchin robe, and he walked slowly
with a gentle air.

"Hello."

I leapt to connect and engage. "It's great to meet you," I gushed,
as if campaigning. "We've heard so much about you. Thank you for
being willing to see us. We're very appreciative."

He just looked at us. "Let's walk down the hall here a bit. There's
a quiet room over here."

That first night with Father John, as we began to talk about the
wedding celebration itself, Linda opened with her concern: "I don't
want the ceremony to mention Jesus, because there will be people of
many faiths, and I don't want them to feel excluded."

"You don't want to mention *Jesus?*" I said incredulously. My mind
raced. Should I fight her on this? And how? "Linda," I said as calmly
as I could. "Jesus is the center of my religious beliefs. And we're going to
be in a Catholic church. We can't *not mention Jesus*. That's a nonstarter."

"Father Appledorn," she countered, "do you know what I mean? Catholics always want to emphasize their superiority and when they mention Jesus, it's all about Catholics telling the world they know what's right and everyone else is wrong. Do you see what I'm trying to say to Tim?"

This Franciscan had known us for only a few minutes and already he was in the middle of a premarital spat, and a pretty profound one. But with the generosity of spirit for which the Franciscans are known, Appledorn took a long pause and said, "I can see you two are going to be an interesting couple to work with! And yes, Linda, I know what you mean. Jesus can seem like a judgmental and non-loving figure if you listen to the way some people talk about him. But let's see if we can find a way around this."

A part of me wanted to power my way through Linda's resistance and demand that the wedding fit my definition of a religious ceremony in the Christian tradition. And a part of me felt I was being totally reasonable in doing so. What could be more reasonable than wanting to call upon the name at the source of Christianity and the name at the source of the spiritual journey that I considered central to my life? But there was another part of me that recognized that Linda's concern wasn't coming from a place of disdain for the gospels but rather from a place of compassion for everyone else who would be in the church on our wedding day.

We left Father Appledorn's small office at the end of the hour in an awkward silence and walked down the narrow hall of the monastery, out past the heavy wooden door, and down the short sloping hill to the parking lot. We walked to our car as if in a "no talk zone," wound into silence by the tension of whom we each thought we were and whom we each wanted to become together. We were creating something new, something that was foreign and unknown. We were beginning the intensive part of the marriage journey—the part where romance and attraction and play yield to constructing a new life together. We were beginning the inner work of deciding what to hold on to and what to let go of as we struggled to create one common life from the distinct and often opposing histories of two. We were trying to express the love that had drawn us from our separate worlds to each other—the kind of love that is beyond any name.

If I'd been paying attention to Zuscha or Lonergan, I would've known I was the one who needed to change. The challenge was right in front of my eyes; after all, I was in graduate school precisely to learn how to express the longing for God in words other than "God" or "Yahweh" or "Jesus." How could I hope to convey to kids in the streets of New Haven that my world had been blown open by a mysterious power that promised life-changing energy and purpose if I couldn't even convey it to the person I loved most? I already knew that my future teaching in public schools wasn't going to be able to depend on the language of Christianity, but I hadn't realized that the first test of my spiritual worldview was going to be our wedding ceremony.

That's where I was able to turn again to Bernard Lonergan. His investigations into consciousness explored not just the ways in which questions of ultimate meaning and value are experienced but also the way in which they are fulfilled. In simple terms, he developed a theology of how to find God: by falling in love. When a person falls in love, he wrote,

One's being becomes a being-in-love. Such being-in-love has its antecedents, its causes, its conditions, its occasions. But once it has blossomed forth and as long as it lasts, it takes over. It is the first principle. From it flow one's desires and fears, one's joys and sorrows, one's discernment of values, one's decisions and deeds.

Being-in-love is of different kinds. There is the love of intimacy, of husband and wife, of parents and children. There is the love of one's fellow men with its fruit in the achievement of human welfare. There is the love of God with one's whole heart and whole soul, with all one's mind and all one's strength (Mk. 12:30). It is God's love flooding our hearts through the Holy Spirit given to us (Rom 5:5). It grounds the conviction of St. Paul that "there is nothing in death or life, in the realm of spirits or superhuman powers, in the world as it is or the world as it shall be, in the forces of the universe, in heights or depths—nothing in all creation that can separate us from the love of God . . ."

As the question of God is implicit in all our questioning, so being in love with God is the basic fulfilment of our conscious intentionality. That fulfilment brings a deep-set joy that can remain despite humiliation, failure, privation, pain, betrayal, desertion. That fulfilment brings a radical peace, the peace that the world cannot give. That fulfilment bears fruit in a love of one's neighbor that strives mightily to bring about the kingdom of God on this earth. On the other hand, the absence of that fulfilment opens the way to the trivialization of human life in the pursuit of fun, to the harshness of human life arising from the ruthless exercise of power, to despair about human welfare springing from the conviction that the universe is absurd.

Here, there was yet another breakthrough for me: the highest aspiration of life was falling in love. That was my first principle. It was Linda's first principle. It was everyone's first principle. We are made to fall in love with each other, with ourselves, and with all things. Slowly—ever so slowly, a light went off in my head. Here, in Lonergan's otherwise dense philosophical theology, was a framing of the code that I hadn't understood: the search for God that I felt in myself and sensed in others could be satisfied by falling in love—not by talking about it or teaching about it, but by falling into it. Believing in God is not thinking God. It's believing that we are happy and true to ourselves only when we give ourselves away to another, to the whole of creation, to love. That's what faith is all about: trusting that you must give yourself away and only then discover the self you were made to be. That's what it means to be made by and for transcendence, to be a being made like God. It means that you are made to give yourself to all things. No exceptions.

The God experience that I so wanted to have and to share was right in front of my eyes: it was in my breaking through to Linda in love.

"At this point," the Franciscan Richard Rohr notes, "it's not like one has a new relationship with God; it's like one has a whole new God!" Words that I had heard before as creeds began to sound like experiences. In the Christian gospels, Jesus says, "the Father and I are one," and all of a sudden I heard him talking about his own experience of unity and love with all things. The Jewish psalmist says, "God himself is my counselor, and at night my innermost being instructs me," and all of a sudden I heard him talking about his experience of a deep trust in the divine. Rohr extends the insight to its fullest meaning: "God is operating with you, in you, and even *as* you." It finally dawned on me that the feeling of being in love was an experience of God. That was fabulous!

Over the course of my studies in spirituality and Linda's and my preparation for marrying, we both started to understand how to bring the parts of our lives together. Understanding isn't the same as doing—the doing would take years. But at least we started to realize we didn't need to know perfect answers anymore. The right questions were enough. The longing of my heart was Linda, and I was hers, too. We'd been in love, but now we needed to fall in love. That meant being vulnerable with each other and letting go of our moorings. It meant becoming believers—becoming "beings in love." We were learning to trust each other and to believe in each other enough to compromise on our most cherished ideas. With faith in each other, we were learning to fall.

At the end of the academic year, Linda Potter and I celebrated the sacrament of falling in love. We tried with everything we had and everything we were to make the ceremony a celebration of the spirit we shared and the spirit we received from our many friends and family. We were married in the 150-year-old chapel at Georgetown University, Linda's alma mater. Presiding was a friend of ours, Father Richard Fragomeni, who made the congregation laugh when he mentioned that Linda and I had a weakness for needing to "discuss everything!" The small, beautiful gothic-revival chapel in the middle of the Georgetown campus was jammed with more than three hundred guests. The New Haven gospel choir the Vernon Jones Singers sang with joyful exuberance, "Blessed Assurance, Jesus Is Mine," and the entire congregation—Christians and non-Christians alike—beamed with enthusiasm. We read the prophet Micah's exhortation to "love tenderly," and we read St. Luke's story of resurrection, where travelers on the road to Emmaus felt the presence of God as their "hearts burned within." And seated on the altar next to Father Fragomeni was the six-foot five-inch Episcopal bishop of New York, Paul Moore, who happened to be Linda's godfather. I don't know that I'd ever heard of a wedding with both Catholic and Episcopal clergy sharing duties in a Catholic church, but there they sat together.

We were in territory that was uncharted for both of us, but we were trying to do what our love called us to do: announce the power of unconditional love in a way that anyone could understand and see and feel as divine. Two days later, we took off on our honeymoon to Nepal and India to explore the ancient holy sites of Hinduism, Buddhism, and Christianity. And when we came home, Linda and I headed back to New Haven together. I was no longer intent on trying to teach English or history; I was intent on trying to show my students how much I loved them and trust that English and history would take care of themselves.

NINE

Social and Emotional Learning

Linda and I moved back to New Haven in the fall of 1986. Linda launched her legal practice as a staff attorney at Yale Legal Services, representing children in neglect and abuse cases. I returned to Hillhouse High School, where a New Haven basketball icon, Salvatore "Red" Verderame, had just taken over as principal, and a fiery educator from out of town, Dr. John Dow, Jr., had taken over as superintendent. In my first week back, a student was shot just a few feet from where I was standing at dismissal. Blood splattered my clothes as cruel evidence of the drug wars that were escalating all around the city. The urgency of change was inescapable. More and more kids were looking for belonging in the wrong places—deadly wrong places. Linda and I were exactly where we wanted to be: trying to do something about it. And within a month, she was pregnant and our family adventure was under way, too.

Over the following years, our first child, Rose, was followed by another, Tim, and then another, Sam, and then another, Kathleen, and then another, Caroline. Our life as a family was enormously full and happy and exhausting. At work, I searched for ways to give students a chance to integrate their inner lives with academic tasks. Red Verderame became my mentor and gave me broad latitude to try to figure out what new ideas might reduce the crushing dropout rate and the persistent violence at Hillhouse. Impatient with the pace of change, Dow pressed Red and the whole team at Hillhouse for new solutions. I reached back to the Comer team at Yale for practical ideas and helped start a Hillhouse "mental health team" and a site-based management team to engage parents and community leaders.

And I kept looking for ways to teach students how to see from within and believe from within, without using those words. I was lucky to meet great educators such as Bridget Hardy, Karol DeFalco, Dee Speese-Linehan, Mickey Kavanagh, Burt Saxon, and Gary Highsmith—all innovators in elementary, middle, and high schools seeking ways to connect meaningfully with their students. We found our way to another Yale professor, Dr. Roger Weissberg, who was writing and implementing new curricula that taught middle school kids "social problem-solving" skills, and we decided to try it in a couple of grades. Another curriculum, for example, taught first graders to develop an awareness of how their words could affect their peers. We taught them the difference between saying something positive, calling it a "warm fuzzy," and saying something negative, calling it a "cold prickly." I'd never seen a first grader discuss "warm fuzzys" and "cold pricklys," and it was fascinating. It was one of the most important lessons I ever saw taught. Middle school students learned to create "stress thermometers" so they could measure their own emotional reactions and thereby be less inclined to act impetuously and destructively. Try to create one for yourself. It's a fantastic way to monitor your own emotional ups and downs. High school students learned to set positive goals that insured nonviolent and healing approaches to interpersonal conflict and community problems. That, too, is a great skill to master.

Without knowing it, we were the first district-level team in the country to try to create a comprehensive approach to what we later named "social and emotional learning." Working with Roger Weissberg, Red Verderame, John Dow, and my fellow teachers, I founded a citywide initiative to promote the teaching of these skills in every grade throughout the entire school system. At the center of all this ambitious effort was Roger's stoplight problem-solving curriculum. During many years of research, he had developed a system for teaching children how to manage their inner lives and interact positively with others. He created a month of lessons that could be taught in an average sixth-grade class and that covered a powerful array of skills and relationship opportunities for children and adults alike. The whole curriculum was encapsulated in the symbol of a stoplight: the red light represented the many skills needed to calm down in a stressful situation and take stock of feelings and goals—the key elements of self-awareness. The yellow light represented the package of skills needed to sort your way through the anxiety and confusion of stressful situations and shape clear and achievable goals—the key elements of self-empowerment. The green light represented the array of behaviors and actions needed to act positively to resolve problems in a way that neither harmed others nor harmed oneself—the key elements of building positive relationships. The underlying lessons were rich in texture and insight, but the stoplight made it seem easy, as it broke those lessons down into six easy-to-remember steps:

When you have a problem:
Stop, calm down, and think before you act
Say the problem and how you feel
Set a positive goal
Think of lots of solutions
Think ahead to the consequences
Go ahead and try the best plan

I watched Karol DeFalco, a master teacher, lead her students in these skills, and I could see that she was teaching kids not only important skills but also powerful experiences of interior discovery—some lessons prompted students to try to trust their peers and adults in an almost spiritual way. I watched children practicing stress management techniques such as quiet breathing, and I could see them learning to find the quiet and peaceful spaces within themselves, much like Pennington or Maharshi taught. I watched kids struggle to set positive goals, which often required forgiveness, and I could hear echoes of spiritual teachings on healing and the prophetic politics of Gandhi and King. I watched children thinking deliberately and reflectively about how to muster the energy to take action in the face of adversity, and I could hear echoes of the World War II–era mystic activist Simone

Weil and the Holocaust survivor Viktor Frankl, who acted in the face of horrific conditions with resolute and self-possessed strength and faith. "Social Development" classes were a combination of emotional self-awareness, relationship skills, values, and inspiration. They were terrific.

More or less. I brought the problem-solving framework to an after-school group I started for students at Hillhouse, the Young Men's Leadership Group, and asked the twenty-five high school young men to learn a shortened version of the program. For a few weeks, our meetings were focused on problem-solving skills and role-playing among ourselves. Doug Bethea, an outspoken and charismatic junior, always wanted to lead the discussions and plan service outings and dances and anything to promote positive activity among his peers. He'd join the other young men in making fun of the simplicity and childlike nature of the stoplight, but then he'd dive into issues of immediate concern. "Some guy dissed you, Lamont, last week in the cafe and you started a huge fight. You think you couldda 'calmed down' before you punched him?" After a short pause, Doug bounced in: "Hell no you wasn't gonna 'calm down' but you shoudda."

Lamont Young was a broad-shouldered, strongly built athlete of a kid with a huge smile and a quiet shyness. He walked through the halls of Hillhouse like a gentle charmer. Girls liked him, his football coach liked him, and he had an older brother, Larry, who always looked out for him. Lamont laughed at Dougie's example of his recent fight, but agreed. "Next time," he muttered. "Next time, I'll call Shriver and have him bring me a stoplight in the cafe. Watch me!" He smiled as if to show he had an understanding of what he should do when trouble found him next. But his tone was honest, too: he grinned, as though admitting that the challenge of being calm amid a conflict was probably more than he could handle.

And so the conversations went. We discussed girlfriend conflicts, parent conflicts, gangs, grades, teachers, clothes, churches, counselors, and more. The guys seemed to welcome the whole idea of having the safe space of the group in which to talk among themselves about their experiences and the tension of school and community life. For more than a month or two, problem solving was the center of the Young Men's Leadership Group, and I was thrilled by the chance it was giving me and the students to open up and try to face the real challenges of life. It wasn't therapy and it wasn't school, either. It was a group of young men trying to discover the source of goodness within themselves and trying to find ways to keep it safe in the world around them. It was intimacy and ultimacy. It was fantastic.

Until it wasn't. One morning, I arrived at Hillhouse to a report of another shooting of one of our students. I went to the main office to ask our principal, Red, what he'd heard from his police sources. He delivered the quick update without emotion: "One of your 'young leaders' was gunned down last night. Shot seven times. A kid named Lamont Young. You know him?"

I was stunned. "Are you sure? I can't believe that! Are you sure it was Lamont Young, the same one in my group?" Red knew enough not to answer me. There was no answer that wasn't already obvious. Of course it was the same Lamont Young. Of course it was the Lamont Young in the Young Men's Leadership Group. Of course he was sure. He just stared down at me over his six-foot-six frame with the wordless look of a man who knew of the brutality of the world in which our kids were living and wasn't sure I had understood it yet. "They shot him seven times at point-blank range, Tim. Believe it or not, he's still alive, but I'm not sure how long he'll last."

"He's still alive? Where is he?"

"He's at Yale New Haven Hospital. I'll let you know if I hear anything else."

I stumbled out of Red's office and back to work—to classrooms, to hall duty, to monitoring the cafeteria, to activities. I was intent on getting down to the hospital as soon as my workday was over and only hoped that Lamont would hang on long enough for me to say goodbye. I could feel a sense of déjà vu come over me as I went through my day: there I was again, confronted by the same heartbreak, the same shock, the same enveloping despair that I'd felt before. Lamont was a magical kid with rock star good looks, a kindness that was unmistakable, and a sixteen-year-old's naïve but eager desire to find his way. I realized I was crazy about him—that he and I and the others in the group had developed an understanding of one another, a trust among ourselves born of confidence, a powerful bond born of mutual affection. It was awkward to think of how all we males had become so close and, though we never showed it openly, so loving toward one another. And now Lamont was dying because none of us had been able to protect him from forces too strong to oppose.

It was about 6:00 p.m. when I arrived at Yale New Haven Hospital and asked to see Lamont Young. I was shocked to find out that he wasn't in intensive care and that there were no family members visiting at the time. I was asked to register with the New Haven Police, since Lamont was a victim of an attempted homicide, and I did so. There were no restrictions on visiting, which surprised me again. But as I approached his room, I could see a cop standing guard at his door, and he checked my identification. I didn't know if he was there to protect Lamont from further attacks or to investigate visitors for information on the crime. Or maybe, I thought, he's just here so that when Lamont dies, there will be a law enforcement official to confirm a killing.

I opened the door quietly, not knowing what to expect. The room was lit by a late-afternoon sun that was pouring in through an uncovered window. At first, I saw only the light. And then I saw an amazing sight: a full human body bound up completely—a leg suspended in the air by slings wrapped thick like a tree; a chest coated in bandages high enough to appear as though pillows were stacked under it; a head fully wrapped in bandages that allowed only small openings for eyes and nose and mouth. Lamont was a still-living mummy with eyes closed and body motionless. As I approached the side of the bed, I began to notice the line of machines connecting him to wires and drugs and began to hear all the beeps and monitors as they kept their ghoulish account of a body in distress.

"Lamont," I whispered. "It's Shriver here. I'm here to tell you I'm so sorry about all this and I'm praying for you, and . . ." My voice trailed off. The body didn't move. Nothing seemed to move other than the lines on the machines and the slow pumps moving drugs from their sterile bags into his wound-littered frame. I tried again. "Lamont. I don't want to tire you, but I want you to know that all of us at Hillhouse are pulling for you. The guys in the 'L' [our short for the leadership group] are all here for you." Nothing. No movement, no sound, no response.

Then Lamont Young's eyes opened up just the slightest bit, and believe it or not, I detected the smallest smile on his covered face. And I could see he was trying to move his lips, so I came close to him. Then he whispered with all his energy, "Thanks, Shrives." And then he drew another labored breath: "Next time," and another breath: "I'll use problem solving."

It was as though I'd heard a voice from the dead, and I replayed it in my mind to make sure it was real. I whispered, "You'll use problem solving? Is that what you said, Lamont? Next time, you'll use problem solving?" He didn't answer, but he smiled. My eyes teared up and I smiled as I gave myself permission to feel the joy of this wonderful kid and my connection with him, despite the horror of the setting. "Next time? Yeah. Next time, Lamont. Next time you'll be fine."

I smiled and reached out to touch his heavily wrapped arm gently. The conditions couldn't have been much worse. He was near death and I was once again confronting my inability to make a difference. But though it seems selfish and obtuse to suggest, I remember feeling that our relationship couldn't have been much stronger. Amid the violence and the physical agony of Lamont Young's fragile life, he was whispering, hopeful, aware, connected. We were together in our little web of life, joined somehow in our vulnerability and our longing. And though I couldn't claim to have helped end the carnage of his life or the anger of those who had attacked him, I could claim something precious still: a friend.

Miraculously, Lamont Young survived seven point-blank gunshot wounds and is now a graduate student at Fordham University. The social development project survived, too. We went citywide to all grade levels with our curriculum, offering teachers as much training as we could. And we created hundreds of after-school activities like the Young Men's Leadership Group that emphasized everything from outdoor education, to early reading skills, to college visitations, to the arts. We were written about in *The New York Times*, and in a long exploration of urban poverty by William Finnegan in *The New Yorker*. The wildly popular book *Emotional Intelligence*, by Daniel Goleman, reported on our work as an example of a cutting-edge school reform effort. Together with a small group of collaborators (Eileen Growald, Dan Goleman, Dave Sluyter, Linda Lantieri, and Mark Greenberg), we coined the term "social and emotional learning." In the years that followed, the field of social and emotional learning entered the mainstream of education reform, proving its value by improving student behavior, teacher satisfaction, and academic performance. With other educators and scholars, we wrote the first book, *Promoting Social and Emotional Learning: Guidelines for Educators*, describing its components and its power.

It was around this time that the Special Olympics movement caught me off guard and came roaring back into my life. Like hundreds of thousands of volunteers around the world, I had been active in my local program in New Haven. I started to see different things than I'd seen before—things that the mystics and Linda and Lamont and Doug and hundreds of other students had awakened in me. When I attended local Special Olympics games, I suddenly began to see the athletes from within.

I met one athlete who gave me a huge hug at a track event, and then noticed him crying later that day after losing. Instead of dismissing him as awkwardly showy, I was struck by how gifted he was in expressing his inner life. At another local event, I walked by a volunteer who was whispering to another about how silly an athlete was acting. Instead of chiming in, I felt the meanness of the comment and asked her to stop. At the Connecticut Summer Games, I watched a group of athletes mount a medal stand and raise their arms and shout cheers in triumph with only two or three of us standing around to see them, and all of a sudden, I was transfixed by how joyful the athletes were despite the fact that almost no one was watching or seemed to care. I'd been around the athletes and these scenes my whole life, but now the happiness and openness and vulnerability started to break through. The athletes were able to be who they were and say what they felt. They were authentic. For the first time, it occurred to me that I wanted to be like the athletes.

It was around this time that Linda and I met Loretta Claiborne, a woman with an intellectual disability who turned out to be one of my greatest role models in life.

Loretta Claiborne was born on August 14, 1953, during that dark chapter in history when having a child with an intellectual disability was a matter of shame. Loretta was the fourth of Rita Claiborne's eight children. Her father was a man named Ben Ritter, but Loretta never met him. He was one of six men who fathered the children of Rita Claiborne, and, like the others, he never lived with her. Loretta only heard Rita describe him as a man who was quiet but treacherous. "He worked in the stone quarry near the Codorese Creek before the war, under the CCC," she told me. "Somebody tried to cheat him there and he shot him in the neck—old Mr. Mott. Mr. Mott survived—but nobody messed with Ben Ritter."

Rita Claiborne met tough with tough. She cleaned houses, worked as a barmaid, and once had a job at the Housing Council. At home, she taught her children the importance of toughness, too. "She was strict," Loretta said. "She knew we were going to struggle like she struggled. So she was hard on us. She had all her Rita rules, like, 'You gotta try twice as hard as another kid 'cause of your color.' And 'Keep yourself clean. Don't you leave my house unless you have clean clothes on.' And 'Life is about choices and options. What you choose will determine what options you get.' And 'Keep your manners. One of these days, you might eat at the White House, and you sure better know how to eat right, because you're a Claiborne.'"

Loretta was different from Rita's other children. In addition to having an intellectual disability, she was born nearly blind and had problems with her feet, which prevented her from walking until she was four. When she reached school age, Rita sent her to Jefferson, the regular public school in their neighborhood of York, Pennsylvania. There was a special-ed school in York, but it was whites only, so little Loretta had to fend for herself in a regular classroom at Jefferson. By the age of twelve, she was still trying to complete the second grade. She'd been at school for six years. She was angry and frustrated, much like my aunt Rosemary had been. "By then," Loretta said, "I'd done nothing but fight with the other kids, get put in the closet by teachers and kept for after-school detentions, then fight some more. One teacher was so mad at me when I couldn't answer a question that she locked me in the closet for the whole day. What she didn't know was that the cookies was in that closet, too, so I climbed up on the shelf and ate myself all the cookies I wanted locked in there. And that just made her go off, but I didn't care. What's worse than bein' in a closet? She couldn't do no worse to me so what did I care. I figured at least I'll get me the cookies."

Social workers, counselors from the local mental health center, and a "Red Cross lady" visited Rita and tried to teach her how to handle her "retarded" child. Rita simply told them: "If God didn't think I could handle her, God wouldn't have given me her."

Rita lived her life in the belly of the whale, but she had faith. When there was just one too many bullies waiting for Loretta outside, Rita would keep her at home. "She'd braid my hair and pull at my skin real hard and tell me, 'You gotta have faith in your heart, child. You gotta have God in your heart, otherwise you won't get by in this world.'"

When Loretta finally finished the second grade, people from the local mental health center came to test her intelligence. When they told her mother the results, they advised her to institutionalize her daughter. "I didn't know it was an institution," said Loretta. "I thought I was going to a private school, and I was excited. Ms. Dorothy next door brought me a box filled with white clothes as a going-away present. I didn't know anything but that I was getting stuff that my brothers and sisters didn't have, and I was getting to go to a fancy school. I got new pajamas and everything."

On May 18, 1965, a social worker drove Rita and Loretta to the Pennhurst State School and Hospital (earlier known as Eastern Pennsylvania State Institution for the Feeble-Minded and Epileptic) in Spring City, Pennsylvania, to put her there for the rest of her life. It was the first time Loretta had been outside of York. "I was just looking out the window of that car with my little white skirt on and my white top and my plaid sweater with pink and blue in it. I was so excited."

The hospital had been built in 1903 on a site called Crab Hill. The first group of buildings was completed in 1908, and the original campus layout was finished by 1921. Not much changed between then and the date Loretta arrived in 1965. The buildings were overcrowded, but the school was serving its purpose, which, three years later, a groundbreaking multipart NBC report described this way: "to ship the mentally retarded twenty-five miles out of town to forget them while they decay from neglect." Pennhurst was a place where people were "deprived of their dignity and self-respect," with "horrible and almost inhumane conditions." Twenty-eight hundred children were found "rotting in their cages, cribs, and beds." The words were shocking—and they could have been used to describe the conditions in dozens of similar institutions at the time.

When the Claibornes' social worker pulled up to Pennhurst, Loretta noticed that although it was supposed to be a school, "there were no children walking around anywhere." A man gave them a tour and pointed to a cottage across a field, and told Rita that was where Loretta would live. From a distance, it looked tranquil. "There was open space everywhere," said Loretta, "and all the people who met me were nice. I told my mother: 'I like it here, Rita. I want to go here.'"

But something about the place seemed wrong to Rita. She brought Loretta home and told the social worker to give her some time to think about her decision.

A few weeks later, a new social worker, Darrell Nixdorf, visited the Claibornes at home. "Have you decided about sending Loretta to the school?" he asked.

"I made my decision," said Rita, looking at her daughter and then back at Nixdorf. "Loretta's going to be educated right here. I ain't splittin' my family up. My kids will stay together."

Nixdorf fumed. "We went through all that work, Mrs. Claiborne, and now this? You know Loretta belongs at Pennhurst, and you know it will be a lot better for you if she goes."

Rita shook her head. "My kid is staying right here."

Loretta never went back to Pennhurst, and she never left her mother until the day Rita died almost thirty years later. At the age of twelve, she was disappointed by her mother's decision. "It was so bad' for me in York at that time and I just wanted to do anything to get out. I thought I wouldn't get teased out there in the country. Those words and those names and all that ridicule, it was just killing me. I thought anything would be better than how I was living."

By the time Loretta reached tenth grade, the school system was experimenting with alternatives to classroom education, and she left school for the last time. They called her program "school-to-work." Special education suddenly meant getting sent to a "workshop" to do "simple jobs like cutting mats and putting covers on boxes and putting bags of chips and nuts into containers." It was much less stressful than being in a classroom, but Loretta still had a lot of pent-up aggression. Sometimes she got into fights at the workshop. Sometimes she ran. "I hated getting on the bus to go to the workshop, so I started running to work. I did like to run—that was about the only thing I liked doing. Of course, they wouldn't let me run on the school track team because I was a 'retard,' but that didn't stop me from running. I'd run with my brother Hank and I'd run home from school and I'd run to the workshop just to get my mind off of things and to be by myself."

One day there was an announcement on the workshop's PA system. "Loretta Claiborne, please come to the office." Loretta was sure she was in trouble, maybe getting expelled again.

But when she reached the office, Mr. Lee asked pleasantly: "How are you, Loretta?"

Loretta was stunned. He had never asked how she was before. She shrugged, then finally asked: "What did I do?"

Mr. Lee handed her a piece of paper. At the time, she was still functionally illiterate. Not one teacher had yet been able to teach her how to read. "Just take it home to your mother," he said. When Rita read the mysterious paper, she "mumbled something about something for her retarded kid. And she mumbled that she had her other kids learning drums and running track and in school programs but what was she going to get for me? And she threw the paper onto the refrigerator, and I thought that was the end of it."

As it turned out, Mr. Lee was seeing more than Loretta realized. He'd seen her running to the workshop and running all over town, so when he heard about a new sports program that was coming to York for kids with "mental retardation," he thought of Loretta. It was clear that Loretta was an unhappy child, and that she hated school and didn't like the workshop much better. But she seemed to like to run, and Mr. Lee decided to try to build on that.

Loretta forgot all about the mysterious piece of paper that was stuck to her fridge. "Then one Saturday in January comes along and Rita comes into my room at six o'clock in the morning to wake me up, hollering about how I need to go to that program and I better get my butt out of bed and down to the bus to go. I told her I didn't want to go, but she made me go.

"So I went down to a church hall to practice running, and I came home and told Rita that I wanted to quit. She turned to me and said, 'Loretta, you start quitting something today and you'll be a quitter for the rest of your life. You're a Claiborne and you're not quitting.' So the next Saturday, and the one after that, she made me go." Saturday after Saturday, Loretta went and she ran: glumly, sullenly, slowly. She didn't understand the point of the exercise. When her coach asked why she was letting the other kids win the races, she told him bluntly: "Because I don't care." She had become more like her mother than she realized: tough, angry, and depressed, without much hope that life would ever be anything but one long struggle. She was also, of course, a teenager.

Loretta didn't know it, but the running practices her mother was forcing her to attend were Special Olympics practices. After a few months, Mr. Lee took Loretta aside and told her that she could go to a "games," if only she would put her fighting hands down and start to use her running feet. "If you try," he told her, "your feet will take you places." Loretta behaved herself during the next few practices, and so in the spring of 1971, she was invited to go to Central Middle School for the first Special Olympics games of her life.

"It was a sunny day. We had opening ceremonies and speeches and a band played for us. When we got there, they gave me a white shirt with black writing on it made by some students and it said Special Olympics on it and I wore it proud! I got to do the standing long jump and the fifty-yard dash—we had yards in those days, not me-

ters. Then I did the three-hundred-yard dash. And then I got a ribbon and I looked around and I loved it. I can remember it like it just
happened." For the first time in her life, people were cheering for her.
She was having fun and, for once, getting a moment in the spotlight,
something only her brothers and sisters and people on TV usually got.
Other people. Something changed in Loretta's heart that day. "Right
there at Central Middle School, something happened. I belonged to
something. I knew right there, I was doing something I loved. No place
else on earth had ever loved me back. But not anymore. At Special
Olympics, I belonged."

The something that happened was, in retrospect, nothing mysterious. A woman who'd felt mostly shame and anger arrived at a place
where she felt love and belonging. In a way, she didn't have to do
anything to deserve it. She felt it as a gift, just like her white T-shirt.
Everything changed, and it's easy to see why: she found her place in
the world. And after a few weeks, it happened again. Mr. Lee announced to the students at the workshop that they were invited to
another Special Olympics event. This time, it would be a two-day
games. They would be going away for an overnight.

"Not me," Loretta snapped. "I don't have the money for all that."

"It's free, Loretta," said Mr. Lee. "Ask your mother for permission
to go to the Westchester games. Make sure to tell her that there's no
charge."

Loretta took another paper home to Rita with all the information
on it, but Rita took one look at the bus trip and the overnight and
had the same reaction as Loretta. "You ain't going nowhere, Loretta. I
don't have money for you to do all these things."

"But look at the bottom of the paper," Loretta begged. "Mr. Lee
told me it says on the bottom of the paper that you don't have to pay."

Sure enough, at the bottom of the permission slip that would allow Loretta to ride the bus to Westchester, compete in games, stay
overnight in a dorm, and attend a dance were the exact words that
Rita needed to see: NO CHARGE.

"Well then," she said, "you can go. But you tell them to be sure
there isn't going to be any charge, cause I am *not* paying for you to go
to that game."

Loretta was thrilled. She packed her things immediately, even though the games were almost a month away. "I was going to be on my own and I had never been on my own before. That was a big woop! And when the day came, I could barely sleep. I was spending my first night ever away from the projects. When I got to the dorm, there was another person in my room and she was nice and we had food and candy. The next day, we woke up to go to the opening ceremony and there were thousands of people cheering me on. All those people around me, and no one called me 'bozo' or 'retard' or 'Clarence the cross-eyed lion.' "

The volunteers at Special Olympics saw something in her that she'd never been able to see in herself. They saw an athlete, not a "retarded" child. Instead of seeing limitations, they focused on expectations. All of a sudden, Loretta was scared, because all of a sudden, she cared—what she was doing *mattered* to all those people in the stands. She'd never raced against so many other runners with so many people watching. So she decided to do what great athletes do: leave it all on the track. She threw herself into the competition—and she won her race, and received the first medal of her life. When she got home, she told her mother she was so happy, she could do the dishes forever and it wouldn't bother her one bit. "There's three hundred sixty-two days till the next Special Olympics," she said, "and I can't wait."

In the twenty years that followed, Loretta never stopped running. There were hundreds more Special Olympics races after that first one, and she collected dozens of medals. Then, in 1978, she entered the Harrisburg Marathon and finished in 3:35—a better time than her coach, Bob Hollis. Mr. Lee had told her that her feet could take her places, and they did not disappoint. She ran another local marathon a few months later, then the Marine Corps Special Olympics 5K in Washington, and then she registered for the oldest yearly marathon in the world: Boston. Not only did she qualify to run the Boston Marathon, which women had been allowed to enter only since 1972, but she finished among the top hundred women in the world. She was on her way to becoming a world-class runner and a superstar of the Special Olympics movement.

At one race, soon after she'd finished the Boston Marathon, a local Special Olympics coordinator asked her to give a brief speech to

This portrait of Côte d'Ivoire athlete Adjara Sylla hangs on the wall in my Washington, DC, office. It was taken at the 2007 Special Olympics World Summer Games in Shanghai. Adjara inspires me every day. (Richard Corman)

My mother on the ocean with her older siblings in the mid-1920s. Rosemary was included—a sister like any other. From left: Eunice, Jack, Joe, Rosemary, and Kathleen. (Kennedy Family Collection/JFK Library)

The family together—one of the last photographs that includes all the children. From left to right: Eunice, John, Rosemary, Jean, Joseph Sr., Edward, Rose, Joseph Jr., Patricia, Robert, and Kathleen. Joe and Kathleen would be gone in just a few years, and so would Rosemary. (Kennedy Family Collection/JFK Library)

My mother, Eunice (*above*, at left), with her sister Rosemary (*left* and *above*, at right). Born with an intellectual disability at the height of the eugenics craze, Rosemary might very well have been institutionalized, but instead my grandparents decided to raise her themselves, surrounded by her family. She was perhaps the most extraordinary of the Kennedy children. Before her operation, Rosemary traveled, played sports, and was a part of everything.

(Shriver Family Collection)

From the start of her brother's presidency, my mother worked tirelessly toward a real political breakthrough in the field of intellectual disability. Her hard work led to this moment, when President Kennedy signed that breakthrough into law, on October 24, 1963. (White House Photographs Collection/JFK Library)

John F. Kennedy helped 5½ million mentally retarded Americans.

Have you helped even one of them?

Write for the free booklet to
The President's Committee
on Mental Retardation
Washington, D.C.

President Kennedy was the first head of state known to have met publicly with a person with an intellectual disability. He's pictured here at the White House in 1962, with nine-year-old David Jordalen of Shrewsbury, Massachusetts, who as a result of this image became a national symbol.
(JFK Library/President's Committee for People with Intellectual Disabilities)

The magic of my mother's eyes (Rowland Scherman)

When I was about three years old, our backyard became a summer camp filled with children who wanted to play—just like me, except all the campers had intellectual disabilities. Many came from institutions where being outdoors or playing was not an option. (Rowland Scherman)

A Day at Camp Shriver

a CARE and SHARE camp

Retarded children and counselors enjoy a ride around the Shriver country place

Mrs. R. Sargent Shriver, Jr., sponsors a camping program for the retarded

A three-week experiment was tried last month by Mrs. Eunice Kennedy Shriver, sister of President Kennedy and wife of R. Sargent Shriver Jr., Peace Corps Director. Mrs. Shriver opened their country home near Washington to 35 retarded children to use as a day camp and provided a volunteer high school or college-age counselor for each, plus four paid employes and her own full-time services. Also, the Shrivers' three children played, lunched and napped with the guests.

President's sister, Eunice Shriver and two of her charges. Emotionally disturbed, the Negro child here rides pony and begins to mix normally.

President's niece, Maria Shriver, joins in a lively patty cake type of game with the retarded children.

Patience at the pool: Mrs. Shriver coaxes Wendell into swimming pool. Terrified of water, he finally stepped in.

Ride for the "Exceptional": Mrs. Shriver drives as Speckles pulls a pony cart across the Shriver lawn.

A poster chronicling the story of the first days of the "revolution" that was Camp Shriver in 1962.

The first ever Special Olympics games. Standing atop the near-empty Soldier Field in Chicago on July 20, 1968, my mother must have wondered if her revolutionary "Olympics" had any chance of catching on. In the years that followed, she would fill stadiums this size many times over. (Special Olympics)

The games were led by Anne Burke (right) and William McFetridge (second from right) of the Chicago Park District, both of whom were relentless despite countless obstacles. Here, my mother hands a check to McFetridge as Chicago Park District Commissioner Marshall Bynum looks on. (Special Olympics)

The first Special Olympics medal moment: this is when "Olympic" came to mean greatness from within.

(Special Olympics)

By the time the Special Olympics World Summer Games were held at Notre Dame University in 1987, nearly one hundred countries and many thousands of athletes, volunteers, and fans had joined the movement. Whitney Houston was the opening ceremonies' headline entertainer, and the show was broadcast on national television for the first time. (Special Olympics)

"Pride (In the Name of Love)" never meant so much as when U2 used the song to introduce Nelson Mandela at the Special Olympics World Summer Games in 2003 in Ireland. (Special Olympics)

My dad embodied the joy of Special Olympics, which he always called "a miracle!" (Richard Corman)

After nine years of dating, Linda and I had the best wedding ever!
(Shriver Family Collection)

Our family happened fast! And Linda insisted that each of our children (from left: Rose, Caroline, Sam, Kathleen, and Tim) play Special Olympics Unified Sports throughout their childhood. Needless to say, they all loved it! (Shriver Family Collection)

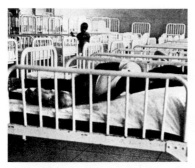

Until much too recently, the most likely future for a person with intellectual disabilities in this country was institutionalization—and that future was a horrible one. One institution was described by its local newspaper as a "vast junkyard of wasted humans." (Center on Human Policy at Syracuse University)

It's the sort of place where Loretta Claiborne (left) might well have ended up, had it not been for the strength and love of her mother, Rita. (Loretta Claiborne)

Instead, Loretta became one of Special Olympics' most heroic athletes, participating in hundreds of games, finishing twenty-six marathons, and winning acclaim from people both inside and outside the Special Olympics movement. Here, she introduces President Clinton to a nationwide television audience and to seventy-five thousand spectators at the Yale Bowl during the 1995 Special Olympics World Summer Games opening ceremonies. (Special Olympics)

The start of the 10K race for Special Olympics athletes from southern Africa in Arusha, Tanzania, in 1998. Billy Quick (front row, far left) and Loretta Claiborne (back row, third from left) joined the runners. Ramadhani Salim Chambo (back row, fourth from left) became my hero that day. (Special Olympics)

Rosario and Eric Marin continue to inspire. (Rosario Marin)

Though little Pearl was never an athlete, her story, and the bravery of her parents, touched the lives of everyone in the Special Olympics movement. (Dr. Dicken Yung)

Marty Sheets was one of Special Olympics' earliest athletes, attending our very first games when he was only fifteen. (Special Olympics)

Frank Stephens, another amazing Special Olympics athlete and blogger, has become the world's leading spokesperson for ending the derogatory use of the words "retard" and "retarded." (Scott K. Brown Photography)

Donal Page (front row, right, with fellow athletes and coaches) stole his nation's heart—and mine, too—at the 2003 Special Olympics World Summer Games Motor Activities Training Program in Ireland. "Grit" never had a better embodiment! (Special Olympics)

I visited Daniel Thompson, a visionary man of faith, at his home in West Virginia. Although he died shortly after this photo was taken, he was full of laughter and peace. (Thompson Family Collection)

My daughter Rose and the world-class swimmer Andy Miyares at our 2010 Global Congress in Morocco. Andy is believed to be the only swimmer with an intellectual disability ever ranked in the top ten by the U.S. Masters. (Diego Azubel)

Everyone at the 2009 Special Olympics World Winter Games in Idaho—including (from left to right) myself, the Irish athlete Ben Purcell, and my son Tim—is experiencing the joy of being fully alive! (Diego Azubel)

In recent years, China has become the largest nation in the Special Olympics movement, with more than a million athletes participating every year. (Diego Azubel)

I got a chance to celebrate with the floor hockey team from Afghanistan at the 2013 Special Olympics World Winter Games in Korea. The bravery of our athletes and volunteers in Afghanistan is beyond comprehension. They have withstood threats, bomb attacks, and every form of adversity, but they labor on and work tirelessly to bring our movement to people with intellectual disabilities who deserve this—and more. (Diego Azubel)

Celebrating my mother's eighty-fifth birthday with my siblings and their spouses. Front row, from left: Maria, Eunice, and Sargent Shriver. Second row, from left: Bobby, Malissa, Alina, Linda, and Jeanne. Back row, from left: Anthony, me, and Mark. (Larry Levin/Shriver Family Collection)

What matters most: Family is both whom you're related to and whom you give yourself to. Here, I'm with the people who have given me the most: (from left) Caroline, Rose, Kathleen, Tim, Linda, and Sam. (Shriver Family Collection)

Maureen Yap (left) was the inspiration for Linda's and her mom, Anne's, Special Olympics Unified Sports team, where Sam (in costume, center) and Caroline (right) and all our kids learned about "the fun that lasts." (Shriver Family Collection)

Caroline (left) and Kathleen (right) have both played on Unified Sports teams with Joelle Packard (center), who is always smiling. (Darian Packard)

The Egyptian athlete Mustafa Mahmoud A. Hamid says it all: Give yourself fearlessly to the game and you will feel fully alive! (Khaled Elfiqi)

the volunteers and donors. Loretta had never spoken in front of people in her life—she'd never even given a presentation in school—but she wasn't intimidated.

"I'm an athlete," she remembers saying. "I'm proud. I ran a marathon and this is what Special Olympics means to me. I ran my first race a few years ago and everywhere I looked, I saw people like me. Nobody called me names. Nobody made fun of anybody. It was all people like me and people who wanted to help and that was all the people who were there. I got a medal and I had the best time of my life. This is a very special thing and I can tell you for sure, it's the best thing that ever happened to me. Thank you."

Loretta Claiborne went on to run twenty-seven marathons. In 1982, she became the first Special Olympics athlete in history to join the Board of Directors for Special Olympics Pennsylvania. After that first little impromptu speech, she went on to speak around the world, teaching the searing lessons of her own childhood and the beauty of belonging. She visited hundreds of schools, teaching thousands of children not to bully one another and to welcome their peers with special needs. In 2012 she was invited to give a TED talk on the subject of fearlessness and intellectual disability. Hollywood made a movie about her life, *The Loretta Claiborne Story*, and it aired on television networks around the world. She still struggles with reading and with many tasks that require school smarts, but not with life smarts. When Rita Claiborne became terminally ill and began to decline, the only one of her eight children she could always count on to help her was Loretta.

Loretta came charging into my world when the legendary governor of Connecticut Lowell Weicker decided to lead the host committee of the 1995 Special Olympics World Games and bring the biggest show in the world of Special Olympics to my adopted hometown of New Haven. At about the same time, my work in the New Haven Public Schools began to collapse. John Dow left New Haven because of his years of confrontation with the political establishment. The Social Development Department I led was just visible enough to be identified with Dow, and the hammer started to come down as soon as he left town. Within months, Roger Weissberg, too, was gone, offered a tenured professorship at the University of Illinois in Chicago. Our funding for preventive social development training was chiseled away and redirected to truancy officers. In the blink of an eye, our work became of secondary importance for the school district. No one ever questioned our results, but more and more people began to question our power to sustain the level of change required to make social and emotional learning stick. The last lesson I learned in the New Haven Public Schools was the most bitter: political agendas often overrule the best interests of children. We in social development were on the outs.

I applied for and was granted a leave of absence from my position as supervisor of social development to work on a Ph.D. At the same time, the governor asked me to devote my energy to the 1995 Special Olympics World Games. And the brash, independent governor was a man to whom few could say no. He was a pioneer of disability rights in the House and Senate of the United States, the father of a son with Down syndrome, and the kind of man who made things happen. It made sense to commit to a year of full-time work for Special Olympics, I thought, and Linda agreed. I never went back.

TEN

Loretta

By the mid-1990s Special Olympics had become a global pheno-
menon with new affiliates in the People's Republic of China, in Egypt,
and throughout Europe, Africa, and Latin America. It boasted close
to one million athletes around the world. Hosting the Special Olympics World Games was nothing like planning the event in Chicago
decades earlier. It was a massive undertaking.

In the fall of 1993, I left my office in the vocational wing at Hillhouse and moved downtown to one of New Haven's only high-rise
office buildings, to be the president of the 1995 Special Olympics
World Games Organizing Committee. An irrepressible social entrepreneur and CEO of Special Olympics Connecticut, Peter Wheeler
was the creative genius behind the games, and he took on the role of
executive director. Within a few weeks, one of the first volunteers to
show up ready to help was Loretta Claiborne.

Can you imagine a better coach for me than Loretta? I was stepping
back into the world of huge events, high pressure, and powerful people.
I was coming from my own small school of the heart in the New
Haven Public Schools, where I'd worked on and off for thirteen years,
trying to understand the still point within myself, trying to understand how to make sense of that stillness, trying to understand what
skills I could teach that would allow me to communicate it to others.
I had been working and living outside of my "family business" for a

long time—with the kids in New Haven, with scholars of religion and psychology, with Linda and our children.

Then all of a sudden I was sitting in a corner office, with a mandate to raise $34 million from private sources, with an eighty-thousand-seat stadium to fill, with hundreds of thousands of spectators to host, and with the president of the United States as our anticipated guest. The world of Special Olympics included more than a hundred countries, and they were all sending teams to New Haven—more than six thousand athletes in all. The scale of everything changed.

Loretta did her best to coach me through it. Week after week, she'd take the bus from York, Pennsylvania, to New Haven to volunteer in the office. She still lived with her mother but would travel to Connecticut for a few days at a time to help with mailings, with the phones, and with preparing agendas for the hundreds of volunteer meetings taking place every week around the city. She was unassuming, quiet, and easy to please. Sometimes she'd just spend the whole day wandering around the office, asking various coordinators and managers and directors if they had any work she could help with. If they did, she'd join. If they didn't, she'd knit in the waiting room and talk to visitors or volunteers.

She happened to be volunteering in the mailroom on the day when we were preparing for our first visit from our boss, Governor Weicker. At the time, the games were still eighteen months away, but that wasn't much time considering the scope of the work that needed to be done. The governor was coming to New Haven to conduct full briefings with the staff and leadership and to evaluate our progress toward our goals. Weicker was tough, impatient, and demanding—a powerful figure who'd spent the early part of his political career fighting Nixon Republicans while leading the business-oriented wing of the Republican party in the northeast. He was a political independent who was known for an independent spirit that bordered on dominance. He used every inch of his six-foot-six frame to lead, intimidate, cajole, and win. In Connecticut, he was known as "the Bear." On this particular day, the Bear was headed to our office to evaluate me and my team. I scrambled around the office, pushing everyone to have their reports ready, their presentations brief but articulate, their numbers accessible, and their plans sharpened.

An hour before the governor was scheduled to arrive, his advance security detail came to make sure the conference room and his desk were ready. At that point, I was on the anxiety express, so I started pacing from office to office. "Can you clean up your desk, Sam?" I said in one office. In the next: "Do you have all your venue maps, Peter?" Then I stormed down the hall barking orders and announcing the governor's imminent arrival. When I reached the mailroom, documents and envelopes were scattered about.

"Can someone please clean up this mess in here?" I fumed. "I've been saying for a week that the governor is coming today, and this whole place still looks like a disaster."

I can't remember the name of the colleague who was in charge, but I brushed past him, only frustrated that I couldn't scream out loud. And as I stomped out of the mailroom there was Loretta, sitting at the coffee table with her knitting. Almost under her breath, she said to me as I passed, "You know, the governor puts his pants on in the morning the same as you."

"I know that!" I snapped. "I know the governor puts his pants on just like . . ." Then I stopped in my tracks, realizing that she'd said something I wanted or needed to hear again. "What did you say?"

"I know the governor's coming, Tim, but he's just a person. That's all I said."

Even as I write this, I'm embarrassed to admit that I really didn't know the governor was just a person like me. I'm even more embarrassed to admit that I'm not sure I understand it even today. I know what the words mean, but I don't know if I really understand it deep in my bones. I was raised in a family where politics was everything, and we spent a lot of time and energy focused on people with flashy titles and the glamour of political success. I guess it was obvious to Loretta why I was a wreck, but it wasn't obvious to me. She was the only person in that office who understood that we were all racing around because we were in the grip of power fear. And she understood it so well that she could identify it and tell me the solution in one sentence: "The governor puts his pants on in the morning, same as you." She didn't follow it up with a pep talk about not being afraid of powerful people, about having confidence in myself, about feeling comfortable in my own skin, blah, blah, blah. Her intelligence about the deceptions of power was so acute that none of that was necessary.

This was the first of several occasions when Loretta coached me on how to see without judging and how to see the beauty of each person—two of the basic gifts of being fully alive. A few weeks after the governor's visit, I received a call from the Yale Alumni Association asking us to provide a speaker for their annual meeting in New Haven. With Yale being the lead university among the hosts for the games, the alumni wanted to learn more about the Special Olympics movement and explore ways to help. The association represented thousands of Yale graduates in Connecticut and around the world. It included some of the world's most prominent leaders in government, business, law, medicine, the arts, and more. Power, glamour, success: being invited to speak to this distinguished audience was a big opportunity to attract donors and press. The amount of wealth in the room would be extraordinary.

We chose Loretta to speak to the group. The meeting was held in an elegant banquet hall in one of Yale's illustrious gothic buildings. I looked across the crowd when I introduced Loretta: mostly white men in pinstriped suits who represented everything Governor Weicker represented and more. They were high achievers, success stories, brilliant thinkers. They had won friends and influenced people. If only we could get these kinds of people to accept our athletes into their world, I thought, we'd be on our way to more opportunity, more inclusion, more dignity.

Loretta began her speech with her life story and went on to describe the joy of running and of discovering herself in the world of Special Olympics. She described what it was like to go out to schools to talk to kids about name-calling and bullying. She described what it was like to find a community of people who saw her abilities, not her disabilities. She described the anger that had infected every cell of her body for so many years but had now left her.

Then she told a story about the previous Special Olympics World Games. "I remember when I was getting ready to go to the World Games in 1991," she recounted. "We were a year away from going to Minneapolis, Minnesota, when our coach gave us a description of what

it would be like. He said that we would stay in dormitories and visit
famous sites on the Mississippi River and compete against the best
Special Olympics athletes in the world. He even made the point of
saying that athletes from the Soviet Union would be coming, and even
though there were always good athletes from there and even though
that country was our enemy, we would compete in fairness and just
do our best.

"And I thought, how could those athletes from the Soviet Union
come all the way over to the United States and not feel scared and left
out? I started to think what it was like when I was scared and I realized that even though they were coming to Special Olympics, they
were coming to a country where they probably thought the people
didn't like them. And I thought to myself, 'That's not Special Olympics. We don't let people feel that way.'

"So I decided to do something about that, and I asked the lady
who lives near my house if I could get some tapes that I could play in
my Walkman that I play when I run that could teach me how to
speak Russian. I said to myself that when those Russian athletes come
over here and if I get to meet them, I want to say something to them
in their own language and help them feel welcome. I want them to
know that in Special Olympics, we don't dislike anyone because of
where they're from or what language they speak or what their religion is or nothing. In Special Olympics, everyone is the same. So I
just decided I would spend a year listening to Russian tapes on my
headphones so that I could show them that in Special Olympics,
they're just like all the rest of us and we want them to feel good about
coming all the way over here to have games with us. And sure enough,
when I met athletes from the Soviet Union in Minneapolis and said
'Privet! Dobro pozhalovat' v nashei strane Amerike' for 'Hello! Welcome
to America,' they smiled from ear to ear."

She then addressed the alumni personally: "That's why I want
you to come to Special Olympics. That's why I want you to come into
my world.

"In our world, we treat everyone well and we tell everyone that
they can be a winner. There are no losers in our world. That's the
world I love. I say God is my strength and Special Olympics is my

joy. I count on them both in my world. So come into my world. In my world, we don't have any enemies like countries do. And in my world, we don't look at what a person can't do; we only give them a chance to show everyone what they can do. That's why our world is the way it ought to be. Because that way, everyone has a chance to belong and there's nobody who gets rejected or left out or excluded. So when the Special Olympics World Games come to New Haven in July, I hope you'll all come out and join our world. You'll see. It's strong and joyful and you can't beat that.

"Thank you."

I was stunned. I'm guessing she stunned the venerable leaders of the Yale Alumni Association, too. Everyone tries to join *their* world. Everyone looks on *their* world with envy and admiration. They're the ones who are the most clever, have risen the fastest, won the biggest prizes. Who was this woman with an intellectual disability, who might not even qualify for a maintenance job at Yale, to tell them they were living in the wrong world? If my first lesson from Loretta was about not being intimidated by power, this took it one step further: don't even try to join the world of the powerful. Instead, create a welcoming world and tell power to come over to it.

In the months that followed, Loretta became a sought-after speaker in New Haven. Local volunteer groups and civic clubs and university departments all asked if she would come to educate their membership on the upcoming games and the messages of Special Olympics. She came to stay with Linda and me frequently, returning home only when Rita was ill or needed help. She was a star everywhere she went, approaching every speaking opportunity with humility, never fussing about her hair, dressed nicely, as Rita would have expected, but never standing out. I must have seen her give dozens of speeches in those days, and never once did she have a note in her hand. I'm not bending the truth in saying that she received a standing ovation every time.

Loretta was fast becoming the ambassador of Special Olympics to the world, and her popularity gave me the nerve to try a new avenue of recognition for her. Yale was hosting the games and was fully immersed in Special Olympics. Perhaps, I thought, the university could

offer Loretta an honorary degree, or better still, invite her to be the
commencement speaker. Had a person with an intellectual disability
ever been given an honorary degree by a college or university in the
United States? I guessed not. Had such a person ever been welcomed
to the commencement exercises of an Ivy League university? I was
sure not. So I called my friend Donald Cohen, the director of the Yale
Child Study Center and a close advisor to the Yale Corporation.

"I think Yale should give Loretta Claiborne an honorary degree
for her pioneering accomplishments," I campaigned. "She's a first in
history—a person with an intellectual disability who's become a world-
class athlete, a powerful self-advocate, a captivating motivational
speaker. She's blazing new ground, Donald. She's exactly the kind of
person that Yale loves to celebrate. What do you think?"

There was long pause at the other end of the line, as Donald tried
to figure out a way to be kind.

"What a sweet idea. It would be wonderful to help Loretta somehow, maybe do something at Special Olympics for her . . ."

"No, no. I'm not suggesting we 'do something' for Loretta. Loretta's just fine. I'm suggesting that Yale do something for Yale by
recognizing her as someone the school is proud to call its own."

"Okay, I get it, but Tim—let's be realistic. This is Yale. Yale isn't
going to do this kind of thing. I'm happy to run it by a few people if
you want; I really do think it's a wonderful idea. But to be blunt, this
is not going to happen. It just won't fit at Yale."

"That's the whole point. No one expects it, but Yale is creative
and smart enough to do something like this."

"Look, Yale is a place that prides itself on intellectual achievement. We can talk to one another all we want, but I strongly recommend looking elsewhere. Yale's not going to end up giving Loretta
Claiborne an honorary degree. She's just not what Yale is about."

In the end it was Quinnipiac University, a rising liberal arts college in nearby Hamden, Connecticut, that recognized how spectacu-
lar Loretta was. Quinnipiac was then emerging as one of the nation's
leading small institutions of higher education, and it had no problem
welcoming Loretta Claiborne to commencement exercises and award-
ing her a Doctor of Humane Letters degree, *honoris causa*. Rita was

unable to make the trip to Connecticut, but Linda and I were invited
to the commencement, as were my parents and children.

The day was a blazing beauty with not a cloud in the sky as "Pomp
and Circumstance" played on the open courtyard nestled against
Connecticut woods and hills. Graduates processed into the ceremony
with typically brilliant young smiles and ribbons of distinction. Parents lined the sides of the procession with cameras and shouts of good
cheer. As the ceremony was concluding and the students were getting
rowdy, President John Lahey rose to give the closing words. He walked
to the podium in full regalia and then asked everyone for just one
more moment of quiet. As the students settled down, he turned to
Loretta and invited her up to the podium, asking if she would be willing to give the benediction. "I know it isn't customary to ask an honorary degree recipient who hasn't prepared for the occasion to speak,
but I am taking the risk nonetheless. Loretta: Would you close our
commencement proceedings?"

With only the slightest pause, Loretta rose and walked slowly to
the podium with a distant expression. "Students, faculty, parents, and
friends," she said, carefully enunciating each word.

"I'm honored to be here . . . This is an anniversary for me. It's
been thirty years and three days exactly since I'd been carted off to go
to Eastern State School and Hospital. I was told that I wasn't going to
be anything but to be put in an institution.

"Today, I stand here amongst you, these students here, and today
I am proud to say, I am somebody. Yes!

". . . And today, though it's too late for me to go to college, today
I am proud when I hear a kid who makes the honor roll. But I am
more proud when I hear somebody who is mentally challenged—like
I did last year back in Pennsylvania, to hear a man go to an institution of higher learning, then going on to be a nurse's aide or what
have you. That wasn't possible in 1966 or '65, when I was supposed to
go to the institution. Today it is, because we have opened up.

". . . [I had] one teacher, she had many students, and this is a life
she changed. If you can change one, you are successful. And I hope
that you have that student that you can be successful with.

"Good luck, God bless, and thank you."

Thousands of students and parents and friends rose in thunderous applause. "I am somebody" never seemed so pure. I'd heard it before, but listening to Loretta, I felt it. Everybody is somebody. She waved haltingly as the applause continued. I knew I was looking at my new role model, and I knew she had a lot left to teach me about how to live that truth.

The 1995 Special Olympics World Games opened a few weeks later. They were my first experience with leading a global event, and I spent most of the time nervous and exhausted. But the games were an amazing experience, too. Towns all over Connecticut hosted national delegations of Special Olympics athletes in the first ever "Host Town" program. Two pioneering doctors, Steve Perlman and Paul Berman, set up health screening centers and launched a world-wide Special Olympics campaign to end discrimination against people with intellectual disabilities in health care institutions and improve care. We held symposia exploring the religious, legal, and psychosocial dimensions of the lives of people with intellectual disabilities, and one of the speakers was the spiritual scholar Henri Nouwen. The games were nicknamed "The Games of Inclusion," heralding the shifting focus of the world of people with intellectual disabilities toward inclusion and respect. The state of Connecticut and the city of New Haven were aglow. The president of the United States opened the games, and several of his cabinet members visited during the week. It was thrilling.

When the games were over, we faced all the work of closing down an office where thousands of volunteers had worked for more than a year. Loretta continued coming to New Haven to help out. Over dinner at night with Linda and our kids, we'd reminisce about all the stories of the games—the beachfront aquatics races, the fierce competition of medal round games in basketball and volleyball, and the surreal finish of the first-ever Special Olympics Marathon, which Troy Rutter from Pennsylvania won in under three hours.

Then Loretta brought up a subject neither Linda nor I was prepared for: "Why don't you move to Washington and take over Special Olympics?"

"No, we couldn't," we answered bluntly. We were happy in New Haven. Our children were all in school there. I was preparing to reenter the school system when the games work was finished.

"You should go to Special Olympics," was Loretta's straight-forward reply. "I think that's the place for you."

That idea was, as the saying goes, a "nonstarter." The last thing on my list of career goals was to succeed my mother and father in a Washington, DC, office, working full-time for Special Olympics. Loretta had an uncanny understanding of what was important to me in life, but on this one, she was just wrong. Every time she brought up the future of the Special Olympics international office, I smiled and changed the subject. It was much more fun to talk about her than to talk about me. I wanted her permission to pitch Hollywood on making a movie about her life, and I wanted to talk about how she felt about Rita's absence from the games. I wanted her to come visit our children's schools to talk to elementary children about difference. I even wanted her to take me on runs—short ones! But I did not want to talk about moving.

At the same time, Linda and I knew that Loretta's advice mattered. More than anyone, Loretta Claiborne was—and remains—fully alive. She knows how to see without judging. She knows how to play like there's no scoreboard. And she knows how to seize the chance to make a difference and accept the risks of trying. She was being what I was trying to be: a person who focused on the elusive intimacy of caring and who fell in love with people she hadn't even met. As much as I tried not to, I had to listen to her.

Eight months after the games, ESPN decided to give Loretta the Arthur Ashe Courage Award—its highest award, given to individuals whose contributions transcend sports. On ESPY night, Linda and I took the train down to Radio City Music Hall in New York to be in the audience. My mother made the trip up from Washington. Loretta herself was hosted in a fancy New York hotel with a limousine at her disposal to take her to and from the theater for rehearsals and the show. ESPN agreed to allocate a few tickets for other Special Olympics athletes and friends of Loretta's who wanted to be a part of the evening. We were Loretta's fan club, and we arrived at the theater flush with excitement, as we walked by baseball Hall of Famer Joe Morgan and tennis greats Venus and Serena Williams and football legends Joe Montana and James Brown. Jeanne Moutoussamy Ashe,

Arthur's widow and a beautiful photographer and human being in her own right, sat nearby in honor of Loretta.

Denzel Washington was the surprise presenter for the Arthur Ashe award. He spoke with an actor's eloquence of Arthur Ashe and his lifelong bravery in the face of racial prejudice and the stigma of AIDS. "Desire. Strength. Heart. In the world of sports, those words are used all too frequently to describe a big play, key moment, comeback victory. But to understand the true meaning of those words, one need only to think of Arthur Ashe. Every day of her life, Loretta Claiborne exemplifies that perseverance and ability of spirit." Then he introduced Loretta with a short video about her life, in which her beloved teacher Ms. Weaver described the bruised child who arrived at her class at the age of twelve, angry but hiding a tenderness within her. It chronicled her entry into the Special Olympics world and her emergence as a runner, as a marathon standout, as a teacher of tolerance and friendship. When the video was over, Washington finished the introduction with the simple words: "Ladies and gentlemen, it gives me great pleasure to present this award to Loretta Claiborne."

Loretta emerged from behind a curtain onto the huge stage. The crowd greeted her with applause, but no one really knew who she was—a middle-aged African-American woman with an average human body and braided hair and a dress from Walmart, and not a single endorsement or contract or scandal to her name. Washington handed her the award and slipped away.

She thanked God. She thanked her teacher, Miss Weaver, and her mother, Rita. She thanked Special Olympics. She thanked my mother. And she concluded her short remarks by saying, "If I could take this award and break it up in over a million pieces, I would love to do that and split it with every Special Olympian. Thank you."

Other winners say similar things. But there was one thing different about Loretta: she meant it.

ELEVEN

Tough World

"Maybe we *should* move to Washington," Linda said one day, cracking open the door to a change of life.

We thought about what we'd be leaving behind and what we'd be gaining. We thought about the effect on our children, on our marriage, on our careers, and more. As we looked at the full picture, everything we could think of told us not to leave. We loved New Haven. Our children had been born there; most of our friends lived there. The kids I'd taught were scattered in virtually every neighborhood of the city, making it impossible to go anywhere without seeing a friendly face. My mentors were there, our church was there, our roots were there. But there was something—and someone (Loretta!)—that told us we needed to go. We decided to move.

Over the course of several weeks in the spring of 1996, we shared the news that we were leaving for Washington and taking up a new role in the Special Olympics movement full-time. What surprised me most about those conversations was the reaction most people had upon learning that I was going to be working for Special Olympics. "That's so nice," was the most common response. The word "nice" came up over and over again.

This irritated me immensely. There was something patronizing and dismissive about that word, and it was inaccurate. Whatever Special Olympics is, it isn't "nice." *Nice* isn't about digging deep into the brokenness and healing of life. *Nice* isn't about the centering intelligence that enables human beings to welcome one another with love. *Nice* isn't about challenging the world to uproot deep and stubborn prejudices that destroy the lives of millions of people. My work in education had always been edgy, tough, confrontational, empowering. I saw Special Olympics the same way, but I realized others didn't. Too many perceived it to be sweet—a break on a Saturday afternoon for "unfortunate" children. Sporting events on Saturday afternoons were indeed a big part of what Special Olympics did around the world, but that description failed miserably to capture the muscular and transformational and empowering moments that I was experiencing.

I saw this lack of understanding springing from discomfort with disability. It was—and is—something to be avoided. Like small children who shut their eyes to make a scary thing go away, many prefer not to look at it directly. If we hear that a neighbor has welcomed a child with a disability into the world, most are still likely to greet the news with discomfort or sadness: "I'm sorry." Some even question why the baby was carried to term: "Didn't they do a prenatal test?"

Almost immediately after starting at Special Olympics, I went on the road to meet with athletes, volunteers, and staff around the world. The first thing I found was that the world hadn't changed as much as I'd thought. Injustice, brutality, indifference, and intolerance were still pervasive. But I also found an indomitable energy source: the parents of many of our athletes, who had learned that, in the words of Shakespeare, "Love is not love / Which alters when it alteration finds." They'd found a way to stay the course of love even when everything was against them. As parents, they were the best teachers a young father like me could have asked for. As social change activists, they were hidden treasures ready to campaign for a more inclusive and just society if given the chance.

For starters, remember where the parents of children with differences come from. Imagine a mother expecting her first child. She and those around her are filled with anticipation. Is it a boy or a girl? Will he be elfin or chubby? Will her eyes be brown or blue? Will his skin be dark or fair? Will he be healthy? Will she be healthy? No matter where that baby arrives—in a small village or a big city, a home or a hospital, the first question is almost always the same: "Is the baby okay?"

On October 4, 1985, Special Olympics mom Rosario Marin heard the answer to that question every new parent dreads: "No. I'm sorry, Rosario. Your baby is not okay. He has Down syndrome." It was the most devastating moment of her life. A minute before, her dream of her new baby son was filled with images of nursing him and teaching him to walk and playing games with him, beaming with pride as he grew and grew. And then, in the blink of an eye, she was lying in a hospital bed, exhausted from labor and seemingly drowning with the words ringing in her ears. Baby Eric was in intensive care. His life was in jeopardy. He wasn't okay. His future was not okay. She was not okay.

Almost every parent in the Special Olympics movement has a similar moment they can recount—like the dad in South Africa who told me that when his daughter was born, the doctor told him she was "a cabbage," or like the mother who was told by her doctor that her baby was "an exchange" for the sins of her past. The author and life coach Martha Beck was told by elite doctors at Harvard Medical School that her child with Down syndrome, diagnosed before delivery, was the equivalent of a cancerous tumor that needed to be excised. These moments are burned into the consciousness of parents who have special needs children. In the overwhelming majority of cases, they had no reason to expect that their child would be anything other than healthy and "normal." And in an instant, their whole view of the world and of their future collapsed. "Your baby is not okay."

Rosario told me what happened next. "I can remember feeling devastated and alone and terrified. I was lying on the bed, and I began to cry and cry and cry. And then I felt myself begin to pray to God for help in this moment. And I know what I prayed. I prayed that the baby would die. I cannot escape it. I prayed that God would take the baby and leave me to go back to my life. I prayed that my own baby would die."

The Nobel Prize winner Kenzaburo Oe wrote a searing and frightening novel in 1964 about a Japanese intellectual, Bird, who finds himself in much the same situation. He is phoned at home and told to rush to the hospital—that his wife has delivered an "abnormal" baby. Bird careens through the dawn-lit streets of Tokyo on his bike on his way to the hospital. He gropes, scuttles, and feels dizzy. He imagines the leaves above the streets soaked with water like deep oceans of green. "If those oceans all at once collapsed, Bird and his bike would be drowned in a raw-green-smelling flood. Bird felt threatened by the trees. High above him, the leaves massed on the topmost branches were moaning in the wind. Blackish grey all over . . . a mean sky that seemed ashamed." Bird has fallen into a grotesque world of terror where everything appears abnormal, freakish, and threatening. He arrives at the hospital to find a doctor who is hairy, obese, and soiled. His mother-in-law is "half buried as if trying not to vomit." The baby is "wretched." He feels himself digging a hole deep into the earth, beyond the reach of light.* Disability can be terrifying.

We live in a world of walls that help us keep unwanted things out. Disability is one of those things we want to keep out. The child is not okay, or "abnormal," or "disabled"—all those are qualities we want to keep on the outside of our walls. But a newborn baby crosses the wall in the most permanent way. The child's presence is like a question: Can you face what seems to be a future emptied of pleasure and satisfaction because of me? Can you, Mom or Dad, live with the reality that your own flesh and blood is terrifying?

Obviously, these questions are immediate, wrenching, and real for each and every parent of a Special Olympics athlete. One of the great gifts of the Special Olympics movement is that it creates communities of parents who have lived this scene and ones similar to it, and it gives them a way to share the stories of how they have worked out an answer to these questions.

One father, Phoenix Zheng, shared his struggle with me in real

---

* The events that *A Personal Matter* describes so poignantly are not entirely fictional: Oe wrote the book soon after the birth of his own son, Hikari, who had a life-threatening brain condition at birth. Doctors told the anxious parents that the operation required to save his life would leave him a vegetable, and advised that it would be more merciful simply to let him die. But the Oes refused to give up on their son. Hikari never learned to use language—but he did learn to compose music. His CDs have sold more than a million copies around the world.

time. His was the most unusual e-mail I have ever received. One morning, I arrived at my office in downtown Washington, DC, and opened the following message in my inbox, addressed to a dozen or so random recipients:

I do need your help
My daught borned in 22th August this year
I noticed her is smaller than other babys and quite hard to feed. The child was examined and confirmed she has Down Syndrome. So tough world.
You know people's Life isn't very well and the attitude of people dealing with Child who has DS is hardhearted. So that there are so high mortality rate of Neonatal baby with DS. People advice us to kill the baby to make sure our life don't get so tough. However, I still don't want to give up.
Could you give me a hand, give me some advice how to cure our pitty baby. Her sile is still so pure.
I prefer to try rather than to kill her by myself.
Could you replay me as soon as possible, I don't how long I can bare the press that peole give us.
Please.
Thanks a lot

I couldn't absorb the words. I read the e-mail again to see if I'd misunderstood the broken English. I read it again and again and again. The words and the meaning didn't change. *Tough world. Hardhearted. People advice us to kill the baby. I don't want to give up. Pitty baby. Pitty baby. Pitty baby. Sile so pure. So pure. So pure. I prefer to try rather than to kill her by myself. Kill her by myself. Kill her by myself. I don't know how long I can bare the press. Please. Please. Please.*

I believe that all prayers are one of two expressions: "please" or "thank you." And I believe that prayer is not just what a religious person says in a church or what a child recites at bedtime, but also the wordless ache of the soul, seeking the presence of the divine in the begging of "please" or the peacefulness of "thank you." I believe that "please" can be directed toward the one God of Abraham or toward the many gods of earth and sky or toward the godless peace of emptiness. And most of all, I believe that same yearning of "please" can be heard not just by a God who is somewhere above us or beyond us, but also by the God within each of us who hears with the ears of the heart and knows when "please" means something far more than a request for a favor or an outcome. In prayer, "please" is a cry for love, not things. And sometimes we get to answer that cry for each other.

I wrote back:

> My name is Timothy Shriver. I have received your request for help and we in Special Olympics want to help. Our goal is to change the hard attitudes that you refer to and replace them with attitudes of happiness and respect for children. But you have a more immediate challenge with a very young and beautiful baby. Please know we will do anything we can to insure that you do not feel that you should harm the baby. We would like to get in touch with you immediately. I firmly believe that your child will grow up to be a wonderful human being and we will do whatever we can to help make that belief come true.
>
> On behalf of the whole Special Olympics movement around the world, I want to congratulate you on the birth of your daughter. I am sure she is wonderful. I know you will be very proud of her for many years to come.

Zheng responded to my e-mail almost immediately.

> Dear Timothy Shriver
> Thank you for help in the hardest time of my life.
> My English is very poor. Please forgive me.
> Whatever happen in the future, I will never forget your help.

On that very day, our leader for Special Olympics East Asia, Dr. Dicken Yung, was in Shanghai with his wife, Meilin, a thirty-year volunteer for Special Olympics. Within hours, they were in a car headed to meet Zheng and his wife and daughter. Dicken noticed immediately that in the first e-mail, the child had not been given a name, a sure sign that the parents had not accepted her as their child yet. He also had the great benefit of common sense and knew that both Zheng and his wife were exhausted. When Dicken and Meilin arrived to meet Zheng, the first thing they did was take him and his wife to a hotel and book them a room, then stay with the baby so the parents could get some sleep. It was a simple act that let the Zhengs know they were not alone, and never would be.

Two days later, Zheng and his wife named their baby Pearl. From then on, Pearl and her parents began life together as a family, and Zheng wrote to me on September 2 as though he was a new man: "I have met with Dicken Yung and his wife. We have a good time . . . I will bring my baby up with all my effort. Nothing can stop me now." He attached a picture of his newborn baby to the e-mail and I sent it to everyone in our office. I could hardly believe the turnaround—the dread that the first e-mail had triggered, the sense of emergency that accompanied my response, the good fortune of Dicken and Meilin's nearby presence and wisdom, the naming of baby Pearl. It all seemed miraculous, and in a sense it was.

I know that many people dismiss miracles as the workings of overactive imaginations or the stubborn delusions of superstitious minds. But "miracle" need not mean a manipulation of the laws of nature and history. It can also be a way of describing a dramatic change of mind and heart at the most fundamental levels of reality. A miracle can be the total deconstruction of a way of seeing the world, where the lessons and expectations of the past suddenly yield to a previously impossible perception of reality. A miracle, in its simplest spiritual form, is an experience of love "flooding our hearts" from a source unknown, of "falling" into a new reality previously unimagined, of seeing the world and others with an inexhaustible joy that is within time but beyond it, too. Zheng and his daughter, Pearl, were a miracle for me and Dicken and Meilin.

The contemporary mystic Jean Vanier is a virtual conduit for miraculous changes of heart. Vanier was born in Geneva, Switzerland, in 1928, the son of a career diplomat who served as the nineteenth governor general of Canada. Jean was something of a prodigy, entering the Royal Naval College in England at the age of thirteen. He served as an officer during World War II, but in 1950 resigned the commission to search for his faith. He landed as a student at the Institut Catholique in Paris, and there met his lifelong mentor Pere Tomas Philippe, a Dominican priest who taught his students not only metaphysics but also prayer and service to the poor. With Pere Tomas, Vanier studied some of the most philosophically complex masters of antiquity and scholasticism, including Aristotle and Thomas Aquinas. These writers challenged him to think deeply, critically, and precisely about the search for meaning in life. He wrote a dissertation titled "Happiness: the Principle and Purpose of Aristotelian Morality," and then he returned home to Canada and the life of a professor.

But Vanier soon returned to visit Pere Tomas, who had been moved to a new post: chaplain at Val Fleuri, an institution for people with intellectual disabilities, located an hour north of Paris. On one occasion, Vanier visited a nearby psychiatric hospital to offer support and care to the patients, and there he met two men who would change his life: Raphael Simi and Philippe Seux. "They were in despair," he said later. They wanted out—to leave the hospital prison to which they'd been banished. They begged Vanier to take them with him. Vanier couldn't bear saying no and bought a small home near the institution. He called it, in French, "L'Arche": the Ark. He invited Raphael and Philippe to come to live with him and thus, in one small house, began an international organization that today includes 145 communities in 40 nations around the world.

"My goal was simply to welcome these men and to help relieve their anguish," said Vanier. "To tell them that I wanted to live with them and that I was choosing to live in a home with them. At the heart of our vision is this very simple message. So many people with handicaps have been so humiliated and so degraded that they live a daily anguish and loneliness. Our vision is different: we want to welcome the stranger—the person who feels like a stranger, an outcast, a person who is not accepted—we welcome you to L'Arche. And our message is that you are more beautiful than you can possibly imagine."

On one occasion, I had the honor to listen to Vanier reflect on the mysterious relationship between the human and the divine. He spoke just a few feet from his home at L'Arche, where he's lived for more than forty years, in a community of people with and without intellectual disabilities who choose to live together and grow in relationships with one another. In the small stone chapel in the village of Trosly, Vanier spoke about the mysterious power of fragility to awaken us to the presence of God:

> In the Bible, we hear over and over again that all human life is fragile, tender, frail. To enter into a relationship with human frailty is to be asked to discover that God is fragile, too. And we find ourselves asking, "What are we to learn from God's fragility?"
>
> First, fragility reveals that God's most powerful words come in tenderness and without any aggression. God's words are "I love you." This is the deep meaning of God. God appears in weakness and tenderness as if looking for us saying, "I love you. Where are you?" God called to Adam and Eve, "Where are you?" And their answer to God was like ours today, "We are afraid." Afraid of what? Afraid of being naked? Afraid of not being successful? Afraid of declining or of feeling lost in a closed world? Afraid of being inadequate or forgotten?
>
> This is the experience of disabilities. In our imaginations, we can look upon a child with a disability and see that the child is the stranger to us, the one who does not fit into our world. So many of the stories of the Jewish people are about strangers, about feeling like a stranger and about welcoming strangers. But our first reaction to the stranger is almost always the same: we are afraid.
>
> But then we hear the prophet's soft voice of love as if calling out from the deep, "I have called you by your name and you are mine." This is the voice of the miracle of love: "Do not be afraid. You are mine, you are mine. If you go through rivers and flames and danger, no burn and no harm will come to you. Do not be afraid. I love you."
>
> This is what can happen with our encounter with the

little baby. The baby is fragile, stranger, tender, and in our encounter, we let ourselves be touched by these gifts and we are changed, softened, loved. The child comes to the places where we are wounded and transforms our wounds. Once you've heard that voice and once you've had that experience, the love power comes to you and you can hear the voice of Isaiah saying "You who used to mourn, rejoice with delight. Exult. Enjoy. I will take care of you and make peace flow, flow, flow."

I quote Vanier at such length because I know of no one else who has ventured so deeply into the mystery of encounter with the fear and strangeness of disability and made it so clear that this journey into and through pain belongs to all of us. Vanier's voice has a way of embracing the voices of so many parents who come to Special Olympics telling us that they once were lost as they tried to face their children's powerlessness, but are now changed, transformed, and found. It also has a way of reminding each of us that nakedness and fear are the pathways to healing.

Rosario Marin, who had prayed that God would spare her the burden of raising a baby with Down syndrome, was given instead a tiny newborn to take home. Six months later, he developed a high fever. She found herself back at the hospital with her son in the intensive care unit for the second time in his short life. Once again, Rosario agonized over this fragile child who was perched dangerously close to death's door. And once again, she closed her eyes in prayer and called out to God from the depths of her soul. But this time, her prayer was different: "Dear God. Please let my baby live." Eric was her miracle, the one she had been terrified to encounter but who had become the voice of God in her life. She couldn't bear to live without him.

There is something rare and unvarnished in the love that parents such as Rosario and Phoenix experience. Unlike almost any other parents, they begin their experience with their children in grief. Their children don't come to them with adorable oohs and aahs, or with the expected rush of congratulations from friends and families. People greet their children with words like "I'm sorry," "Tough world," as Zheng wrote, or—in the grotesque and surreal world of Kenzaburo Oe—"wretched." Right from the start, these parents often grieve the painful loss of what they thought they would love, and they grieve what they thought would be lovable. They begin the journey in pain and survive it by learning that what they feared would be unlovable is the opposite.

Spiritual writers have for centuries written of the way in which deep love so often emerges from experiences of loss and vulnerability, and for this reason, they teach, vulnerability is not to be feared. Saint Francis experienced his first conversion when he confronted the feared leper of his community and kissed him. After his kiss, he notes a profound change: "When I left [the lepers], that which seemed bitter to me was changed into sweetness of soul and body; and afterward I lingered a little and left the world." It is difficult to capture exactly what Francis means when he says that he "left the world," but it is clear that he touched a different dimension of reality, and the sweetness was a source of healing and new life within his soul and body. He was no longer afraid. The psalmist writes of this same transformative power when he cowers, "hard pressed and falling," but then finds that he, the rejected "stone" who was broken and discarded, has become the priceless "cornerstone." And he exclaims: "it is wonderful in our eyes" (Psalm 118).

On one Special Olympics trip, I visited a small institution for people with intellectual disabilities outside of Cape Town, South Africa, where about fifty adults with severe disabilities were housed. I was there thanks to the generosity of a hundred of the world's most gifted musical artists, who'd raised almost $100 million for Special Olympics by selling Christmas music. Under the leadership of my brother Bobby and the legendary music team of Jimmy and Vicki Iovine, stars such as Stevie Wonder, Jon Bon Jovi, Stevie Nicks, and B. B. King had given the proceeds of their recordings to support bringing the freedom and joy of Special Olympics to the world's poorest citizens. And in Cape Town, as in thousands of other communities worldwide, we put their generosity to work.

The conditions there were poor, with several men and women in each room, concrete floors, dark halls, and limited facilities. Most of the residents had complex needs that their families were unable to care for at home. My colleague from Connecticut, Peter Wheeler, had joined our global team and traveled to South Africa to help raise the profile of our movement and he'd found his way to the institution, called a "Sanctuary." He'd introduced the Special Olympics "Motor Activities Development Program" to the residents there, a series of simple activities designed for people with very severe challenges. On the day of my visit, dozens of the residents joined me in the small common room of the facility and gathered in lines and circles to show off their skills. Small events are "Special Olympics," too, and they take place by the thousands all over the world. I was there to observe and support this one.

Several of the athletes arrived in the common room in wheelchairs. Most were not able to use language to communicate. Their caregivers pushed their chairs or helped them with their walkers or simply held their hands as they came into the room. The pace of arrivals was slow and deliberate. There was no rush. No one had anywhere else to go.

As I watched a group of the residents throw bean bags and kick inflated balls and perform the lifting and lowering of the brightly colored sheet, I sat next to a resident who was there only to watch, not to participate. His disabilities were too severe even for these basic activities. He was seated in a wheelchair with his head resting against an enveloping cushioned headrest that protected his neck and shoulders. His hands were drawn into his body, thin and missing muscle, knotted tight and unmoving. His head was cocked slightly to the side, his mouth just open, his eyes fixed ahead but not moving to follow the activities. The games being played in front of us were rising in enthusiasm with an occasional cheer and loud noise popping from one or another of the athletes as they became more and more animated by their tasks. The room was lighting up and smiles crept onto the many faces that were assembled.

The young man sitting next to me did not move, but the woman at his side began to massage the knotted muscles of his neck and shoulders, gentle and absent-minded, watching the games. I thought to myself that she must be his mother. She watched the other residents play but her hand worked on his neck unconsciously and with tenderness. I leaned toward her.

"My name is Tim Shriver. It's so nice to meet you here."

"Nice to meet you Mr. Shriiiva," she answered in a beautiful South African lilt.

"Please call me Tim. And this is your son?"

"Yes. This is Daniel."

"Nice to meet you, Daniel." I gestured toward him. I reached out and touched his motionless hand. "Thanks for inviting us all to come here to the sanctuary."

Daniel of course did not respond. Neither did his mother. I turned to her to strike up a conversation.

"I was wondering how things are going for you here in South Africa. We in Special Olympics want to be helpful in promoting sport and even more, in promoting change in the country. How are things for you and Daniel today?"

"Things are fine, thanks," she answered simply and without the slightest attention to my question.

"That's wonderful," I replied. But I had another agenda. I wanted to learn about the problems in South Africa so I could formulate plans for advocacy and change. "But I think we have an opportunity to challenge the leaders here to do more for people with disabilities. What could be done differently, in your opinion?"

The games in front of us continued, as did her massage of Daniel's head and neck and shoulders. "Things are fine, thanks, Mr. Shriiiva," she said again.

"Well, I've studied the situation here and I know the schools don't have adequate resources for children with special needs. Even this sanctuary could use some better facilities. I know you must have endured a lot of challenges trying to raise Daniel. Could you share some of your experiences with me?" I wanted to know what was wrong and in need of changing. I was in my own world, thinking politically, seeing only the lack of financial resources, the corrosive neglect of political leaders, the insidious effect of stigmatizing public attitudes. She was in another world.

"Thank you, Mr. Shriiiva. But Daniel and I are fine."

"Fine? Isn't there something better that could be done?"

She finally turned to face me. "You know, Mr. Shriiiva, I will say it again. Daniel and I are fine. Perhaps you don't understand so let me tell you. Daniel has taught me something that most parents never learn. Daniel taught me unconditional love. Every day, I am grateful to him. I'm sure there are many things to change, but as for Daniel and me, we are fine."

I had heard words such as "unconditional love" many times in my life. I had fallen in love with Linda and had never felt anything like the excitement of her and me together. I had read Lonergan's writing about God's love as a love that has no conditions for its fulfillment. I had felt the grief of lives lost and knew grief had its source in love. I had seen five children born and growing, tiny ears emerging miraculously, fingers stretching to grasp my hand, a bicycle ridden for the first time with peals of exuberance.

But somehow, I had never quite heard before what she said to me that day: that most parents never learn unconditional love. I wondered whether that was true, and more troublingly, whether it was true of me. Had I loved my children with conditions? Had I calibrated my love for them, even unconsciously, in a way that was based on how well they lived up to my expectations? I had never seen a moment quite like the one next to me that day. It was just those gentle maternal hands on that broken but beautiful body, the two of them so completely together, no games being played, no discussion being undertaken, no task being completed. I couldn't look at the two of them for long—I had to look away. They were so intimate, so united, so peaceful together. I felt I was intruding with my abrasive questions and my arrogant ambitions. Love is unconditional, I realized, otherwise it isn't love.

I asked myself again: Was I capable of unconditional love? As much as I wanted to answer with a full-hearted "yes," I knew that I couldn't, but I wanted to figure out how. Now at least I had my role models—Daniel and his mother. Unconditional love isn't a thing you can figure out. It's a gift given and received in equal measure.

•

Every now and then, Zheng sent me pictures of little Pearl and I shared them over and over again with everyone in my office. Pearl became a living symbol of all that we wanted to create in China and around the world: she was hope from the experience of despair; happiness despite challenges of body and mind, unconditional love. When Pearl was almost two years old, I arranged to meet her and her parents at one of our Special Olympics games near Shanghai. The three of them came to a community center together and we took pictures. Pearl was strong enough to stand while holding the side of a table. We cheered as she looked up at her mother with an astonished expression. She was adorable.

Those two years had not been easy for Pearl or her parents. Like a high percentage of children with Down syndrome, Pearl had been born with serious heart defects—no left pulmonary artery, a hole in her heart, and several other dangerous congenital abnormalities. Pearl was often hospitalized and even at home she was often sick. Caring for her was a struggle, and her little life always seemed in jeopardy.

"Frankly, I often feel exhausting of caring Pearl . . ." Zheng wrote me when Pearl was almost three. "We can't sleep well, Pearl always cry at midnight and we have to leave work to take care of her as she is so bad physical. So high medicine fee . . .

"So many times give up is come out in my deep mind, we are really tired. However, when she smile at me, all bad thing just disappear. As my poor English, I don't know how to descript this feeling, I just know, that's call love, and I think that may be the true core of Special Olympics."

In 2005, little Pearl died after a failed heart operation. She was only three years old, but her death sent waves of grief throughout the Special Olympics movement. Thousands of us had followed her life, her first hours, her "sile so pure," the inspiration she gave her father to believe that nothing could stop him, her ability to make "all bad thing just disappear." I wandered through the halls of our Washington, DC, office building. In office after office, people were weeping over the loss of a child they hadn't even met. We posted Pearl's picture on our international website.

"God bless you and your families and litter Pearl," Zheng finished his last e-mail to me. As I wept with my colleagues that day, I took a picture of "litter Pearl" and put it in a silver frame in my office. What was it, I wondered, that drew us so close to her life? The picture was black-and-white and a little fuzzy. It showed Pearl wrapped tightly in warm clothes and a hat, only the small features of her face visible. But her eyes held on, as if telling me to stop running and stay with her, to stop racing away to bigger ideas and grander tasks. Pearl was a teacher of how to love from within. We met only once. I never heard her speak a word. But her presence had made me a better father and a better man.

TWELVE

The Fun That Lasts

More often than not, parents and friends of people with intellectual disabilities say that they have more fun and happiness around those people than around others. The more time I spent with them, the more I, too, discovered that they had a lot to teach me about how to have fun. But to get the full message, I had to leave the sidelines of volunteering and advocating to play Special Olympics Unified Sports. And I'm proud to say, the first time I played on a Special Olympics Unified Sports team, I won a gold medal!

"Unified," as it's called, is a chance to get off the sidelines of Special Olympics and onto the field. The founder of Unified is an affable and passionate Special Olympics leader named Beau Doherty who had started his career working in institutions as a recreation coordinator. "It was pretty grim. I remember more than a few times when I had large groups of residents and was told to clean them up by hosing them down. I can't say I'm proud of that work but it did teach me one lesson: I had to get those folks out of those institutions and into the community. Anything was better than life in those institutions."

Beau started working for Special Olympics Massachusetts when he was twenty-five years old. Seared with the memories of what life was like for people with intellectual differences when they were isolated, he became obsessed with doing whatever he could to promote their integration. At Special Olympics Massachusetts, he pioneered the idea of creating teams where half the competitors would be people with intellectual disabilities and the other half would be non-disabled "partners." In 1992, Beau became the executive director of Special Olympics Connecticut, and he put his ideas to work by coaching a newly formed softball team that included me.

At the end of our first season, on a sunny day in New London in early August, our team cruised to an easy victory in the Special Olympics Unified Sports State Softball Championships over the incumbent champions, Waterbury. I played an errorless second base in the final game and was high-fiving my teammates for hours after we were awarded our first gold medals. Our rivals were none too happy about being dethroned. Everyone thinks that Special Olympics athletes are sweet and kind and don't really care about winning. Wrong! Whenever we ask athletes what they like most about being a part of the Special Olympics world, medals almost always rank at or near the top.

The following season, our New Haven team again looked like the favorites. We had a diverse range of talent: power hitters who were cops by day, gritty outfielders who had competed in Special Olympics their whole lives and ran down almost anything, and a steady battery of pitchers and catchers who kept the ball around the plate. When Waterbury came down to New Haven for our first regular-season game of the spring, we knew they were going to play us hard, but we felt unbeatable.

One of Waterbury's power hitters was Tony Marino. He'd competed for several years and was a real trash talker. When Waterbury was at the plate, you could hear his constant chatter calling for hits and runs. When we were at the plate, he'd snarl the old playground taunts: "*No hitter, no hitter, no hitter.*" He was both tough and funny, and our team answered him in kind.

When he came up to bat the night of our first regular-season game, I was ready at second. Or at least I thought I was. A few pitches went by for balls and strikes, and I think I must've fallen victim to a position player's worst mistake, which is to let your mind wander. In any event, on the next swing of the bat, Tony crushed a smoking hard low line drive directly toward me. But unlike any line drive I'd ever fielded before, this one had sharp backspin on it, and as I crouched down to catch it, it rose up like an inverted curve ball. Before I could get my glove up, it smashed into my mouth at full speed. In an instant, I was on my back, dizzy and afraid to touch my mouth for fear that my teeth were all gone. The ball had hit me hard, and blood was all over my face. I was conscious but dazed and embarrassed. By the time the umpire called time out, my teammates were hovering over me with ominous looks in their eyes.

Tentatively, I reached toward my face and to my surprise, all my teeth were there and none of them seemed to be pointed in the wrong direction. The blood appeared to be coming from my lip, which was bountifully swollen but still in roughly the right place. My nose was in one piece despite a few grinding noises when I tried to move it from side to side. All in all, I began to come to my senses with the relieved conclusion that my face was more or less intact. I stood up, wiped the blood onto my sleeve and regained my position at second base, telling everyone that I would be fine. And standing there on second was Tony Marino, looking at me quizzically, and perched in position to run to third.

I wasn't sure how he'd ended up on second or where the ball had gone after it careened off my face, but with everyone slowly returning to their positions, he and I were standing in the middle of the field in our own space. "Nice hit," I said to him, conceding the obvious.

"We're going to kick your ass in States this year, buddy."

I looked at him cockeyed, not sure if my ears were working. Had he somehow missed the sight of me flattened on the infield, bloodied by his blast? He was a Special Olympics athlete, and I just *knew* that he'd meant to say something charitable. I kept looking at him, waiting for the expected kindness that transcends competition.

"You heard me. We're gonna win States this year and you ain't got no chance!"

Finally, I smiled, not at him, but at myself. He wasn't a "Special Olympics athlete" or a "person with intellectual disability" or a "sweet kid with a lot of heart." He was a softball player, nothing more and nothing less. When the game was over, there would be time for les-

sons and friendships, but while the game was on, we were competitors. And the only thing on his mind was winning.

I snapped back to the game. *Focus, focus, focus.* There was a runner
on second with nobody out. Batter up. A ground ball hit to me was a
play to first. Game on.

I've long remembered that moment because it reminds me that no
stereotype fits people with intellectual disabilities. Some like to think
that everyone with a disability is kind and open or sweet and gentle
but that's no more true of this population than it is of any other.
Stereotyping isn't wrong because it's politically incorrect; it's wrong
because it's factually incorrect. Labels are designed to group people
together for one practical need or another, and we use them all the time
for perfectly reasonable purposes. We group people by age to determine
who votes and who doesn't. We group people by gender for restrooms.
But none of those groupings define the person, and most groupings do
something far worse: they create assumptions and prejudices.

Tony Marino is a person with an intellectual disability, but as it
turned out, he was also an aggressive rival and a cocky competitor who
wanted to have fun and win. Most important, he was uninterested in
faking how he felt. It may be that he experienced a moment of concern when he saw me knocked down, but that was overridden by his
excitement about the game and his focus on winning. And unlike
most people, he didn't decide to hide his desire to win in order to conform to anyone's assumptions of what the socially "correct" feeling was
in that moment. He was focused on kicking my ass and having fun
doing it!

I've heard similar stories over and over again from thousands of
people who have been surprised and disarmed by the emotional hon-
esty that often radiates from people with intellectual differences.
Most of us are afraid to be emotionally honest much of the time.
We're afraid that our feelings will prove embarrassing to ourselves or
hurtful to others, so we hold them in or edit them through socially
acceptable filters or blurt them out in gossip. So the circle goes on
and on—unstated feelings lead to unstated feelings and we miss the
important stuff and instead have conversations about nothing or the
weather or some celebrity breakup.

Not so in the world of intellectual difability.* At a Unified summer camp called Camp Pals, volunteer counselors and support staff spend a week playing sports and living together and taking trips and all the while, hearing exactly how all of the campers with Down syndrome feel all the time. And it's a riot! "There are so many problems in the world and there is so much BS in the way people act toward one another," said Felix Llanos, a young man who worked with the campers with Down syndrome for a week in a variety of support roles. "But not here. Here, there's none of that. Here people wear their hearts on their sleeves. One camper is scared of thunder and he just showed it and I was like 'Wow, man. That is so cool that you can just be who you are.' People out there in the streets—man, the world is so screwed up sometimes—people try to get over on the next person or compensate for themselves by putting up a front and it's all just so many lies. But here, everyone is just themselves."

As Llanos spoke, I remembered one evening when I was at the World Economic Forum in Davos, Switzerland, where thousands of the world's most powerful and wealthy people convene every year to "improve the state of the world." I called my daughter Rose after one especially exhausting day to report on my efforts in selling the story of Special Olympics to the world's most rich and famous. I was telling her how tiring it was, and she, a spiritual intuitive herself, kept pushing me, asking me what it was that made me feel so depleted. "I guess it's that these folks are wound so tight that they take the joy out of me."

"I guess," Rose said, "those are the most scared people in the world. I guess it's understandable that they'd be unable to have much fun."

"You're right, Rose. They have a lot to be afraid of."

"The most scared people in the world" is not the way that the

---

* "Difability" is not a typo, and yet it is not a generally accepted word either. I use it often, however, to jog my consciousness out of the "dis" mind-set that so often includes subtle assumptions of lack of ability and negativity. "Dif," on the other hand, invites the recognition that there are a million abilities and that each of us has many different ones. Some advocates in the disability world do not like the word "difability" because they are concerned that it diminishes the rightful pride that people can and should take in who they are, "disabilities" and all. I understand this sentiment and respect it. At the same time, I think using the word "difability" can help.

World Economic Forum advertises their elite guest list. Most of us assume that the people with Down syndrome at Camp Pals better fit that description. Then again, maybe not. Llanos was onto something when he said that most people "out there" put on fronts and pretend to be something they're not while everyone at camp "is just themselves." What's more scary than having to fight every day to prove superiority and gain massive wealth and act like someone different from who you are in order to feel safe and secure? And what could be less scary than being strong enough to be just yourself?

Most parents try to create an environment in their homes where their children can feel free to be "just themselves," and Linda and I were no different. We tried to raise all five of our children—Rose, Tim, Sam, Kathleen, and Caroline—to know that their home is one where they can always be exactly who they are. We also tried to make sure that "being yourself" never translated into "being spoiled and entitled" by constantly reminding them that however much we loved them, to be a creature of infinite value doesn't mean that you're superior but only unique. Together, we tried to teach that all people are beautiful and we tried to deepen that lesson in prayer and practice it in welcoming relationships. Welcome and prayer: it was our own little formula.

But like most parents, we couldn't make those lessons come to life in the abstract, so we got help. Beginning when Rose and Tim were still in elementary school, Linda and her friend Anne Yap decided to form a Special Olympics Unified Basketball team in our neighborhood. Almost from birth, our children attended Special Olympics games and events, so the idea of sports with people with differences was not new to them. And we had the added advantage of living next door to Anne and Dean Yap, who had three beautiful children, one of whom, Maureen, has Down syndrome. Maureen was the same age as our son Sam, and they attended school together. But after school, Maureen was also very good at eluding her parents' watchful eyes and sneaking into our backyard to play on our swing set. Among the many joys of living next to the Yaps was the chance to look out the window at random times and see Maureen pushing herself gently on the swing set with no one around, a slightly curious but content look on her face. She was mischievous, and she was a delight.

While our children and the Yap children were still very young, Loretta came to talk to their classes about what it means to have an intellectual difference, and she delivered her most pointed message: "Names hurt." She was two decades ahead of the anti-bullying campaigns that have recently spread around the United States and other countries. "You may not realize it," she told the students, "but when you call someone a 'retard' it hurts, and it hurts for a long time. If you hurt my arm or my leg, it heals fast, but when you hurt my heart, it can last forever. So," she often finished her talks, "I'm asking you all to turn on your head before you open your mouth and remember that there's a person inside everyone who's got a special need and don't make fun of them or bully them and whatever you do, don't use the word 'retard' to make fun of anyone. Sticks and stones may break my bones but names hurt for a lifetime. Thank you."

Needless to say, having Maureen in class and spending time with Loretta helped our children sensitize their peers—and often their teachers and other parents, too—to the cruelty of language. Time after time, Timbo (as we called our son) would come home from play dates saying that he'd heard a friend's mother call someone a "retard" and he'd felt paralyzed, not knowing what to say to a grown-up. By the time he was about eight, he and Rose had learned. "I had to ask Mr. Dyer at gym class not to call students 'retards' when they drop the ball in class, Dad," said Rose. "I don't think he listened to me but I did speak up." Similarly, Timbo confronted his friends on the playground so often that they finally dealt him the most irritating of rejoinders: "Okay, Timbo! We get it. We won't say that word around you." He knew that was the worst kind of dismissive comeback, and it only made him more frustrated. "It's not for me that you shouldn't say the word. It's because it's mean." Some listened, but most were puzzled. Our kids were getting an early education in the deep-rooted and hard to reverse stigma against people who are intellectually different. Most of their friends just didn't see a problem.

But nothing can teach a lesson like play, and that's where their Special Olympics Unified Team came in. In the third year of our basketball team, with Rose now thirteen, Tim twelve, Sam eight, Kathleen seven, and Caroline four, Linda and Anne Yap scheduled a series of games with a new Unified Team from a special school one town away. The opponent was Katherine Thomas School, a small day school for children with learning disabilities and various levels of autism in Rockville, Maryland. KTS, as it's called, is one of those places that's hard to find and feels less like a school and more like a multidimensional education and rehabilitation facility when you arrive. It is located in a small office park just off the interstate behind an Adventist hospital. The doors are industrial, the halls narrow, and the environment vaguely clinical. The level of care for students is outstanding and the staff world-class, and the fees are as high as thirty thousand dollars for the high school program. Most of the children who attend KTS are there because the regular school special education program isn't able to support their needs.

Beginning in January, our band of eight-to-twelve-year-olds, which included my brother Mark and sister-in-law Jeanne's children Molly, Tommy, and Emma, would play weekly scrimmages against KTS—one week they'd come down to our local gym at Blessed Sacrament School in Washington, and the next week we'd haul out onto the highway to KTS's gym. The kids on both teams played through the season with good cheer, but basketball is a difficult game for young children and is even more difficult for those who have challenges. As a result, the scrimmages only faintly resembled basketball. Dribbling was occasionally done properly; repeat shots were allowed on each possession so that each player would have several chances to find the net. The score wasn't kept and time wasn't monitored. Both teams substituted regularly, with partners playing more the role of helpers than competitors. One morning after practice ended, Linda took off with the girls to run errands, so Timbo and Sam and I headed for home—just the boys. Three men in a car on a cold weekend morning can easily fall into mindlessness. The pattern in our car was familiar: turn up the radio, zone out, and drive home. But as we coasted along the interstate, something was gnawing at me. I

wondered what my kids were really thinking about their Unified mornings. Their friends from school weren't with them at KTS, and the
game wasn't the kind of competition that would lead to great stories
of athletic triumph. I was starting to think that maybe I was unwit-
tingly forcing my kids into guilt-induced duty, the exact thing that
I wanted so desperately to avoid. We hadn't ever talked about their
Special Olympics volunteering from the point of view of what they
wanted—we'd simply launched into it and brought the kids along.
At some level, I wondered if they were wishing this whole Special
Olympics thing would go away so they could be relieved of the extra
responsibility.

So I did what most kids can't stand: I broke the silence and started
a conversation.

"So what did you guys think of the game today?"

"It was fine, Dad," Tim answered.

"No, really. Don't just say that because you think that's what I
want to hear. I really want to know what you think of the whole experience." I wanted to probe their thinking without using words that
would prompt or suggest answers, but I couldn't resist. "You've got to
be thinking at some level that you don't want to be out at KTS at that
small gym, don't you?"

Pause. Neither boy answered.

"Aren't you?" I persisted.

"Dad!" Sam blurted. "It was fine. Relax!"

Another long pause. The car droned on down the cold highway as
the radio blared. I looked at both of the boys and they had already
zoned out again, staring out the window, listening to music. So I decided to increase the stakes. I turned off the radio.

"Dad! Why did you do that? Turn the radio back on. What's the
matter with you?"

"I'm asking you a question, and I don't think you're giving me an
honest answer. I'm asking you about this whole Unified Sport thing
and what you feel about it and if you're just doing it because you have
to or what. So I want to hear what you really think—honestly think—
or no radio."

There is a pause that seems like minutes but is only seconds, in

which these two boys look at me as if I am the most irritating person
on earth. Exasperated, Sam pivots in the front seat toward me, raises
his hands like an Italian chef, and says, "Look, Dad. Let me explain it
this way. If you were to tell me that next weekend we were all going
to Disney World, I would say that would be the most fun we could
possibly have. We would have a blast and it would be fantastic. But
there's one problem: as soon as we would get home, it would be terrible because the whole thing would be over and everyone would be
depressed."

I'm puzzled. I have no idea what he is talking about or why Disney World has come up. We've never been. He doesn't draw breath
and continues.

"When we go to Special Olympics and we play with the athletes
and cheer for Matt and D.J. and Maureen and Peter and Joelle and
give them high fives, it's fun in a different way. It's the fun that lasts.
It doesn't go away. Get it?"

I'm in shock. What did he just say? Did I hear him say, "the fun
that lasts?" Where did he come up with that? I don't say anything. I
don't know what to say. Another long pause.

"Dad!" Sam almost yells, interrupting the empty space. "Now
please turn the radio back on!"

"Did you just say, 'the fun that lasts'? Did I hear you right? Did
you just say that and come up with that point right here in this car?
Do you know what that means? Do you understand what you just
said? What does it mean, by the way? What did you mean by 'the
fun that lasts'?" I rambled and mumbled and tried to stop doing
both so I could let "fun that lasts" into my mind and heart. I
looked out the windshield as the big curve of the Washington belt-
way approached and my exit was in front of me. Neither boy said
anything for a moment. And then Tim complained, "Come on,
Dad. That's not fair. We answered your question. Now turn on the
radio!"

The boys were onto something bigger than I imagined. In those
three words, "fun that lasts," Sam articulated what thousands of people involved in Special Olympics games had felt, but which I at least
had never heard expressed so brilliantly. As I thought about Sam's

expression, I kept trying to unpack it and understand what had led him to say it. What part of his Saturday-morning practice had led him to believe he was in the midst of something "that lasts"? What part of the relationships he had with the athletes had made this whole thing seem fun to him? What experience had led him to see that there can be more than one type of fun? How had he learned that there is a type of fun that is enjoyable but temporary and often frustrating? And how had he come to see that fun could be recast as a state of joyfulness that endures and is never disappointing?

My sense is that the key to understanding what our children understood lies in the mysterious relationship between helping and being helped. How many times have we all heard the expression, "I got back more than I gave"? Philanthropists announce it at gala dinners; civic organization leaders announce it at community gatherings; religious leaders announce it from the pulpit. Everyone says it as if everyone understands it. But try asking someone to explain what they got back, and the result is usually a lot of blank stares.

"Like what?" I ask. "What did you get back?"

The initial answers are frequently the same.

"Well, the athlete [or the 'patient' or the 'victim' or the 'child' or whoever] had such a wonderful time and she or he seemed so happy [or 'better' or 'appreciative' or other positive attribute]." The answers are almost always framed in terms of an experience of the person getting helped. I have asked a question to the person who does the helping—and they answer in terms of the beneficiary of their service. But then I persist.

"I see. But you've just told me that the person you helped appeared to be happy or appreciative, but I thought you said that *you* had received something in return. What did *you* receive?"

The next wave of answers typically focuses on participation. People repeat the same message about the person who was helped—that he or she was happy or grateful or appreciative. But then they add something like this: "I was happy to be able to be there when the person I was helping was happy," or "I was happy because someone else was happy."

I push again. "That's wonderful. But I'm still a little confused. If

I told you that I was happy last week, I don't think you would automatically be happy, would you? In other words, I thought you said that you received something from this encounter that was different from what the other person received. But so far, you've only told me about the other person's happiness and not much about what you received. Was it just that you got to watch? Or did you actually receive something from this experience?"

At this point, virtually everyone I've ever asked—and I've asked a lot of people—has the same reaction. They take a deep breath. They sigh, and they go quiet.

And then what follows is a story about what matters most. One man told me that before going to a local Special Olympics event and volunteering at the check-in table, he had never understood how to face adversity with a strength that comes from within. "I heard them say that oath—how does it go again? 'Let me win' and then they say that second part, 'but if I cannot win, let me be brave in the attempt.' I think that about sums it all up," he said to me. "I mean I just felt that I could live like that, too. I could face whatever comes my way and just focus on being brave and doing my best. Those kids were all out on the field and I looked at them and I realized that they were all facing much bigger challenges than I ever had. But they were being brave. That's what I got back. I got back what it means to be brave and I can't put a price on that. I guess you could say I helped them that day by showing up and volunteering for a few hours. But they helped me believe in myself again. They helped me believe that I can be brave."

These kinds of experiences flow like rivers when you stop to ask people the meaning of giving and give them enough time to answer. I was at a dinner with a woman in her seventies, and she was describing helping in a different context—she visited cancer patients in the hospital. I went through my questions about what she got back and the usual answers emerged, but when I pushed a third time, her eyes began to well up. "There was one woman I visited for many months before she died. I suppose what I got back was that I mattered to her. You know I've been married all these years and my son is grown up and I've had so many experiences, but I don't think I ever mattered to anyone the way I mattered to her. When I would arrive at the hospital, she looked at me in a way no one had ever looked at me. She said to me one time, 'You are an angel to me,' and I tried to tell her 'No,' that I was just lucky to meet her and I wasn't anything special, but I cried and cried later that day because I'm embarrassed to say that I had never felt needed like that before.

"Do I sound pathetic?" she continued. "I hope not. But I guess that's what I got back, now that you ask. I got back the belief that I mattered to someone. I don't know what she received from me, but I can never thank her enough for helping me to believe that I mattered."

There is clearly a mysterious element to these "helping" encounters, but the mystery is not new. The Greeks had an expression, "give up what thou hast and thou wilt receive." Jesus suggested that we find our lives in losing them. The woman who saw the eyes of a cancer patient and found her own value and worth, Sam finding a source of fun that he otherwise could not find—these are only recent installments in the universal human quest to capture in words what so often eludes words: how it is that there is a beautiful and fun part of ourselves that we can find only in giving ourselves to others, especially to those in the greatest need.

We live in a time when individuality and self-advancement and competitive selfishness have been elevated nearly to the status of a religion—where more and more, we're conditioned to believe that we are alone; solitary beings destined to make sense of the world only by making sense of ourselves. We're on our own. We feel we have to fight to win at school, and fight to win at work. We're fighting to be popular, to lose weight, to stay young. We're even fighting to be happy and to avoid the most dreaded outcomes: loneliness, despair, defeat.

Viktor Frankl was among the first modern psychologists to suggest that modernity need not be a trap of individuality. He wrote and practiced medicine after the Second World War and with the unique benefit of having known firsthand how people had found "meaning" in their lives despite the terrifying and desperate conditions of Nazi death camps. Frankl survived, but of course, millions did not, and it was in the face of the horrific evil and despair that Frankl discovered that human beings have a "defiant power" to seek and find meaning in one another. In countless lectures and interviews, Frankl discussed his bestselling books, *Modern Man in Search of a Soul* and *Man's Search for Meaning*, but in discussion, he went even further than he went in writing. "Human beings are not primarily and originally concerned about intra psychic problems . . . they are normally, fundamentally, originally, primarily and basically concerned about something or someone out there in the world . . . Human beings survive . . . for the sake of a cause to serve or a person to love." In another interview, he went still further: "Human beings are motivated by a spark—by the search for meaning . . . Human beings are fulfilled when they are recognized by another as a subject, not an object to be used but as a subject to be appreciated for his unique gifts. And the highest level of relationship is love when we see in the other person, not just the subjectivity of the person but the unique subjectivity of that person, the beauty of that person . . . Unconsciously," Frankl added, "[we] harbor a directedness toward transcendence."

Frankl's message isn't far from Sam's. The Hindu master Pandit Rajmani Tigunait frames the paradox of service in interiority: "Compassionate service helps to alleviate the pain of those who are suffering. But its greater value lies in purifying the minds and hearts of those who render it." One could debate the meaning of "purifying" for years, but one thing seems certain: for many of us, it is when we give ourselves to others who are vulnerable that we lessen our fear of being vulnerable ourselves and we open up. In Frankl's language, when we exercise our human ability to see the unique in one another, we become freed of our loneliness, our despair, our sense of being trapped in our own tensions. For a yoga master and meditation leader such as Tiguanait, when we render compassionate service, we become able to ease the distractions and illusions of separateness that the mind creates, and we can see more clearly and more purely the beauty and unity of ourselves and all beings. In the end, giving really is receiving, and the most important thing we can give away is fear and the most important thing we receive in return is our fearless self, loved by others, fully alive.

Sam's insight adds still another element to this picture: the power of games. The philosopher Friedrich von Schiller tried to understand the human experience of the body and the spirit and came close to Sam's insight: "[Man] is only completely a man when he plays." Schiller was trying to express the belief that a different type of consciousness emerges in play. What the mind cannot grasp from ideas or thoughts, he theorized, it intuits in imagination and play. I can just imagine Schiller in the gym at Katherine Thomas School, with all his erudition and knowledge of Greeks and Romans and medievals and moderns, trying to find the words to explain the aesthetics of the children running and laughing and bouncing their balls in chaotic and beautiful dances of play. I think he might have given up and agreed that Sam had it right: it's the kind of fun that lasts.

A few years after my midday lesson in philosophy at the hands of my two sons, my daughter Rose and her high school friends started their own Special Olympics Unified Bowling program. They were social entrepreneurs before the term was popular and created their own weekend team, with more than thirty athletes and partners. It was inspiring to see someone so young create something so powerful. Clearly she understood the fun that lasts and wanted more of it. And she and her siblings and friends were also the target for the next surprise: a call from the film producers Peter and Bobby Farrelly.

The Farrellys wanted to know if Special Olympics would collaborate in the making of a film about the athletes. They were friends of my brother Anthony and involved in many fund-raising events for his wonderful program, Best Buddies, so I knew they were good people. But at the same time, I was wary, since their brand of filmmaking was what one might kindly call "adolescent humor." They'd made such hit films as *There's Something About Mary* and *Dumb and Dumber*, films soaked in bathroom humor and the occasional joke at the expense of a character with intellectual disability. They were great at making teenagers roar with laughter (and making me roar, too), but I couldn't see how any film they might make would be appropriate for a movement like ours.

But after months of discussion, Peter Farrelly managed to convince us that his vision was sincere and serious: "I want to make a movie that is funny, but I also want to make a film that shows the human side of Special Olympics athletes. I know there are a lot of movies that tug at people's heartstrings and tell emotion-drenched stories about people with intellectual challenges, but I don't think that's the whole picture of what goes on at Special Olympics." The film was called *The Ringer* (2005), and in it, a lifelong loser, played by Johnny Knoxville, sneaks into a Special Olympics dorm, feigns an intellectual disability, and tries to win a race and a bet. I visited the set in Austin a number of times, and during one of the lunch breaks, I walked a few blocks with Bill Chott, a skilled improv actor who was playing a Special Olympics athlete. "I don't know how to tell you this, Tim," Bill said, "but working on this film, I feel like I'm getting back so much more than I'm giving."

There it is again, I thought, giving and receiving. Needless to say, I pressed Bill. "What do you mean?"

"This is just the best set I've ever been on—it's as simple as that. We've got about fifty Special Olympics athletes around us all the time and they just make the set the best I've ever been on. They're always having a good time and enjoying everything."

"I hear you. But that's what they're doing. You said *you* were getting back a lot more than you gave." I know I sound like a broken record. "What about you? What makes this set so different for you?"

Although Bill and I had just met, I could see he was already frustrated with me. In my head, I was preparing for the three-part discussion and looking forward to what Bill might tell me once I'd broken down the routine responses. But instead of the usual pattern, Bill went silent and just kept walking.

"Bill. Did you hear me? I was asking, what makes this so special for *you*?"

"I don't know what you're looking for me to say, man. I don't know what else I can tell you. But let me tell you this. On this set, I get twenty hugs a day. I've never been anyplace like this. That's about the best I can explain it. Twenty hugs a day. And I like it."

You need to be fearless to hug people—and you need to be recklessly fearless to hug people twenty times a day. In the Unified world where you play as you are and you try with all the energy God gives you, and you hug people you're happy to be with, you can feel safe and seen and light and fun. That's an energy worth celebrating.

By the way, Waterbury did beat my team, New Haven, in the State tournament that second year. Tony Marino was right. They kicked our butts. And I'm not embarrassed to say, it was a blast.

THIRTEEN

I Am So Proud

It would be a huge mistake to assume that the Special Olympics school of the heart curriculum ends with love and fun and trust and hugs. Life requires more than that, and we all know it. It requires grit. One day, a colleague sent me a short essay that started me wondering what we really mean when we talk about "grit." It was written by a Special Olympics parent who was also the chaplain of the United States Army Base at Fort Leonard Wood, Kansas. He was writing about watching his daughter, Elizabeth Carlson, race for the first time. I read his piece to myself:

> I remember the day perhaps too well. It was the first time for my daughter Elizabeth to attend a "Special Olympics." She was very excited. She didn't know my love of athletics and competition, but she did know the excitement of the crowds and the feeling of importance of being in the 50 yard dash.
>
> Even saying dash forces me to deviate from the normal paradigm of speed, sleek runner, world-class times; and understand running from the world of a child who never crawled, a child who caught herself with her head when the teetering which became walking was painfully, yet perseveringly practiced . . . I don't want to reminisce too much but that day . . . it is still etched indelibly in my memory. I knew

the world of "special" children. I knew and know the world of
expectation, of hope for new performance plateaus, the predisposition of "boxes" which we tend to need to classify human
beings as we strive to define them in reference to "normal" . . .

Yet this day was different. I recall her lining up with five
or six other athletes. There was anticipation in the air. There
were officials and whistles and flags and tapes to break at the
finish line. And then the race began. My daughter who never
crawled, who never walked as my other five children walked
so strongly and so perfectly . . . was running.

Today I put on hold the fear that running always leads to
falling. Running never was "right" for her and I watched and
watched as she ran and ran. She won. Elizabeth won the race.
I rushed to her and embraced her. I could feel her entire being surge with feeling as we shared her moment of athletic
victory . . . the memory of that day, of my precious, special
daughter running will last forever!

"Liz," "Lizzy," "Elizabeth Christine Carlson," I love you,
I'm proud of you, you're special. God gave you to us to cher-
ish forever. Thanks for the courage you have given to all of
us, the strength, and the desire to try, to never give up and
yes . . . to run.

When you read something like this, you know it's trying to communicate with your heart, not just your head. And when that same
reading leads to tears, you know it is trying to free some part of your
heart that is yearning for its message. Chaplain Carlson wasn't just
writing about an event. He was writing about a relationship between
himself and his daughter where the strength and the love between
them had given one of them, Lizzy, the strength and the grit to be
unafraid to try something monumental: running. More than anything else, he was writing about a moment in which he'd learned that
she wasn't afraid to fail, that no matter how difficult it was for her to
walk or run and no matter how likely she was to fall and get hurt,
she was tough enough to try. He must have known that his belief in
her was what made it possible: he'd found a way to tell her through

words and through love that he saw something in her that no one else saw and maybe something that she didn't see, either. That's what made her able to risk it all in the race. She knew she had her dad with her. And as a result, she had grit.

The dictionary definition of "grit" is full of words that describe Lizzy Carlson: "courage, spirit, resolution, determination, nerve, guts, doggedness." As I read her father's account, I could almost feel her willpower rising. I could sense that she'd found a courage she might not have known she had. I wondered if she'd prepared for that moment or anticipated it. I wondered if she'd had to force herself to make the effort or if the guts had come naturally to her. Who was this Lizzy Carlson who had climbed this enormous mountain of a challenge and run this race and won?

A hundred years ago, the great psychologist William James puzzled over the rarity of the person who does what Lizzy did:

> Men the world over possess amounts of resource which only very exceptional individuals push to their extremes of use . . . Compared with what we ought to be, we are only half awake. Our fires are damped, our drafts are checked. We are making use of only a small part of our possible mental and physical resources.

James's question of whether or not most of us ever push ourselves to the extremes of our capability the way Lizzy Carlson did at Fort Leonard Wood has been taken up today by teams of researchers who are trying to understand grit and what role it plays in our lives. The University of Pennsylvania researcher Angela Lee Duckworth, building on the work of other positive psychologists such as Mihaly Csikszentmihalyi and Martin Seligman, has been studying the lives of people who achieve at the high end of their respective professions to see what psychological trait most fully contributes to their success. Duckworth and her colleagues have studied a lot of traits that we commonly associate with success: intelligence, for instance. Most people assume that the more intelligent you are, the more likely to succeed you are. To some extent, that's true. Cleverness can take you far in the world.

But Duckworth and her colleagues have found that in the long run, grit influences success more than IQ or any other single personality factor. The research defines "grit" as having two parts—one is perseverance and the other is passion for long-term goals. Interestingly, grit is not the same as self-control, nor is it the same as the need for achievement as validated by others. People with grit often pursue their goals against the grain of others' expectations, often do so with persistence despite risk, and yet have a strong capacity for human connection and collaboration. When Duckworth evaluated groups of high-achieving people such as Ivy League students, West Point cadets, and National Spelling Bee finalists, she found that grit was a better predictor of success than anything else. And in a finding that is of special importance to the world of Special Olympics, grit is not correlated with intelligence. You can have a really high IQ and not have much grit. And similarly, you can score poorly on an IQ test and be a star when it comes to grit. Grit requires both the capacity to see the goal and the capacity to not see the frustrations associated with trying to reach it, but it does not require school smarts.

Lizzy and her father clearly have faced their share of disappointment, but then again, who hasn't? The difference between Lizzy Carlson and most of us is that disappointment usually leads us to fear trying again. And what's the effect of that fear? A discouraged person or, worse, a defeated one. Why believe in the audacity of a dream when disappointment looms? Better, it seems, to stay away from risky situations and reduce the chances of failure; better to live within the range of what is reasonable, what is safe. If running leads to falling, stay home.

But as we all know, that's not the pathway to a fulfilled heart. We know there's something beautiful and special within each of us—something we know is good and we want to believe we can share with the world. The Lizzy Carlsons of the world remind us to take *another* chance and try again. And we need to remember that her gritty effort came with her father's love and within a community of support. If we're going to pursue our dreams, if we're going to muster the grit and optimism necessary to bring those dreams to life, we need to silence the voices in our heads, and around us, that tell us not to try.

When I first read Lizzy's father's account of her race, I took the text to a meeting of the international board of directors of Special Olympics—a group composed of Olympic champions such as Bart Conner and Nadia Comaneci, corporate leaders such as Muhtar Kent and Jay Emmett, entertainers such as Vanessa Williams and Jon Bon Jovi, disability rights leaders such as Deng Pufang and William P. Alford, and Special Olympics revolutionaries such as Stacey Johnston and Florence Nabayinda. At the opening of the meeting, I told the board that I was actively in search of a deeper understanding of the source of Special Olympics' power to change lives, and I read the whole of his essay. When I finished, I looked up to see a room of thirty global leaders stunned into silence. Then one of our most powerful corporate champions, Mark Booth, at that time the CEO of the media giant BSkyB of Europe, spoke up. "I spend my whole life in meetings with tough businesspeople, and I spend my whole life never showing my emotions to anyone. Then I come to Special Olympics and I cry. I don't know whether I'm embarrassed or overjoyed but I know I'm a better man here. And I know it makes me want to have the kind of guts that Lizzy Carlson shows us all."

I wish Mark had been able to come with me to Arusha, Tanzania, to witness another brilliant lesson in how to develop the "kind of guts" that makes us all better human beings. Arusha is a small city located near Mt. Kilimanjaro in the high altitude plains of Tanzania. Tanzania is a country of enormous contrasts. It has some of the world's most beautiful destinations, and is one of the world's ten poorest nations. The Ngorongoro Crater is home to Africa's most diverse and concentrated range of species; Lake Victoria is the world's largest tropical lake and the source of the Nile River; the city of Dar Es Salaam is among the best deep water ports on Africa's east coast; and off the coast, in the beautiful Indian Ocean, sits Zanzibar, one of the most exotic islands in the world. But Tanzania's grinding poverty has gone largely unchecked despite decades of optimistic reform efforts. The father of the nation, Julius Nyerere, was among Africa's greatest independence leaders who brought charisma and hope to the liberation of his country from European control in 1961. But his strategy for development was rooted in socialist economics that failed miserably.

When I set out for Tanzania in 1998 with my mentor, Red Verderame, and athlete leaders Loretta and Billy Quick, more than 75 percent of the population were living on less than one dollar a day. One of those people was Ramadhani Salim Chambo, a young man who met us with Tanzanian flowers and a hug at the Arusha airport when our plane from Amsterdam landed at midnight on the single, barely lit runway. He was twenty-three years old, or thereabouts: I would later find out that he was born sometime in 1975, but no one in the family could remember the exact date. Most of the passengers who had gotten off the plane with us were headed to Mount Kilimanjaro, but we were headed in the opposite direction, toward town, where Special Olympics Tanzania was scheduled to host the first-ever invitational 10K race for Special Olympics athletes from around southern Africa. Almost thirty athletes were invited to the multinational race, and a larger group of local athletes was also going to be included in competitive runs of shorter distances. Ramadhani and his coach helped us gather our bags and board a minibus bound for our hotel in Arusha. But halfway to the town, the bus driver suddenly pulled over to the side of the unlit, one-lane road. There was no sign of light or life. I assumed the van had broken down. After twenty hours of travel. Just what I needed. Great.

But no one else seemed perturbed, so I couldn't help but ask, "What's happening?"

"We're dropping Ramadhani off," said the coach.

I looked out into total darkness. I looked for a path. For a friend or parent who might be meeting Ramadhani. Nothing. There was absolutely nothing but a couple of hundred yards of open field bordered by woods. The door to the van opened up, and Ramadhani smiled at me and waved without a word, climbed out, and headed for the wall of trees in the distance.

"He lives in a village on the other side of those trees," his coach said. "This is as close as we can get in the van. He'll be fine."

I asked the coach to stop him. Couldn't I offer him a room at our

hotel if he needed a place to sleep? Or couldn't we drive him directly
to his home? The people on the van regarded me as if I were some
sort of cute, perplexed animal. He was fine and he was off into the
darkness.

If I had followed Ramadhani to his village, I would have found
what those in Tanzania considered a typical life for a young person
with an intellectual challenge. Ramadhani's mother, Khadija Sha-
bani, worked the fields, and sold handmade goods and vegetables to
earn money. On a few occasions, her husband had worked in a repair
shop in Arusha. In more than four decades of work, she had never
earned as much as a single dollar for a day's work.

When I spoke through an interpreter to his mother, Khadija, she
was blunt: "I am proud," she told me, "that Ramadhani was never tied."

"Tied?"

"Many parents who have boys like Ramadhani tie them up in the
closet or in the yard so they don't cause any trouble to the others in
the village," she said. "Ramadhani had so many problems, you see.
His birth was a difficult one. Maybe Ramadhani was sick because of
how he came. Maybe I had a fever when I was carrying him. I don't
know. But he didn't speak. His mouth was always full of saliva and it
was so hard to keep him clean. And the other children would not
play with him so he became naughty at times and quarreled with
others. But I refused to tie him and I just tried my best to stop him
from being naughty and keep him clean and tell the other children to
leave him alone."

When Ramadhani was eleven years old, a social worker visited
his village and explained to his mother that a new school was opening for children like him and that she could take him to the school
and they would try to help him learn some things. "I was so happy. I
couldn't read but I signed the paper the lady gave me and Ramadhani started school. By that time, he was almost always clean and
when he started school, he became less naughty. Some days, he
helped me with some work too. The other children left him alone and
that was better for us all. I became happy with how this boy was
growing."

At around this same time, a smart young man named Frank

Macha worked as a manager in the largest stadium in the former capital city of Tanzania, Dar Es Salaam. Macha was an up-and-coming professional in Tanzania's sport community with experience managing national soccer matches and large sporting events. His dream was that world-class sporting events featuring international stars would someday come his way.

Instead, what came was an invitation to visit the local Special Olympics competitions in Dar. "Mr. Madai [chairman of Special Olympics Tanzania] came to my office one day and asked me to come to see this special sports event. I knew nothing about this," Macha said, with a bellowing laugh. "I told him I would come to the event, but I had no idea what he was talking about. You see, you must understand that these children were . . ." Macha's voice trailed off when recounting his assumptions. "Let me say it this way. These children—I didn't know about them. I thought they were not, let's say . . ." Again he struggled for the words. "I thought they were useless.

"But when I arrived at this track event in Dar and I saw the children and they were running about and doing their races, I thought to myself, Oh, my God! Can you believe what I'm seeing? I mean it. I said, Oh, my God! and I spoke to the almighty right there to say: This must be your work, my God! Maybe I can't say it right in English, but I must tell you that I saw God calling at me on that day and telling me, 'This is your work.' From that day, I told Madai that I would be with him for the rest of my life."

Often people ask me how Special Olympics has been so successful in growing to reach millions of people in more than 170 countries around the world. It's simple. Special Olympics grows because people like Frank give themselves to the athletes. They volunteer, willingly and without force, to give their time and their hearts to something that is captured in words such as "Oh my God!"

Volunteers like Frank Macha are a massive and often untapped force for social change for one enormous reason: when they feel the moment of belief, they follow it, and fall in love with pursuing it, and commit to it. Frank Macha unlocked his own grit, saw his goal, and gave himself to it. We say that volunteers "believe" in their causes and "believe" in their capacity to make a difference, and I've seen enough to know that's true. But I also know that believing is something that lives not in the head but rather in the soul. The word "believe" probably comes from the Old English *belyfan*, or "to hold dear," "to love." We almost always associate "believing" with something religious or spiritual, and maybe that's appropriate since the most central religious and spiritual experience is being in love. But the root of the word also helps explain the meaning of volunteering: when you're a believer like Frank, you've fallen in love with people such as Ramadhani and given yourself, not just your time or your money. Frank gave himself to the athletes of Special Olympics like a person who falls in love. That's what a "volunteer" does: a volunteer does something for love, not money. And when you act from your heart, there are few obstacles that can stop you. Believing is itself a form of grit: it's giving yourself completely to a destination, or a person, or both. That's Frank Macha.

Frank didn't just feel the belief; he traveled all over the country, running workshops and recruiting volunteers. And one of those people he recruited was Nellie Mollel, a coach who attended one of Frank's first training sessions near Arusha. Inspired by Frank, Nellie went to the special school that Ramadhani attended and suggested that a Special Olympics program was needed at the school. And, following Frank, she volunteered her services to be a coach. Ramadhani was one of her first athletes.

He was thirteen years old at the time. She trained him to run a hundred-meter race. He never missed a practice; his running kept improving. And that wasn't all. "Ramadhani became more and more clean and tidy after he started to run with the coach," recalled his mother. "I laughed with him and told him, 'Ramadhani, you are becoming a sportsman now!' He smiled when I said these words to him." For the first time, she was feeling proud of her son. For the first time, he was feeling proud of himself.

Not long after my arrival in Arusha, it was time for the invitational 10K race and all the runners from the neighboring countries showed up on time for the start. Another group of athletes—those from Arusha, including Ramadhani—also showed up and were awaiting the chance to run in their events: a 100-meter and 400-meter race scheduled to be run after the 10K. The stadium we were using filled with spectators (in part because the streets of Arusha were cluttered with the unemployed and those with no place to go). I saw Ramadhani approach the starting line for the 10K, but then I heard his coach tell him, "No, Ramadhani. This race is too long for you. And you have no shoes on your feet. You cannot run this race. We have a shorter race for you later."

But Ramadhani swatted the coach away. And when the gun sounded, Ramadhani set off with the other runners, one lap around the track, then out into the jagged streets of Arusha. I watched as the coach went over to Frank Macha to express her concern about Ramadhani. I heard Macha assure her a van was trailing the racers and it would pick up Ramadhani when he tired. She turned to an expressionless, diminutive man, dressed in a sport coat that hung from his shoulders, several sizes too large. This, I came to learn, was Ramadhani's father. The coach explained what was happening. The father nodded.

For more than thirty minutes, as the runners raced through the town, there was no activity in the stadium. Then the lead runner, Joseph Mateuzu from Zimbabwe, entered, rounded the track, and finished to cheers in a time of thirty-four minutes. Amazing! One by one, the runners returned. The limit time was one hour. Anyone not finished by then would be picked up by the van.

As the hour approached, most of the runners had made it back and crossed the finish line. A lull returned to the crowd. Then—at fifty-nine minutes, just one minute to go—the final runner charged into the stadium. Ramadhani. He was the only runner left for the crowds to cheer. He rounded the outer half of the track, then came around the back stretch, turned down the final hundred meters. Down that final stretch he ran, and the crowd began to cheer. He ran, head high, chest out, his feet bare, and with all the energy God gave him he crossed the finish line of the 10K in last place before a cheering crowd and a standing ovation. There was some confusion on the track, as no one could quite believe Ramadhani had made it, but there he stood, panting heavily, with that smile his mother saw when she called him a "sportsman."

Frank Macha ran over to me. "Tim, I am so proud. I am so proud."

And I looked over to the side of the track. Ramadhani's father stood frozen. Tears streamed down his face as he regarded his son with pride.

Ramadhani might not fit the perfect scientific definition of grit—effort combined with a razor-sharp focus on goals. He might not score highly on the subtests that measure it—after all, he isn't even verbal and the measures wouldn't be accurate in assessing him. But that one element of grit that often goes unnoticed—the capacity to persevere for a goal even when failure or disappointment might occur—there, Ramadhani would have something to say. Because on that day he amazed us all, less by what he did than by who he was; less by his skill and his speed than by his spirit and his relentless effort; less by his time in the race and more by his bravery in pursuit of the goal. His father wept with pride for his boy who had nothing: no real education, no real job, no real breaks in life. But his boy finished a race that no one thought he could. He was the gift. He was the grit.

Frank Macha, man of faith, cried, too, on that day. "Glory be to God," he said. He didn't need anything more than Ramadhani to prove it.

FOURTEEN

The Heart off Guard

No matter how inspiring people such as Lizzy and Ramadhani are, I'm always left to wonder why I can feel so alive around them and then, a minute later, feel like the light has gone off. Is it possible, I wonder, for people like them to change a whole society? Is it possible for a whole nation to experience the massive energy of grit and heart that they embody, and change? Or are the lessons of the heart always bound to be personal and individual moments where two or three feel it but the rest don't? Is it possible to bring a whole country awake to the beauty of every person, or just myself?

I got my answer in 2003. In that year, the Special Olympics World Summer Games moved outside the United States for the first time, and Ireland became the first other country to host the huge event.

Led by Mary Davis, a thirty-year Special Olympics volunteer, Ireland mounted a nationwide campaign to raise the money and volunteers and energy to host the world. Though Ireland is smaller than Massachusetts and has an economy that's tiny by comparison with its European neighbors, Mary convinced the prime minister, Bertie Ahearn, and the president, Mary McAleese, to join together and commit the entirety of the government to the cause of the games. Mary rallied the villages and towns across the country to the ideals of Special Olympics like a boxer determined to punch way above her weight.

The music entrepreneur Ossie Kilkenny called on politicians and artists. The young business maverick Denis O'Brien agreed to chair the board. Volunteer applications poured in by the thousands as schools, universities, churches, and sports clubs committed to staffing the games. Irish companies vied for the chance to be sponsors as the Bank of Ireland launched a nationwide fund-raising drive with donation boxes at their 310 branches. O'Brien's Sandwich Shops pledged contributions for every purchase of their triple decker sandwich. The most powerful sport organization in the country even made an unprecedented offer: the Gaelic Athletic Association, proprietor of the fabled Croke Park Stadium, in which only Gaelic sport had ever been allowed, offered it as the venue for the Opening Ceremony.

In 2003, however, there was another Irish story playing out—one with a long and bloody narrative: "the troubles." Ireland was—and remains—a country with a painful history of being divided between north and south. Ireland's is a story of centuries of violence and separation along religious and cultural lines, which resulted in the nation being split between the Republic of Ireland in the south and the British government controlling Northern Ireland. In the twentieth century, decades of random killings and paramilitary attacks and state-led police operations and mob flare-ups had left the people—north and south—simmering in hate and soaked in pain. The pro-British Unionist leader the Reverend Ian Paisley referred to Catholics as rabbits and vermin, while the leader of the underground Irish Republican Army, Gerry Adams, was often accused of being responsible for bomb attacks. The British government was responsible for security in the north and maintained it through the feared tactics of the Police Service of Northern Ireland, which was suspected of targeting Catholics for extralegal investigation and even torture. Even though Catholics and Protestants—unionists and republicans—lived in the same cities and towns in the north, and had for centuries, the fear and loathing that separated them was all but absolute. Political or peaceful solutions were out of reach.

But for two decades, both Northern Ireland and the Republic of Ireland had participated in local and national Special Olympics activities together, so when the Special Olympics World Games athletes arrived in Ireland and fanned out across the island to stay in host towns for a few days before the start of the event, all towns were included. The United States, long a strong supporter of the republican position in the conflict, was chosen to visit Belfast, the capital city of Northern Ireland and the center of unionist power. So more than five hundred American Special Olympics athletes arrived on June 16, and they went first to Stormont, the capital buildings of Northern Ireland's United Kingdom government. They met their hosts, then fanned out across the north for a few days of host town welcomes and celebrations prior to their trip to republican Dublin.

On the fourth day, having visited historic sites such as the King's Hall and been given a reception by the lord mayor of Belfast, the entire U.S. delegation came together again to head south to Dublin. There was time for one last picture. They gathered on the steps of Stormont, where for the first time in history the commissioner of the Garda Siochana, the Republic of Ireland's top law enforcement officer, and the chief constable of the Police Service of Northern Ireland stood together, each in full uniform. Something had begun to change. Not just on those steps but across the land. Stories began to emerge of a country cracked open by the presence of the athletes of Special Olympics. Gerry Adams later told me, "The arrival of Special Olympics athletes was an historic moment in the history of Ireland. From the King's Hall to Croke Park, they had a non-sectarian appeal. They took us out of ourselves and showed us how to rise above conviction. We applauded them spontaneously on the streets across the nation. We applauded because we needed them more than they could have possibly known."

In historic Croke Park, the opening ceremony kicked off the games and seventy-five thousand people never seemed so joyful. A thousand Riverdancers performed, filling the stadium with the percussive rhythm of national pride. President Mary McAleese declared, "*Céad míle fáilte* [One hundred thousand welcomes] . . . We have long been looking forward to this day . . . Ireland is famous for its welcomes, but never in the history of our country has there been a bigger or better welcome for anyone than the welcome prepared for the world's best special athletes." War in Afghanistan had been rag-

ing, yet six young athletes from a Kabul orphanage marched into the
stadium to the loudest cheers imaginable. Muhammad Ali, Jamie
Lee Curtis, Pierce Brosnan, and Ronan Tynan joined the celebration.
And, fittingly, my mother, who had accompanied her brother President Kennedy to Ireland almost precisely forty years earlier, spoke for
the last time to an Opening Ceremony audience.

As she spoke, she was surrounded by the twelve Special Olympics
"Global Messengers," and she stayed onstage as the world's most
famous rock and roll band, U2, launched into their legendary song
"Pride (In the Name of Love)." Midway through, Bono disappeared
backstage, reemerging with Nelson Mandela. Continuing to sing,
Bono proclaimed Mandela "the president of everywhere and everyone
who loves and fights for freedom . . . and freedom is what tonight is
all about. Freedom from anything that holds you back," and together
with the athletes and my mother, Mandela stood and waved to the
crowd. When the song ended, he helped punctuate the ceremony
with his own resounding message: "The Special Olympics give telling testimony to the indestructibility of the human spirit and of our
capacity to overcome hardships and obstacles. You, the athletes, are
ambassadors of the greatness of humankind." Moments later, the
torch arrived, having traveled from Athens, across Europe, and across
Ireland. The runners were preceded into the stadium by an honor
guard of uniformed officers of the Republic of Ireland, the Garda.
But the Garda were not alone. They were accompanied by the Police
Service of Northern Ireland, whose officers marched in Croke Park for
the first time. Together, the two forces saluted the flame of hope, and
together they were cheered. There were tears to go around.

The Nobel Prize–winning poet Seamus Heaney was born and raised
in Northern Ireland. He knew how intractable societies, with their
traditions and biases and histories, can be. But in his play *The Cure at
Troy*, Heaney saw the possibility of change:

> *History says, don't hope,*
> *On this side of the grave,*

But then, once in a lifetime
The longed-for tidal wave
Of justice can rise up,
And hope and history rhyme.

Heaney did not venture an explanation for what can trigger those transcendent moments when hope and history rhyme—what combination of longing and healing, bravery and pain come together to create a breakthrough where despair yields to justice. But I suspect he would have agreed that it requires someone or something that can pierce the assumption that conflict is inevitable, and inspire us to want to live at peace. And I think he would have also agreed that such a breakthrough comes when someone does something disarming enough to make a whole nation see itself and its "enemies" differently. We're all waiting for the once-in-a-lifetime moment when the world changes and we realize that we're all in it together. We're all hoping that the fun that lasts and the grit that makes it possible and the inspiration of those who believe in both—that all those will become the way we live, not an exception to the way we live. But how?

No one—Bono, or Muhammad Ali, or even Nelson Mandela—could have answered that question more definitively than Donal Page, a young man whose road to the games was as unlikely as anyone could imagine. Donal was born in County Galway, the sixth of the eight children of Sean and Mary Page. Sean is a dairy farmer. He's up most mornings at five and works the day through. There is never a day when the animals don't need care.

Donal was born on October 6, 1984, and was a happy baby, "the happiest of all the eight that we had," remembers Sean. But on the morning of Good Friday, 1985, when Sean woke up to check on the livestock, he found little Donal feverish and sick-looking. He called to his wife and checked Donal's temperature, and all of a sudden, the baby became unresponsive. Good Friday is a holiday in Ireland, so the parents knew that most medical offices would be closed. But by 7:00 a.m., they were so worried that they drove their little baby to the doctor's home. On the way, Mary, holding the baby in her arms, began to cry. "He's dead, Sean."

By the time they reached the doctor, Donal had begun to breathe again and the doctor sent them straightaway to the children's hospital, but he held out little hope. When they arrived, the emergency medical team filled them with despair: "We'll do what we can, but he'll surely not last more than a few hours." As the hours ticked by, Donal improved a bit but didn't regain consciousness. He had convulsions every few hours. But he lived through the day, and miracle of miracles, by Saturday, he started to improve. "He baffled them," said Sean. "They didn't know what to make of him, but he was doing better so I went to church for Holy Saturday to do my devotions. When I returned to the hospital, things had gone wrong again. They told me he was dying and to call the priest, so the priest came and we had him confirmed right there in the hospital. He was convulsing and limp and there was nothing in him. But somehow he survived until Easter morning. It was then that he had his worst convulsion, and the doctor told me for sure, 'He's gone this time.'"

This pattern of despair continued for seven days. The doctors identified Donal's condition as Reye's syndrome, a rare but often deadly infection that can cause damage to the liver and brain. The doctor who attended to him at the hospital remembered that Donal was the "worst case" he'd seen in his almost forty years of practice. But Donal Page slowly started to improve. Within two weeks, the medical team pronounced him to be "out of danger," but they also reported the status of his functioning: his brain had been subjected to such severe trauma that he was blind and deaf and had intellectual disabilities. In the space of those two weeks, Donal had gone from being a healthy baby boy to being a child with severe enough challenges that he would depend on around-the-clock care for the rest of his life. "We brought him home, anyway," said Sean. "Me and the wife just decided that we would take him home and do what we could."

There was nothing easy about their decision. "For the next twelve months, he would be fine one day and the next day, he'd be in the hospital again. Right there from the start, Mary gave her whole life to him—that's never changed. Her whole life is devoted to Donal. And over the months, he would gradually improve a bit here and there, but we'd be never knowing what was next. When it came to his first birthday, we says to ourselves we'd better celebrate because we don't know if there's ever going to be another one. And the other children were quite young so they all had to take second place to Donal. The first years were very difficult."

Sean Page recounts these moments without a break in his voice. As he spoke to me on the phone from his home near the small village of Portumna, I could hear the long groans of cattle in the background. Sean knows the land and its rhythms, birth and death, care and feeding. He trades in the raw milk and has no role in the processing. He speaks with that same freshness: raw and simple and clear.

"Do you ever ask, 'Why me?' " I said to him.

"We're lucky enough," was his answer. "Donal's with us."

In the years that followed, Donal could be in and out of the hospital at any time. When Donal was sixteen, Mary suffered a stroke, making the care of Donal that much more challenging. As the other children grew up, "they were a great help. They never complained and I'd even say that growing up with Donal helped them a bit. They understand the differences in people better than most," is Sean's way of putting it. "They know family.

"When Donal was five, we took him up to see a doctor in Dublin because I thought Donal was getting a bit better. But the doctor in Dublin told me that Donal would always be deaf and blind. But that's because that doctor didn't give him any time to let him show what he could do. I could tell ya for sure that he could see a bit and hear a bit, and I told everyone in our village that the doctor in Dublin was an arse. And the doctor in my village told me I was right, and that's because the doctor here spent time with Donal and me in the kitchen, and walked around, and watched him. That's what Donal needs—a bit of time, and then he's a good child."

By the time the Special Olympics World Games came to Ireland in 2003, Donal Page was eighteen years old. Beginning at the age of five, he'd attended a local school, where the teachers did the best they could. Then, at the age of eleven, he enrolled at a special school where there were several teachers with special training in the care and education of a child like Donal. When his special school started a local Special Olympics program and volunteers came in to teach the students simple activities and games, Donal was always included. And when the school heard that Donal and two of his friends were selected to attend the World Games, there was cheering all around.

The morning after that triumphant Opening Ceremony, reports of amazing feats of athletic excellence began to stream in from fields and gymnasiums across Dublin. At golf, Conrad Zastrow from South Africa played a scratch round. At power lifting, Amal Zeynalove from Azerbaijan lifted a personal best 303.9135 kg in the deadlift. And for the first time in Special Olympics history, when times at track and field and aquatics were analyzed, a stunning piece of trivia emerged: more than one hundred performances by Special Olympics athletes would have been good enough to qualify for the 2000 Sydney Olympic Games themselves! All over Ireland, the athletes of Special Olympics were being cheered into victories they could never have imagined possible.

Dublin was also home to another first: it was the first World Games where athletes with the most severe challenges were given a chance to compete in the same "Motor Activities Training Program," or MATP, that I'd observed in South Africa with Daniel and his mother. MATP is an official "sport" of Special Olympics and is designed to prove the central belief that everyone has a gift and deserves the chance to show it. No exceptions. While the skills of MATP athletes may be the most modest ever to be counted as sport, the athletes themselves rarely disappoint.

The RDS hall in downtown Dublin was designated for the MATP events and a few dozen athletes from nearby towns and villages were selected to show off their MATP skills. One of those athletes was Donal Page.

Donal left early in the morning of Thursday, June 26, on a school bus with his two other mates, his longtime coach Celia Hobbs and three other staff members. His parents arranged for a friend to look after the animals so they could drive up to Dublin to watch their son compete. They left before dawn. "We surely didn't want to be late not knowing what it was going to be like getting into Dublin and all," remembers Sean. "So we arrived at the RDS and of course it wasn't opened yet so we went around Dublin a bit and had a cup of tea."

By the time they returned to park at the RDS, what they saw was nothing short of amazing. The car park was packed and there was already a line of spectators queuing up for the MATP events. None of the other Special Olympics venues in Dublin were full at midweek, but for the first-ever World Games Motor Activities demonstration day, the hall was bursting with energy. "Sure I had no idea that there were going to be so many people there," Sean said, "so even though we were still early, I said to the wife, 'Let's go, Mary, and find our-selves a spot inside. We don't want to be out here when Donal's time gets called.'"

As good fortune would have it, I was lucky enough to be on my way to the RDS at the same time as Sean and Mary. My focus was on welcoming the president of Ireland, Mary McAleese, to the event and explaining MATP to her.

To be honest, I was slightly intimidated to be hosting the presi-dent, so I was a little edgy. And beneath my anxiety about hosting a president was another fear that I would never have admitted to any-one: I was worried that the events would be disappointing to her—maybe even sad. We were so grateful to her—for her wonderful Opening Ceremony speech, and for the extraordinary support she had shown the Special Olympics movement. I was thinking that it maybe would have been better had she attended track and field, where so many athletes were performing with such unexpected skill. If she were there, she'd see great races, well-trained athletes, a display of grit and perseverance. I could just imagine her leaning over in the midst of the races and saying something like, "Oh, my! I had no idea the athletes would be this impressive! Isn't the runner from Lebanon amazing? And isn't that women's relay team from Panama fast?" And I would be able to answer, equally excited, "You know, Madame Pres-ident, I am just as amazed as you. Every time we hold these World Games, the athletes rise to higher and higher levels of achievement. It is so thrilling to watch!"

But I was sure that conversation would never take place at MATP. I could just imagine what might go through her mind: "What am I doing watching people pushing bowling balls around when I should be at my office handling matters of state?" And what could I say that would make MATP sound more interesting or exciting? What I was failing to anticipate was the person who would embody "thrilling" more than any other competitor I'd ever seen in my life.

When Mary McAleese, the president of Ireland, entered the RDS hall and took her seat in the front row of the stands, she was greeted by a huge ovation from the more than 1,500 fans filling every seat behind her. She was popular in the warmest way; the people of Ireland loved her. Just after we sat down, and before I could start the requisite small talk, the announcer blared, "Next up, Donal Page from County Galway. Will you join me in welcoming Donal to the stage, where he will perform the 'grasp and release.'"

The crowd applauded warmly. From behind the stage, a young woman came pushing Donal in his wheelchair to the center of the riser. I could see that Donal had only the most limited control of his arms and that his body was slightly contorted in the chair. But I also couldn't help noticing the face of the woman pushing him, her broad smile, her glittering eyes as she looked out to the crowd. She was Donal's coach. She positioned Donal in his wheelchair in front of a small table, and she came around the front to set up a small beanbag. Once she secured the chair and the bag, she leaned over to speak to him in his ear—last-minute instructions and encouragement. Donal's challenge was to reach over, pick up the beanbag, lift it, and move it to the other side of the table. She placed her hands on his shoulders, then down on the bag as if to capture his attention and make sure he understood. With that, she stepped off the riser and headed toward the back of the stage from where she'd come. But she paused midway and turned to watch Donal perform from a safe distance.

"Start," barked the announcer, and Donal began his task. I was close enough to Donal to see his eyes, and I could see him scan the crowd with a slight hint of a smile. His gaze moved around the hall. It was as if he was taking the whole of the place into himself; as if he was saying that he wouldn't connect with that beanbag until he'd first connected with the people around him. The crowd was quiet. I knew nothing of his story, but it was hard to imagine he'd ever been in front of thousands of people before. At the same time, he'd lived his whole life learning how to communicate without words or motions, and he was doing that right there on that stage. There were no words and only the slightest of movements. But he was gathering us, taking us in, collecting the energy in the room for the task ahead.

After a minute or so, without the slightest hint of Donal's picking up the beanbag—a minute that seemed like an hour—he turned his head downward to the task at hand and, to my relief, started to focus on completing his assignment. Silence has an uncomfortable power in a room of thousands, and while I practiced it in prayer, I was ready for it to end in the arena. And Donal, it appeared, was ready to do what he had come to do. As his hand started toward the bag, one fan in the crowd shouted an unmistakable cheer—"Come on now! Let's see it!"—and a rustle of encouragement moved through the room.

If I had been apprehensive about the MATP event before it began, I forgot all about it. The moments of silence had brought my full attention to Donal. And with my attention, I felt a bond emerge between him and the crowd of which I was a part, and I was all in, focused completely on pulling for him to pick up that bag. Donal was now leaning into the challenge, but even though he tried and tried to move his hand to pick up that beanbag, he just couldn't do it. Another minute went by but his body simply wouldn't cooperate. All of us assembled could tell he was giving it his effort, but there was no movement in his arm, no grasping in his fingers. Try as he might, the level of difficulty was just too high. Thousands of people were watching him and we were frozen in disappointment and empathy. He just couldn't do it.

But after another minute or so, Donal's hand moved. His father remembers thinking, "If they just give him time, he can do it. I was remembering all those doctors who gave up on him and told me he was blind and deaf and could never do a thing. They didn't give him time. I was just hoping that the crowd there at the RDS would give him time, 'cause sure I knew he could do it." Time—that's what passed, second by second, and into several minutes with only the slightest movement of his arm. But the crowd stayed with him, and after the arm moved, a few fans started to applaud and a few more shouts came from the bleachers: "There you go, lad! Now grab it!"

And so slowly, deliberately, and with a level of effort I'd never seen before and never seen since, Donal Page pushed his arm to grasp that beanbag, and the crowd exploded in cheers. It had taken him almost ten full minutes to get his arm and his hand lowered onto that bag, but the place reacted like these were World Cup finals and the home team had just scored a goal. Applause turned to stomping, shouts turned to enthusiastic howls, and whistles rang out from the crowd. Donal looked up—just a glance—and continued on his task.

Donal Page took eighteen minutes to complete his MATP demonstration of the beanbag lift. Alone on the stage, in front of the president of his country and thousands of fans, Donal Page did what almost no one believed he could do: lift a beanbag and move it about twenty inches from one side of a table to the next. He did it with a combination of effort and focus that left us all in tears. We were all standing for the last five minutes or so, cheering, shouting, clapping, yelling, laughing, crying, and crying some more. I never once had to lean over to President McAleese and say something insightful. I never once had to worry that the competition would be unsuitably sad. It was, quite simply, the most inspiring athletic achievement any of us had ever seen. If grit had a definition in 2003, it would've been a picture of Donal Page. And if grit has the capacity to change a nation, it lies somewhere deep in the abundance of grace and strength that Donal Page revealed to his country at the RDS in Dublin. "They gave him time," his dad recalls. "That's all he ever asked for—just a bit of time. And with a bit of time, I knew he could do it."

Late that night, the bus carrying Donal and his teammates returned home to Portumna. They were accompanied the whole way by a police escort of the national force, the Garda. The flashing lights of motorcycle officers signaled celebrities on board, and the roads were cleared of traffic to let the bus pass by. When they finally arrived home after nightfall, a final surprise greeted them: the town square was full. News had spread of the great achievements in Dublin. Donal was lowered off the bus with his medal around his neck, and the square filled with cheers. "That's a day we'll never forget. There was Donal in the middle of the town and the lights flashing and him and his medal and everyone congratulating him and telling him, 'Well done,' and Mary and me—well, we felt a light in our son that we'd never felt before. He's a good lad and we always knew it. But there he was, and this was his day, and God, he was glorious."

Over the course of those two weeks in Ireland, the athletes amazed crowds again and again. There were so many moments of athletic greatness we couldn't keep track. But in my mind, none of those moments outshone Donal's.

In a later poem, Seamus Heaney wrote of a drive along the Irish shore and the beauty of the inland swans and the color of the sea and the movement of the light on the stones. As he paused to take it in, he realized it was just a moment—

> *Useless to think you'll park and capture it*
> *More thoroughly. You are neither here nor there,*
> *A hurry through which known and strange things pass*
> *As big soft buffetings come at the car sideways*
> *And catch the heart off guard and blow it open.*

That was Donal's gift to me and Donal's gift to his family and to his village of Portumna and to the great nation of Ireland. He caught our hearts off guard, and with his grit and his fearless effort, he blew them open. Ireland will never be the same.

FIFTEEN

Humility and Simplicity

No matter how many times someone like Donal Page catches my heart off guard and blows it open, I still find myself waking up a few days later to reality. In the "real" world, I remember, Donal is a sympathetic figure but not a person who can lead a nation. Donal isn't in control of power and influence like real leaders are. "Real" leaders climb the ladder and gain control of companies and countries and societies. They're ambitious and hardened and tough and make decisions based on the interests of individuals and groups—and based on their own interests, too. I can't expect someone like Donal Page to be on a par with politicians and captains of industry and scholars and generals. He's an inspiration, of course, but he isn't a "leader."

And every time I think that way, I try to remember it's wrong— that there are many kinds of leaders and that all the greatest leaders have one thing in common with Donal: they lead from the heart. And no one showed me the meaning of real leadership—and Donal's— better than Nelson Mandela. If there was ever an individual who had the credibility to understand what it takes to be a leader, it was Mandela. And thankfully, he explained his secret to me.

Mandela's story is the stuff of legend. He grew up under one of the most repressive regimes of the twentieth century, South Africa's apartheid government, which imposed a system of race-based segregation that disempowered and oppressed the majority of its citizens.

In the 1960s, Mandela led efforts to resist this system. He was arrested and stood trial, while many of his companions were tortured and killed. Despite an international outcry, Mandela received a life sentence and spent the first eighteen years of it in the brutal Robben Island prison, surrounded by the icy, shark-infested waters of the south Atlantic. Mandela was forty-six years old when his sentence began, and like all the prisoners, he lived in a tiny cell with only a single thin blanket and a straw mat for bedding, and no indoor plumbing. He was subjected to hard labor and given little opportunity to communicate with friends, political allies, or family. During the majority of his imprisonment, he was allowed to write and receive a letter only once every six months. Once a year, he was allowed to meet with a visitor—for thirty minutes.

After twenty-seven years, the nightmare ended. On Feb 11, 1990, the shackles were released, and Nelson Mandela walked down the driveway of Victor Verster prison in the town of Paarl, near Cape Town, to his freedom. Mandela insisted on walking out of the prison alone, and the image of him striding down the abandoned prison road remains among the most powerful of the twentieth century. He was met by thousands of supporters and massive worldwide media coverage. He paraded to Cape Town and addressed millions around the world from the balcony of City Hall. Along the way, the world noticed his resolute posture, his singular stride, his dazzling, enveloping smile.

In the years that followed, Mandela mesmerized South Africans with his commitment to reconciliation. He met with and befriended the prosecutor who had led the case against him. He was elected president of South Africa in the first free elections in the country's history and entered the parliament with his arm around former president de Klerk, the man who'd led the previous, racist regime. As he sat in the chamber that had once enforced the brutality of apartheid, Mandela cheered the newly elected members of parliament, even shaking the hand of General Constandt Viljoen, the leader of the nine-member white separatist delegation. Together with his fellow antiapartheid hero Archbishop Desmond Tutu, he formed a national truth and reconciliation commission to work toward granting amnesty to all who had committed atrocities during the years of oppression. He became not only a hero of political justice but a global icon of freedom, forgiveness, and peace.

If there was ever an individual who understood leadership, it was Mandela, and like people all over the world, I wondered over and over again how he did what he did. What was the secret of his leadership? How could he look into the faces of those people who had beaten him, denied him his own children, murdered his brothers and sisters in the struggle, and then put his arms around them? How does a man endure so much suffering and return it with friendship?

During Mandela's presidency, Special Olympics' movement in South Africa was small and poorly known. Hundreds of thousands of people with intellectual disabilities were stigmatized, their existence seen as proof that their parents were cursed or guilty of sin. Parents reported keeping their children hidden so as to avoid the mockery of peers. Orphanages were filled with babies and children with many different challenges, abandoned by families too poor to raise them. The AIDS epidemic added to the problem, as the disease contributes to developmental delays and disability.

So, needless to say, in the post-apartheid era, all of us in Special Olympics were eager to increase our visibility and effectiveness in South Africa and enable people with intellectual differences to be a part of the country's newfound focus on equality and justice for all. Beginning in 2000, my indomitable colleague Peter Wheeler flew there several times to talk with our local volunteers and scope out the possible level of support we might be able to get from government, media, and business. His goal: to come up with a breakthrough event that would grab the attention of South African media and create the traction necessary to grow Special Olympics not only throughout the country but across all of sub-Saharan Africa. And in South Africa, there was really only one breakthrough figure: Nelson Mandela.

When Peter called me in Washington to say that he had reached out to former president Mandela's team and had found them receptive and open to helping launch a national campaign for Special Olympics, I was ready to dance on a tabletop. "We've got to get them a proposal," he reported. "They're willing to ask Madiba [South Africans often called Mandela by his clan name], but we've got to get them a plan."

In the days that followed, we mapped out an audacious if achievable scenario for a major event: we would ask former president Mandela to launch a Special Olympics campaign for inclusion and acceptance from his own prison cell in Robben Island. There, in the place the world had come to see as the epicenter of discrimination and intolerance, we would ask Nelson Mandela himself to light the Special Olympics "Flame of Hope," our most powerful symbol of the freedom we aspire to achieve for all. And from that cell, with Mandela himself carrying that flame of hope accompanied by Special Olympics athletes, we would announce a campaign of national awareness, sports, joy, and inclusion. We would then "run" the flame off of Robben Island and into Cape Town and up to the seat of government, Pretoria, where we would present it to the leaders of the country with a call to action: change South Africa to make it a place of tolerance not just based on race or ethnicity but also based on "difability."

Peter submitted the proposal and the waiting began. But it wasn't long before the word came back from Mandela's staff: "He wants to do it! He'll go to Robben Island for Special Olympics." We were ecstatic: the world's most loved and recognizable hero of freedom was going to join our team! The planning began in earnest.

A few short months later, Linda and I and all our children, together with my sister Maria and her entire family, landed in Cape Town for the launch of "African Hope 2001." Our delegation was led by Ricardo Thornton, a Special Olympics athlete from Washington, DC, who had spent many years of his life locked up in institutions. Like Mandela, Ricardo had been "incarcerated." He had been held against his will for thirteen years, from 1966 to 1979, until he was finally freed and, against all odds, got married, found a job, and moved into his own apartment where he and his wife, Donna, raised their son. Ricardo was joined by Theo Tebele, an athlete from Botswana, and of course, there was Loretta Claiborne.

The first stop of "African Hope 2001" was the prison camp at Robben Island. Together with about two hundred volunteers and supporters from Special Olympics South Africa, we rode the ferry from Cape Town harbor out to the cursed island and then started the short walk from the dock to the prison door. We walked in nervous disarray, the younger children racing ahead, all of us looking down the path at the prison wall, the morning glare shooting darts off the stony ground and into our eyes. There was little conversation. The walk was short enough—just a few minutes—so nothing needed saying.

As we approached the prison, the door swung open and there was Mandela, awaiting our arrival like a host awaiting guests for a banquet. It was morning and his eyes were alight with anticipation. "Welcome!" he bellowed, and began bantering playfully with the children and greeting each of the athletes with that mesmerizing smile. We walked through the narrow prison door into the courtyard a few steps away. The inside of the prison was dim with walls of concrete and stone. Mandela continued his welcome. "What sport do you play?" "Are you ready for a match?" "You're a champion? Is it so?"

Within a few minutes, Mandela led Ricardo, Loretta, Theo, and another local athlete, Danielle September, down the prison hallway to his old cell. He entered the barren cell with the athletes, and as they held a torch, Mandela lit it. The world-famous photographer Richard Corman captured the moment. In all of the photos, Mandela is smiling from ear to ear.

I followed Mandela and the athletes as they carried the lit torch out of the cell, down the dark prison hallway, and out into the courtyard, where a crowd of Special Olympics athletes and volunteers and press had gathered. This was the courtyard where Mandela and other prisoners had lined up daily to do hard labor, breaking stone and hauling loads. I kept glancing at him to see if being in that cursed place brought back the pain. I kept waiting for signs that the dark memories were surging back.

Our short program started. Ricardo spoke about what it meant to grow up in an institution, not understanding why he could never leave. "We would just go about our day after day. We didn't know nothing else, nothing about what was outside or how people lived or if people cared about each other. We didn't know why we were in there and forced to live like that but we knew it was a bad place." He described what happened eight years after he was released: "By then, my wife, Donna, and me were married and wouldn't you know she was pregnant and going to have a baby." Huge smile. "But a lot of people said we was wrong to do that, that people like us shouldn't have a child and we didn't know how to take care of a child and I guess they were right in some ways because we didn't. And then when we were in the hospital and the doctors were helping Donna, and the baby was finally born, and they handed little Ricky to Donna and she was crying and she looked up at the doctor and asked him, 'Doctor, when my baby grows up, will he love me?'" The crowd in the court-yard was hushed. "That's why we all need to be free so we can know that we can love each other and not worry that we're so bad that not even our own children will love us."

Ahmed Kathadra, a fellow prisoner of Mandela's and, by then, the curator of the Robben Island museum, hurried the program along because of the heat. Mandela smiled through it all, playfully ges-turing to people in our audience, happily posing for picture after picture, speaking only to say that the athletes of Special Olympics deserved, like everyone else, to be free.

It struck me that day that Mandela was leading the same move-ment that the athletes of Special Olympics were leading as well. His words echoed the message I'd heard from Loretta and so many others: "To be free is not merely to cast off one's chains but to live in a way that respects and enhances the freedom of others." Like Mandela, our athletes were victimized by the projection of threat and fear—in his case, the projection of threat and fear was attached to skin color, while in our movement, it was attached to a score on an IQ test. The Nobel Prize–winning economist Amartya Sen wrote a powerful book, *Iden-tity and Violence: The Illusion of Destiny*, that laid out the scholarly ar-gument of why Mandela and the athletes of Special Olympics belong in the same movement. Identity, Sen argues, is about many things. Think of anyone you know and you can probably think of dozens of ways of defining their identities. A person might be a woman, an American, a Republican, a doctor, a soccer player, a mother, a wife, a daughter, an aunt, a poet, a gardener, and so on. In another person's many identities, we often find common ground. We have something in common with that person because he or she is in some way like us. Friendship and solidarity come from sharing some dimension of identity with another.

But the opposite can also happen: our many identities can be reduced to a single one. Violence and stigma, according to Sen, result when social and political structures narrow identity and reduce a group to a singular identity. We become only that "Republican" or "Black man" or "retard." And once we have become reduced to a "choiceless singularity of human identity, [it] not only diminishes us all, it also makes the world much more flammable." We no longer share things in common. We live in different worlds.

Singularity doesn't just make the world more dangerous; it also adds to the likelihood that our empathy will be short-circuited. As the noted psychopathologist Simon Baron-Cohen has found, empathy can be explained as easily as "our ability to identify what someone else is thinking and feeling and to respond to their thoughts and feelings with an appropriate emotion." Empathy is a key capability for all of us, helping make relationships possible, communication clear, and violence less likely. But we all know of countless examples where empathy has seemed totally absent—where cruelty and violence were perpetrated on helpless victims while the perpetrator lacked any empathy whatsoever. We often wonder how it's possible for such cruelty to exist—the savagery of the Holocaust, the random violence of a vicious criminal act, the capricious killing and raping by warlords, or the callous dehumanization of a person with disability. Baron-Cohen offers the psychological correlate to Sen's "singularity." "Empathy erosion arises from people *turning other people into objects*" (emphasis original). When you treat another person as an object, interacting with them as though only your own side of the story mattered, then your "empathy has been turned off."

That's what had happened to Mandela, and that's what had happened to his fellow leaders who stood with him on that day in the prison courtyard, Loretta and Theo and Ricardo and Danielle. They were placed in what Sen calls a "set of rigid boxes" and the labels on those boxes were used to turn them into objects and to justify making them seem strange, loathsome, and dangerous. South African "whites" (a singular descriptor) loathed South African "blacks" (another singular descriptor).

Similarly, Loretta and Theo and Ricardo and Danielle were loathed by "normal" people (an all-encompassing positive descriptor) because of their "disability" (a singular negative descriptor). South Africa became defined by a "primal way of seeing the differences between people," as did most communities where people with intellectual disabilities live. In both cases, there was a massive empathy turn-off. And the price paid for those empathy turn-offs was the suffering of millions of people and nearly the loss of Mandela, Loretta, Theo, Ricardo, and Danielle.

Who wouldn't have understood if Mandela had had an empathy turn-off of his own and excluded whites and nationalists from his government and agenda? But he never returned hate with hate. He never put anyone else into a rigid box. As the event wound down at Robben Island, I realized that I wouldn't have the chance to ask Mandela the question I'd longed to ask: How had he become so forgiving? The crowd pushed us toward the doorway of the prison, and it was time to return to the ferry and carry the torch to Pretoria. As we neared the door, I looked at him, smiling and thanking everyone, showing no residue of the painful memories of that space, no bitterness or weariness, and I was left to wonder: How does a human being do that? And what do I need to do to live like Mandela?

In the following years, we made repeated requests of Mandela, and over and over again, he said yes. He came to Ireland for the 2003 World Games. He recorded public awareness videos. I thought there was nothing else he could do for us—he seemed to have done everything. So imagine my surprise when I received a call from his office in 2004 telling me that Madiba wanted to dedicate his eighty-fourth birthday party to Special Olympics and to hold a huge festival to celebrate the gifts of our athletes. Peter Wheeler flew down months ahead and again created an event to mesmerize the nation. This time, he planned a full-day celebration in Limpopo Province, where more than five-hundred school-age children with and without intellectual disabilities would come together to meet, play games, learn about difference, and celebrate the birthday of their hero, Nelson Mandela. Limpopo is a rural province, both poor and remote. It is far from the centers of South African power, Cape Town and Johannesburg, and unknown for any distinctive attractions. I suppose that's why Mandela chose it for his party. For our part, we were happy to bring the Special Olympics message to those who needed it so much.

The birthday arrived and this time, my mother was able to make the trip. Across the fairgrounds, sports games had been set up. You could chip golf balls, kick soccer balls, toss bocce balls. The children with intellectual differences arrived on school buses and fanned out across the grounds going from game to game. Hundreds of children from orphanages raced around the field, their eyes intermittently bulging with excitement and then falling back down toward the ground into what was surely a learned inwardness. There were children of all colors from mainstream schools there to meet them. Both children with intellectual differences and those without played together and stopped in special tented "classrooms" to discuss the challenges of overcoming discrimination and share openly about how much misunderstanding existed. Large white pads were used to capture all the ideas the kids were sharing about how to change their country. Parents were invited to come and share their hopes and dreams as well. "We do not believe our children are cursed," one mother of a child with intellectual disabilities insisted. "We love our children."

No matter how much we all expected Mandela, it was still as though we gasped for air when he appeared. By the time he arrived, tens of thousands of local residents had swarmed the bleachers, and a huge cheer arose when he paraded into the center of the stadium on a golf cart. Even though he was not on foot, the same demeanor he'd shown in his departure from prison was unmistakable. In the stands, the murmur of excitement quickly turned to cheers. "Amandla!" the crowd chanted as the golf cart inched toward the stage. *Power!* The response was equally strong: "Awaaytu!" *To the people!* "Amandla!" *Power!* "Awaaytu!" *To the people!* The chanting intensified as Mandela walked slowly up to the stage in his beautiful paisley African shirt, his signature red AIDS ribbon on his lapel, and his generous and triumphant smile beaming its way naturally across the field. There was no jumbotron, no gaudy decoration or signage or lighting. There was just a small stage, hundreds of children with intellectual disabilities, thousands of supporters, and that wildly welcoming smile.

There were a few short speeches by athletes, a musical performance or two, and the requisite remarks from the governor of the province and other government officials. Through it all, Mandela sat next to my mother, smiling, the two of them whispering back and forth. My mother was never happier than when she was with a president, and this particular former president was in a class all to himself. She was beaming like a little girl, glancing over at me occasionally with a wink as if to say, "Can you believe it?" A young boy with Down syndrome came without permission and sat down between them. My mother looked over to me as if to ask who had invited him up to the stage. I laughed and shrugged my shoulders. Whoever he was, he had chosen the right time and place: seated on the lap of Nelson Mandela next to Eunice Shriver in front of hundreds of cameras and thousands of fans. I never caught his name, but he is in every picture of the day. Perfect.

As the festivities continued in a mix of chaos and spectacle, I remember wondering about Mandela and my mother, both in their eighties, both having seen their share of suffering, both resolute in their desire to wage the fight for freedom, wherever it took them. On that July 18, the fight had taken them to a celebration in the park and then to a birthday cake that looked as big as the field itself. Mandela blew out the candles with a gang of our athletes. Together, he and my mother released white doves. Our athletes clamored to touch him and take pictures. The stage was overrun with cheers and appreciation. The hidden children were in the open. The cabbage child was a smiling beauty. The scorned parents were on the stage with the star. *Amandla! Awaaytu!*

As I reflect back on those moments in that stadium, I remember best the brief remarks my mother made later in the day to a small group at lunch. She didn't like to speak extemporaneously and usually labored over her speeches for weeks. But after the huge festival was over, about a hundred of the day's leaders withdrew to a function

room to eat and celebrate, and my mother rose to speak spontaneously. "Someday soon, President Mandela and I won't be watching
you from here. We'll be watching you from somewhere else," she said
as she looked above the eyes of the audience as if focused on a point
in the distance. "But I hope you remember that we'll be watching
and we'll be keeping an eye on you and we'll still be doing all these
things that we're doing today. And I want you to remember all the
mothers who are still fighting and trying to find things for their
children, and even if we're not here, we're going to be still helping
those mothers. So don't think you can stop just because we're not
here . . ."

She had never before spoken about her own death or taken the
perspective of eternity. She spoke with her lips tight and her lower
jaw jutted out in between breaths. That jaw often came forward in
moments of stress and became to all of us a primal signal that she
was focused on something serious and hard. Her jaw often moved
around like an emotional compass in a magnetic storm. When it
came out, it was a telltale indicator that she was someplace the rest
of us were not, and when it softened an instant later, she was ready to
come back, with a decision and a plan to fight. It was as though her
face was mapping her path from analysis to resolve. She only shared
the resolve. And on that day it was clear: "I'm not here for long but
you'd better stay the course." I could feel the expectations renewed.

Resolve has its role in social change, and very little good in the
world has come without it. "Power is taken, not given," said Frederick
Douglass, and a man who could watch slaves at work while he clung
to his own precarious freedom could hardly be questioned. A woman
who had fought so hard for eighty years could hardly be expected
to stop, so it was no surprise that my mother's view of the afterlife
included a full measure of fight and resolve. Even heaven was not
exempt from the struggle. It was a perch from which she could conduct the earthbound battle for dignity. Even there, she would be
peering at mothers all over the world as they picked up their phones
to call for help for their children. And even there, the fear of those
awful words, "There's nothing for Rosemary. Nothing," would keep
her vigilant, angry, demanding. It was a battle without an end in

sight and the inevitable end of her life wasn't going to stop her from leading it.

By the time she made her brief remarks, Mandela had left the fields at Limpopo, but before leaving, his staff had issued an invitation: Would we be able to meet with Madiba the following day for tea? Needless to say, that was an easy invitation to accept.

Mandela's home was nothing that I expected. There was no dramatic driveway leading up to a grand entrance—no swarm of security officers, no touches to the architecture that would've spoken of legend. The driveway was small but welcoming, the entrance pretty but family-size, the house decorated with colors and art, but not memorabilia or monument. It was a gracious and elegant home. My mother and I and our leader in Africa, John Dow, and his wife, Gloria, were invited to come into the sitting room and make ourselves comfortable in the same way one might expect for any home.

Mandela entered the room with his usual demeanor—a little unsure on his feet, light in his gaze, excited by every introduction. He flirted with Gloria Dow about her beauty and joked that he wished he had known her in his younger days; he joked with my mother about her energy and laughter. He spoke easily about how happy he was to have been with our athletes on so many occasions. We recalled our times together. Robben Island? "Oh yes, that was a good day," with a lilt in the "good" as if to call our attention to the point. His birthday? "Well, you know, it's not a happy day for me so why not make it a happy day for someone else!" And then a huge smile. Your knees? "The doctor tells me I can't walk on them but they are still working no matter what he says!"

For many years, I'd been trained how to act in meetings such as these. The presence of Mandela meant that the primary dynamic was to listen to him. The presence of an assistant marked the meeting as an official one, even if held as though among friends. I guessed that our time would be limited to thirty minutes, maybe a bit more. Current topics in politics were always of interest. *What do you think of the current elections? Of the news coming from the Middle East? Of the economic crisis?* These types of questions were ideal for politicians, giving them lots of material on which to opine about what should be done. These meetings were always memorialized with pictures—and most of the time, the most important part of the meeting was the picture taking. Discussion was usually very brief and rarely allowed to go beyond current events, gratitude, and mutual accolades.

But on this occasion, I was churning inside, trying to formulate a different type of question: I wanted to know how he'd become the kind of person he was. I knew people of resolve and fight, people of dedication and relentless energy, people of gentleness and compassion, people of laughter and warmth, people who lead. But there was something about him that was all of those things wrapped into a package that was more than any of them. I wanted so badly to ask him a question about himself but I couldn't figure out how without flouting the unstated rules of the meeting. I was so flustered I couldn't even come up with a way to ask him anything obvious.

Then it just blurted out. "Madiba, I know this sounds ridiculous, but can you share with us how you came to be the way you are?" Oh my goodness, I thought, that sounds so silly. So I went on to try to alter the puzzled look he gave me. "We've all followed your career and read your book and seen you speak many times, but I still can't understand how you lead with so much positive energy." Please stop, I told myself, you're sounding more and more like a sycophant. "When we went to Robben Island, I couldn't help but think of all the pain and horrors of that place." Like he needs me to tell him that! "But everywhere you go, you carry yourself with an infectious smile, a sense of openness to everyone, no traces of bitterness or impatience." Except now. "I'm sorry to ask such a strange question, and I don't know quite how to say this, but how do you do all that?"

Finally, I stopped. Thank God. I didn't look at my mother or at the Dows or at Mandela's assistant for fear that I would collapse in a heap of humiliation. I just kept my eyes on Mandela, as if to beg him to be joyful once more despite the impetuous guest that he'd somehow allowed into his home. And thankfully, he obliged.

"You see, all of us who were in prison are the same. We all have the same way about us. Because in prison, we all learned two things. First, we learned humility, because when you are trapped there, you realize that the struggle isn't about you and is much bigger than you.

You're only in prison because you believe in the struggle and you believe it is important—more than you. And when you're there for all that time, you realize it very deeply. And that is really humility and that humility brings a kind of freedom. You're not so worried about yourself anymore—freedom not to worry comes from humility.

"And then we also learned simplicity. You see, in prison, you learn to be happy and content with so little and you realize that you need almost nothing to be satisfied.

"That's it. Humility and simplicity. That's what we learned—all of us—and that is what makes all the difference. You must lead with humility and simplicity."

Wooooooooow, I thought. That's huge. I want that! And before I could control myself, I was blurting again: "Madiba, isn't that what we all want? But no one wants to spend twenty-seven years in prison to get it—at least I don't. How do you recommend the rest of us develop those qualities without going to jail for half of our lives? Any advice for me?"

I felt as if I was on a middle school version of a soap opera, asking predictable questions of a wise character that were not very thinly veiled questions about me. How embarrassing. I could hear myself reciting a squeaky and self-absorbed version of myself: "How can I beee liiike you, o wise leader?"

But again, he indulged me.

"You must find it as you can, Tim. You are quite lucky, though. You have the athletes of Special Olympics all around you. I think they understand this very well. They are leaders, too, I think. It seems so. Is it?"

The rest of the trip is now a blur in my memory. I don't remember how the conversation ended and I don't remember how I answered Mandela. We have a few nice pictures to remember the meeting, snapshots of the celebrity-meets-hungering-mortal type. In all the pictures, Mandela beams as usual.

But the keepsake of that meeting wasn't the pictures. The sacred breakthrough of that trip took place for me in those few choice words: humility and simplicity. It's all about the humility of knowing that there's something bigger than you, and you can find freedom in that.

It's all about the simplicity of knowing that you need so little to be happy, and you can find freedom in that as well. I could hear echoes of Loretta's speech at Quinnipiac College: "I was given so little but I am with you today, and I am so happy." I could hear the echoes of the basketball at Katherine Thomas school as I watched my children move across the floor with Eli Johnson and Matt Ficca and Lucy Collins, slowly, easily, working their way to a basket or two a day. "Dad! There's another kind of fun and that's the kind that lasts." I could hear them all in Mandela's exhortation to work for freedom with humility and simplicity. I was beginning to see how a leader becomes a forgiver: by giving him- or herself completely to the deepest values of the human spirit. I was beginning to understand what led him to our athletes. He understood them. In a way, he was just like them.

I'll never be able to answer fully the question of how Mandela found the strength to lead, the simplicity to be happy, the humility to forgive. He wasn't a religious man, although during a discussion with our youth leaders in Dublin, he did bring up the subject. He noted that he had begun to think about religion and was curious to find that part of it that was a force for peace. As if beginning a new chapter in his eighties, he wondered, "What is it in religion that people are looking for?" I don't know where that inquiry took him or if he remained interested in the topic for long. But it's clear from the historical record that Mandela didn't get his humility and simplicity from being a part of a religion. As he said, "I learned it in prison."

But it's not a coincidence that religious experiences and prison experiences are often described using similar language. Monks have their "cells," and religious retreats often call for "solitary" experiences. Jailhouse "conversions" are common. Many religious orders call for sacrificing the "freedom" of independent life to live in obedience to others. Many religious followers go voluntarily into their roles, of course, and prisoners don't. But both kinds of experiences remove people from social contact and isolate them, often with limited comfort and food and stimulation. In both cases, the choices and pressure of the outside world are all but eliminated. And in both cases, people are forced to live in isolation and solitude and try to learn from the detachment they teach.

For a precious few, that detachment leads to unimaginable finds. The kind of humility and simplicity that Mandela describes is not uncommon to people who sacrifice themselves for a person or a cause and endure isolation and loneliness because of it. Martin Luther King, Jr.'s greatest writing was from the Birmingham jail. Great spiritual writers such as Julian of Norwich and Theresa of Avila wrote from behind walls. Gandhi denied himself food and led a revolution from his hunger. They each marshaled the power of humility and simplicity—to paraphrase Gandhi, "the weapons of the strong"—to be irrepressible leaders for change. In each case, with the sacrifice came strength. Ironically, they gave up their self-determination but found a deeper self-awareness. And even more ironically, the victims of oppression became architects of forgiveness.

Not all people who go to prison emerge like Mandela. Not all families that include members with intellectual differences find their way to peace and forgiveness, either. Not all people who embark on religious quests find themselves bathed in love and tolerance. Despite Mandela's suggestion that each of his fellow prisoners learned the same humility and simplicity that he learned, many a man or woman subjected to imprisonment turns bitter, resentful, enraged.

But that doesn't deny the possibility that many people who undergo great suffering and isolation learn a unique way of leading from within. What they lose or voluntarily give up in comforts and possessions, they gain in authenticity and interior strength. "Hunger, toil, and solitude are the means," wrote the fourth-century spiritual master Evagrius Ponticus, and "the proof of (the kingdom of God) is had when the spirit begins to see its own light, when it remains in a state of tranquility . . . and when it maintains its calm as it beholds the affairs of life." There is a ring of Mandela's prison-learned "humility and simplicity" in Evagrius's description of the pathway to seeing one's own light. And there is a ring of Mandela's leadership style in Evagrius's description of the one who maintains calm amid the affairs of life.

Was that the source of Mandela's leadership? Had he found his way to his spiritual center, which in turn gave him a leadership power that prison bars could not contain? Had he found a way to lead without needing to demonize or seek revenge because he had seen his "own light"? Most of all, had he become the world's great political peacemaker because he trusted that same light to be in others? Was that what enabled him to build a government around the otherwise politically and morally reckless premise of sharing power with those who had committed crimes against him and even crimes against humanity itself?

I think so. I think Mandela was very much like Donal and Loretta and so many others who endure "hunger, toil, and solitude" and emerge as leaders with humility and simplicity and light. They all share an intuitive if not explicit sense of being a part of something much bigger than their egos or their personal success. They lead with a focus on the big goals and not on their self-interest. They acquire power in order to share it and not to accumulate it. They help us move beyond the singular identities that so often divide us, and point to a common spirit that unites us. They create bonds among groups rather than divides between them. They take huge risks by forgiving their enemies.

So as it turns out, Donal did know the secret of leadership after all: he was humble and simple, but he was also tough beyond description and joyful in triumph. He was just like Mandela: when people saw him, they saw a better version of themselves. He made people want to be better—and what more could any leader hope to achieve? I only hope we'll find a new generation of leaders who understand how to lead from within, as Mandela did and as Donal did, too. And I also hope that I will have the courage to dwell less on talking about how much I admire the likes of Mandela and Donal and more on learning to pay the price necessary to follow them.

SIXTEEN

Fully Alive

If Loretta and Ramadhani and Ricardo hadn't convinced me to live with my heart cracked open, Mandela tried again. Still, that's a hard lesson to hold on to, and I bounce around all the time. One minute, I'm feeling the openness of complete trust, but the next, I'm back working hard to win in the world that Thomas Hobbes described as a "war of all against all." But then I get inspired again and fall back into feeling the safety and freedom that is the ultimate secret to being fully alive.

But as William Shakespeare wrote in *Hamlet* centuries ago, "there's the rub": we don't actually know what the "ultimate" lesson is. We don't know if our lives are sustained ultimately by goodness or sustained by nothing at all. We don't know what dreams will come after we close our eyes and cross the line from life to death. If death is darkness and nothingness, then perhaps life is darkness as well, and there is no reason to trust anyone. If that's the case, then being fully alive means just fighting for everything you can get until you die. But if death is a transition to energy and light and joy we can't yet fully imagine, then life, too, should be lived in that light and joy and trust. If the universe is harmonious and inviting us to live with the love and fun and grit of the athletes of Special Olympics, then it only makes sense that we learn how to face death with that same confidence and love.

But how?

How can any of us really trust that there's a benevolent universe when there's so much pain all around us? Isn't it wiser to try to protect ourselves from getting hurt rather than trusting one another? And doesn't it make sense to insulate ourselves from the discomfort of vulnerability and death for as long as we can?

When I think like that, Jean Vanier becomes an insightful guide. He reminds me it's possible to hug people when you meet for the first time, to hold hands with people you barely know, and to smile into the eyes of people you've just met, as if to say, "I love you." He can do all that, because he's figured out that if we want to understand trust, we must first practice it. Here's how he explains it.

> Our happiness comes from creating places where we welcome the strangers of the world and live the compassion that says "you are more beautiful than you dare believe." Our goal is to end the tyranny of the normal because normality implies that some are welcome and others are to be rejected. It sends a message that there is a certain way you should be and that you will only matter in the world if you become like others who are normal. This specter of normality is the source of fear. What could be worse than to tell someone to be another? The only real normality is the tenderness and compassion of God. If we can make that the "normal," then we can trust each other to be as we were created: beautiful, fragile, but loved.

When I heard Vanier speak these words at the age of eighty-four in the small chapel just a few feet from where he founded L'Arche more than forty years earlier, I could feel the presence of so many athletes of Special Olympics who had told me in their own way of the terrifying "tyranny of normality." But Vanier's message isn't simply about how to help those who have been excluded and mocked because they are not "normal." It is also—and maybe more powerfully—a message about how to learn to trust that we are each in the care of ultimate goodness. "The pedagogy of L'Arche is the experience of loving one's enemies. We must learn to love whatever appears to be the enemy. Tragically, people with disabilities are often treated as an enemy, someone to be feared, avoided, loathed."

I was puzzled at first by this version of an "enemy." Not many people would refer to a person with an intellectual challenge as their "enemy." What was it about them that led Vanier to use that word? I'd always thought of my enemies as those who had done something wrong—deeply wrong to my country, my family, myself. Cruel people were enemies and violent people were enemies, but people like Donal or Ricardo or Ramadhani? They weren't enemies. Hitler was an enemy.

But Vanier's spirituality was focused not only on the "enemies" "out there" in the world but also on the "enemies" within each of us. "The enemy is all the things we fear and disability is a symbol of many enemies. When we see disability, we see the enemy of vulnerability, the enemy of physical illness, the enemy of weakness, and the enemy of despair and death. At L'Arche, we are trying to learn how to love in a way that transforms all of these. In L'Arche, we are welcoming all of you—your brokenness, your victimization, your anger, your fear—so that you can live in a community of intimacy, and gentleness; so you can live, give life, receive life, reveal yourself to others . . . To learn the love of the enemy is to lay down all arms and say, 'I am unarmed!' I fought the most terrible battle—the battle with my enemies and the battle with myself. I have no need of arms anymore. I am no longer afraid. I can live at peace now."

Vanier sounded much like Brother David Stendl Rast, who describes the meaning of faith: "Faith . . . means ultimate trust in the power of God."

Who wouldn't want that kind of faith? No one. Who knows how to get it? That's tougher. In the fall of the year 2000, I met a Special Olympics athlete who turned out to be the best role model I've ever had in the experience of ultimate trust, Daniel Thompson of West Virginia. Our paths first crossed when out of the blue Daniel wrote me a letter after watching *The Loretta Claiborne Story* on television. "The movie made me feel like I knew where I come from . . . I was not picked to play any games—or when they had to pick someone, I was the last one picked," he wrote. "Loretta has been through what a lot of us have been through," he continued, "and it hurts too. I can only hope that someday we can see the world change and people love us for who we are."

I found the combination of pain and vision in Daniel's letter remarkable, and I wrote back immediately. I asked him about his background, his sports interests, about what had motivated him to write his letter, about what his goals were in life, about his experiences in Special Olympics. But what I was really trying to ask him was what had led him to be hopeful. And how had he learned to frame the hope of the future so clearly and insightfully as being free of fear—a time when "people love us for who we are."

Daniel and I exchanged dozens of letters, then hundreds of e-mails, and he became a spokesperson for Special Olympics and a leader in my brother Anthony's great organization, Best Buddies. Over the years, here's what I learned about Daniel Thompson's faith.

Daniel was born on June 28, 1961, in West Virginia. He was sick right at birth with multiple organ failures and multiple surgeries. Early predictions were ominous, but as he told me years later, "the doctors fixed me up right there at the beginning. Right from the beginning, I surprised people." He surprised people by surviving, but that didn't make it easy. He had problems in development, didn't walk until he was four, struggled with speech into his elementary years, and was in and out of the doctor's office all the time. But he made it out of diapers and joined peers of the same age in elementary school and proved all the doubters wrong by graduating from high school with those peers. "One teacher did put me in the hallway because I couldn't understand stuff, but most everyone was good to me. My friends were good kids."

In 1999, Daniel was selected by Special Olympics West Virginia to go to the World Games in North Carolina to compete in his favorite sport, bocce. In his own hometown of Bridgeport, West Virginia, he'd won more than ten medals in bocce competitions, and he'd learned the Special Olympics oath ("Let me win, but if I cannot win, let me be brave in the attempt") by heart. But he'd also come to his own conclusions about what the words of the oath mean. " 'Let me

win' doesn't mean let me win. The oath means let me try my best
to win. 'If I cannot win' doesn't mean I cannot win. It means to try
and be a good sportsman about yourself. And 'let me be brave in the
attempt' doesn't just mean let me be brave and attempt. It means let
me do what I can and let the outcome be what it may and let me be
happy about it. That's what the oath really means, you see?"

Time and again, I noticed this beautiful tension in Daniel. On
the one hand, he would always emphasize the importance of effort, of
doing one's best and trying hard. He would tell me stories about how
he worked hard to learn to read and how much his grandmother had
helped him. He told me about his first computer, and how he learned
to send e-mails and use an Internet browser. He told me about the
time he moved into a group home in a new neighborhood where the
residents had organized a petition to keep him out. "I went and gave
a speech at the senior center and my speech touched one of the neighbors that was doing the petition and she came to talk to me . . . Now
she's changed her mind and she came to work for people with disabilities! She was just afraid." He was a fighter in every sense, focused
on his goals, determined to use everything in his power to achieve
them, resilient in the face of setbacks.

But he had learned something else playing bocce, too. One of his
favorite stories was about the time one of his opponents, Rachel, a
young woman from Lincoln County, beat him out for the bronze
medal in a state championship. "I was so happy for her," he reminded
me again and again, because he knew that it was hard for me to
understand how a man as tough and determined as he was could be
happy about a loss. "I keep trying to tell you, Tim," he'd say with
a playful smile, "she hadn't won anything for five years and I'd won a
gold and a gold and another gold and three silvers and she was about
ready to give up. I could tell that she wanted that medal so bad and I
already had a bunch."

"But, usually," I said, "winning just makes competitors want to
win more."

He looked at me as if I was a little child trying to understand the
magic of Silly Putty or the mischief of Curious George. "Sure I
wanted to win a medal. But you gotta remember the other, Tim. It

made me happy to see her winning that medal. I don't know why people take all those steroids and things just to try to win so hard. All you need is to go out and do the best you can. You don't need garbage in your system. That won't make you win nothing. You just need to give it your best. And that day Rachel did better than me and she was so happy and I was just as happy as she was."

Daniel Thompson had learned to balance his desire to win with his faith that he didn't need to win to be happy or fulfilled. Over the years, he became one of my favorite guides in how to try to achieve that balance myself. Like him, I wanted to perform at a high level in my work, but also like him, I wanted to believe that I could trust the outcome regardless of my effort. I became annoying to my friends and family, because I'd forward his e-mails to them so often and suggest they, too, follow his advice. At home, I'd quote Daniel about this or that issue, as he always seemed to have a perspective that combined his razor-sharp instinct about what was important and worthy of effort with his deeply peaceful capacity to accept the outcome of whatever came his way. My brother Anthony asked him to help grow the Best Buddies movement, and he responded by becoming one of the best speakers and advocates for the national Best Buddies gatherings. He'd show up at Anthony's gala dinners in a tux and a smile and, over and over again, deliver a short talk that would stun the gatherings of stars and tycoons. At one point, my daughter Kathleen made a sign for me to hang over my desk: "Daddy, if you feel stressed out, just repeat, 'Don't Worry, Be Daniel.'" Kathleen was tuning in to the way Daniel's sense of trust and harmony could spread to me almost magically. Years later, she wrote her college application essay in tribute to another athlete, Peter Mullins, who captured this same combination of exuberance and trust and titled it "Speechless." Even at eighteen, she was already attuned to the great balancing act of ultimate trust and ultimate effort.

In the spring of 2007, everything changed. Daniel wrote me one of his typically unassuming e-mails updating me on his activities in the local Special Olympics and Best Buddies programs and then added one other item: "I wish I could tell you good news but it's all bad. I have to go next friday for more surgery . . . Well the tumor they took out of my bladder two week's ago I found out yesterday from the doctor was colon cancer . . . I'm not sure of the outcome yet. I'm putting it in the Lords hands as I told my Bible Study group at church. I know you might be crying one reading this but don't okay i've not cried as of yet and don't plan on it as I'm like Daniel in the Bible in the lion's den i have faith in my doctor . . ."

The news stunned me. I called him on the phone in the way that people do when they get news that is bad in a big way. "What happened? Are you sure? Do you have a good doctor? What about treatments? There must be something that can be done. How did this happen? You seemed so healthy and fine just a few weeks ago . . ."

Daniel answered in simple, calm words. I was fixing; he was being. I tried to claw my way to an alternative ending; he tried to reinforce the truth. "The doctors told me that I was probably doin' the right thing by not having all the chemos and everything. So we'll just see how it goes. Right now, I feel okay." I spoke to his doctor, who reinforced the message: treatment was unlikely to help. The cancer was too advanced. Daniel's decision made sense. Later I saw the words Daniel had written to his doctor: "I have told Mr. Tim Shriver as well as my church and my family I feel good about my mind not to do any treatments of chemotherapy as I want to be able to enjoy what life i have left like take long walk's on warm days. And go place's with out fear of getting sick . . . I want to live my life till the end feeling good and not being sick all the time. So their you have it . . ."

Daniel was dying. He was okay with it. I wasn't.

A few weeks later, I drove to West Virginia for the second time to see Daniel. A few years earlier, I'd driven down at his invitation to attend the opening ceremony for the West Virginia Summer Games. We'd marched together in the parade of athletes, and I'd given a short speech to open the games in which I'd quoted Daniel. We were surrounded at those games by the Knights of Columbus, chiefs of police, the president of West Virginia State University, and thousands of athletes, parents, coaches, and volunteers. "Oh, my lands, Tim!" Daniel said over and over again as I told everyone we met about how brilliant he was and what a visionary he was. It was a party and we'd had a blast.

This time, the drive across western Maryland and over the Appalachians and into the rocky hills of central West Virginia was for a different sort of ceremony.

Highways hug the earth in West Virginia and wrap themselves around mountains and valleys and rivers as if weightlessly suspended among natural things, plying pathways that sit crisply above the mysterious layers of wood and life and soil and rock below. Trucks rumble by from time to time, but the roads have the quality of an intruder in that part of the world, emerging from one hidden corner of mountain and disappearing beyond another. After four hours on the road, I reached Daniel's exit and pulled off Interstate 79. I wished I could go on and on above the earth, not having to stop. I looked at the narrow road ahead of me, leading up the side of the hill toward Daniel's home, and I thought of the poet Seamus Heaney again: "Useless to think you'll park and capture it / More thoroughly. You are neither here nor there, / A hurry through which known and strange things pass . . ." I wanted, at that moment, to hurry through.

I drove a few hundred yards, weaving up a hill and tightening my grip on the wheel—"be careful coming around the corners, Tim. Some of the kids around here don't remember that there's two sides of the road!" I counted the driveways and houses as I'd been instructed, eventually turning right onto a dirt driveway, then again, onto a lightly overgrown grassy driveway. I came to a full stop in front of an aluminum-sided single-story ranch house with a nice view of the hill below, a small barn to the left, and nothing much else. Daniel emerged from the house wearing baggy knee-length blue-jean shorts, white socks, a gray sports shirt, and his big, round, tinted glasses. He walked toward the car slowly, steadily, amiably, like Ed Sullivan with a grin. "You made it!"

I had worried the whole drive about how to act naturally and what to say to Daniel about the dreaded intruder—his cancer. There was no hiding my purpose: I was coming to say goodbye to a dying friend who was young. As much as I wanted to see him, I didn't want to face him. But within moments, the scene changed. "Let's go for a ride," Daniel said, and suddenly Daniel Thompson and I were zooming away on two giant all-terrain vehicles his brother kept in the garage. Daniel had no idea that I loved go karts and mini bikes and riding in the woods. Growing up in Rockville, my dad had allowed me to have a go kart, my older brother Bobby a mini bike, and my younger brothers Mark and Anthony a glorified golf cart known as "the Dune Cat." When we were kids, we rode these machines as often as life would allow—around our backyard fields with dozens of dogs chasing us, in timed races against one another, into the woods in search of adventures, and, one time, right into the swimming pool that doubled as Camp Shriver's aquatics venue.

All of that came back to me that September afternoon as Daniel and I became two little boys revving our engines and riding as fast as we could along dirt roads into the hills. We'd stop as Daniel pointed out childhood landmarks. "See that abandoned shed?" he asked. That's where he'd escape to, camping out and watching the big red-tailed hawks overhead, the deer all around, and hearing nothing but the sounds of the woods. Then we were off again, across an open field, then careening down the side of the hill in low gear to save the brakes and handle corners better.

Every image I remember about our ride, I remember as being bright and crisp. The road was rough and in high definition. The ATVs were bright and loud. If Daniel had trained for a lifetime, he couldn't have done a better job of capturing my full attention to prepare me for our farewell. I could have ridden those ATVs all afternoon, but time was short. "Let's get something to drink, Tim," Daniel said. "Come on in and I'll show you the house. And I want you to see my medals and a lot of things you're going to like for sure!"

For the next two hours, we talked and talked. I asked Daniel about his childhood, his many illnesses during infancy, his friends at school, his discovery of Special Olympics, his family, his life. "Did you struggle a lot when you were in school?"

"Nope. Everyone was good to me except for maybe one or two people in high school. But most of the other kids are from right around here, too, and we grew up together and they could see that I wasn't so good in my studies but that didn't bother nobody."

"Do you remember being in the hospital a lot?"

"Nope. That was mostly when I was little and my mother told me about it but I don't remember none of it. From all I could tell, the doctors just kept taking me in and patching me up. One time it was my kidney and another time it was my bladder and another time it was my brain and they told my parents that I wouldn't live past five but here I am and none of that never bothered me. I can't even remember any of it!"

"What about working? What's it been like trying to get a good job?"

"Yessir, I've had good jobs! I worked at Walmart for a while, but I left after a year because I couldn't handle the pressure. That's the only time I really needed money. A lot of the workers at Walmart, they even gave me money and then I got my social security and I went back to the store and I went around to the employees and tried to give them back the money they had loaned me, because I kept a record—but they didn't want back their money, which was totally amazing, you know."

"You've never had much money, but somehow it doesn't seem to bother you. Is that right?"

"I've had plenty. You gotta look out for others, too, when it comes to money. Look at Leona Helmsley. She said to one of her maids one time by accident, she said, 'Oh, I don't have to pay taxes. Only little people do.' She was just focused on money. Like Donald Trump. I'm positive that one of these days, it's going to catch up to him. If I could, I'd say, 'Donald, you may have a life of fame. You may have a life that you think is good and stylish. But, Donald, I want you to think of being in a dark, dark space, nothing around you, no telephones, no cell phones, no iPods, no computer, no nothing, no friends. Nobody ever comes to visit you. You have nothing. You are just all alone, all by yourself in a little dark corner and there's a chair, and that's it. That's what living with disabilities is like.

"'And then all of a sudden, you wake up and you got mail and you got a friend and you got people who want to play with you. Then life gets all full. So therefore, Donald, I feel you should donate and help and give your time and effort. You'll feel better and you'll feel happier and you could even get a tax deduction, too!'"

The mention of the dark spaces brought images to mind that

I didn't expect. As he started to talk about dark spaces, I thought first of the quiet of contemplative prayer and the tranquility of being drawn inward and toward the big emptiness. But as he spoke, I realized he was speaking of that other dark space—the space of nothingness where nothingness is not an open door but a brick wall, a prison of aloneness that I'd heard so many people mention but not with Daniel's raw directness. "No nothing" was not a description of an inner peace but rather of an inner despair. I realized that beneath Daniel's guileless positivity lay a history of loneliness and isolation. I thought of the terrible poetry of the prophet Isaiah as he describes the suffering servant: "He was despised and rejected by people. He was a person of sorrows, familiar with suffering. He was despised like one from whom people turn their faces, and we didn't consider him to be worth anything" (Isaiah 53:3). I was struck by how powerfully that image from the Hebrew scripture matched Daniel's reverie about the dark spaces. He, too, had been a man of sorrows. He, too, had been a man from whom others hide their faces. Daniel's faith had not come without cost. He knew the meaning of "all alone."

But I was still puzzled. He was describing an experience of loneliness and despair but he'd come through it and landed in a place of trust and happiness. "You have to take it in," he explained. "You have to let it draw into your heart. You have to experience it. You have to relax your mind. You have to let that darkness draw into your head to understand, you know?" There was nothing impulsive about Daniel's take on the dark spaces and the journey to belief. He was deliberate and focused about it. He had "let it in."

"So sometimes, things don't turn out well," I said.

"Right."

"Like you having cancer."

"Mm-hmm."

"That's not—"

"Right. I mean, I wish they would have caught the tumor on time and I wish they would have gotten that from the bladder and it not spread to my liver and lungs but it did. And there's no turning back the clock. There's only to go forward and I chose not to have chemotherapy because the doctor said that if it made me sick then they would stop it and then it would only guarantee me maybe two more years. And my grandmother, my dad's mother, she had radiation and was guaranteed six months with radiation, and she only lasted six weeks. So you know, I take all that stuff into account in my head, and I prayed about it and I prayed about it. And I talked to my senior pastor at church about it and a couple other people, and then I came up with the decision that it would be best if I just relax and not done any chemotherapy and just live in peace with myself and just not do it. And after that, I was able to sleep really good, so I've made the right decision."

"But this didn't turn out the way you wanted it to."

"No it didn't."

"So how do you—I mean, most people—I mean, you know it's disappointing. It's heartbreaking when things, I mean . . ."

"Yeah."

"Somehow you're able to pray on it?"

"Mm-hmm, right. Because I have faith . . ."

"Right. So when you prayed, how did you pray on this?"

"I said, 'Lord, give me the guidance as to which way you wish me to go.'"

"Do you feel like the Lord spoke to you?"

"Yeah. I feel like the Lord spoke to me and told me, hey, you know, don't do chemo because this will make you sick and then—because chemotherapy is poison, you know, and it destroys part of your organ. It could have even destroyed my heart murmur. I have a heart murmur, and it could have affected my heart valves and stuff as well as my life and my kidneys and all."

"So did you ever ask God why God put you in this position?"

"No. I never asked why God put me in this position."

"Do you ever want to ask God that question?"

"No. I have no reason to. The Bible tells us there's a time for everything. You know, there's a time to die, there's a time to live, there's a time for everything."

"Did you ever get asked by anybody who didn't have any faith how do you get faith? What if I don't believe?"

"I'd tell them they need to—that God is real. And they need to find God and figure it out."

"And if somebody were to say to you, how do you know God is

real besides what the Bible says, do you have anything in your life
that tells you—that confirms for you that God is real?"

"You bet. Me! Because I was able to prove to teachers and some
grade schools that thought I would not amount to anything, because
I did amount to something in my life. And when I go, I will leave a
legacy behind. Just like all the plaques I have here and awards, the
award from my church, what they gave me, and I also have a distinguished rescue award and Special Olympics camp award from where
I helped out a lot and, you know, I have a lot of things that I will
leave behind . . . because I was able—because God just, you know,
when I was down and out and needed help and I didn't want to ask,
God took me and led me to the right places and the right people. I
mean, you know, God led people—God led me to the right people to
help me out so that I wouldn't have to worry. I mean, I have had
miracles happen."

"Mm-hmm."

"You know? And I have friends right now who are praying that
my cancer will go away on its own, which I think is good."

"Do you think it's going to work?"

"I'm not sure. It's up to God. Whatever God chooses for my life,
it will be."

Daniel and I talked on and on. We were in the basement of his
house—a full basement of one large room with every inch of wall
space decorated by a Special Olympics medal or a certificate from
a local Bridgeport church or civic association. There were a few
bookcases—cubes that you get at a container store—and they were
mostly full of scrapbooks and photo albums from his many adventures with local organizations, and with Best Buddies and Special
Olympics around the world. From time to time, he'd point out a
keepsake and digress into a story about how he'd won it. "Here's my
medal that I won at the State Games in Charleston . . . Here's the
computer that I use to send all those e-mails that you send to everyone . . ." He was proud to show off the markers of his life, but as
quickly as he'd point to them, he'd put them down gently and casually, as if moving on. He seemed to love them all, but he didn't hold
any of them as if they mattered all that much.

I mustered the courage to press him to open up to me at an even more personal level. "How did you get to the point where you experience God . . . ? Do you remember the last time you really felt God's presence?"

Immediately, he returned to cancer.

"Well, when [I was in the hospital] I woke up and I knew my pastor was in the room, in the recovery room, and I woke up from my surgery and the nurse gave me my hearing aids and stuff and I experienced God trying to help me to wake up, you know, and I knew something was wrong when I saw my CPR band taken off and then I knew something was wrong when I seen my two brothers come and both of them have power of attorney. You know, they were like—and my niece was crying a little bit and I knew something was wrong and I was like 'Okay, God. What's going on here?'

"They wouldn't tell me, you know. Well why would the whole family be there for? I knew that God was, you know, keeping me in peace and giving me comfort and guidance to get me ready for what was going to be told to me.

"And then when my doctor told me [about the cancer], I took it better than what my family thought I would."

"Did you go to a dark space?"

"Huh?"

I couldn't help but wonder if the news had drawn him back to the depth of aloneness and fear.

"Did you go to a dark space?" I repeated.

"I relaxed in my mind. I floated off into a dark space."

"Is that the same dark space you spoke of before?"

"No. It's two different dark spaces. The one dark space was loneliness stuff, you know, but the other space is where you go to give yourself peace of mind, a chance to relax, and to reenergize yourself and to think about stuff and life in general, you know?"

"Is it sometimes easier to have your faith when you're in that dark space?"

"Yeah. Because you know you're not alone."

"In the first dark space, you're alone?"

"Yeah. Right. You have nobody. But in the second dark space, you're not alone. You have faith. You have the Lord. You build happiness, you know?"

"Mm-hmm. There's no way you could be in the first dark space now?"

"Nope."

"And if everybody left you?"

"Nobody is going to leave me."

Daniel Thompson died a few weeks after my visit to West Virginia. He was reduced in a matter of days from a walking, talking, upbeat young man to nothing. He was raised in a faith rooted in the Bible and he died in that faith, too. But he didn't just read the book; he sought the presence of the God to whom the book referred. He opened his heart to see the spirit come alive: he believed that love is more powerful than hate; he practiced that trust is more powerful than fear; he knew that faith is more powerful than doubt. He lived it all the way: life is more powerful than death. "Whatever God wants for my life, it will be."

As I prayed for Daniel in the days following his death, I kept thinking of the verse that is repeated over and over again in the Psalms and the gospels and in the writings of the early Christians: "The stone the builders rejected has become the cornerstone." There was a paradox in Daniel's life, just as there is a paradox in the text of the psalm: what you think is broken is, in fact, perfectly beautiful. The beauty is the work of the divine and can be seen by us mere mortals if we use the eyes of love, and then the broken is transformed into something "beautiful to behold." With our hearts tuned to this beauty, we begin to see beauty in all things and then just beauty itself. Daniel had heaping amounts of struggle and pain, but he had learned, like Vanier, to love the enemy of the "dark spaces" and found his way through them to heaping amounts of triumph and laughter. He was as determined to change the world as any other great social activist. But he was equally focused on trusting that his destination was in the hands of the maker of that same world. The ultimate truth came from seeing the world as he saw it from the quiet, dark space: with trust, peace, gentleness. He was a cornerstone of faith and trust.

Two years after Daniel died, my mother followed him to the light. Her last Special Olympics event was the World Games in Shanghai, where Hu Jintao, the president of the People's Republic of China, joined with her in celebration of people with intellectual disabilities. Just over ten years earlier, a senior leader of that same country had called for the elimination of people with intellectual differences, but amid fireworks and tens of thousands of volunteers and a television audience of more than one hundred million, Hu declared those days to be over. "The Chinese government and people will use the occasion to promote the well-being of people with disabilities in China, and work with governments and peoples in other countries to improve the well-being of people with disabilities in the world and contribute to the building of a harmonious world of enduring peace and common prosperity," he proclaimed. My mother was eighty-six at the time, and bone thin, and living on the other side of several strokes. She was no longer running games or delivering speeches. But maybe as a result, she was having more fun than I'd ever seen her have at games before.

The ceremony dazzled the crowd. There were thousands of drummers; magnificent, staged adventures depicting the search for unity and harmony; enormous fireworks and light shows; and stars such as Yao Ming, Yo Yo Ma, Lan Lan, and Jackie Chan. Tens of thousands of Chinese volunteers embraced the mission my mother had fashioned from her own childhood. When she was recognized from the stage, she stood up, and eighty thousand cheering citizens of China stood up, too, waving in welcome, support, and gratitude. I spoke briefly to the crowd and called on the spirit of Lao-tzu, who wrote that "the way of heaven is to benefit others." From where I stood on the field, I could see my mother's face on the giant screen as people cheered and cheered for her.

Shanghai was a long way from Brookline, where my mother had heard the lonely voice of her mother saying the words that would animate her life: "There is nothing for Rosemary." It was a long way from the heartbreak of Rosemary's operation in Washington, DC, and a long way from the summer camp in Rockville, Maryland, where my mother had spent hours upon hours in the pool trying to teach lonely children to swim.

But the distance from where she grew up to where she died was short. Her life ended in a hospital room with a view of Nantucket Sound, where she'd raced sailboats with Rosemary and all her siblings as a child, where she'd returned in the summer to raise her own children by the sea, where she'd laughed with her brother on the night when he was elected president of the United States, and where she'd gone to comfort her mother when he was murdered. Toward the end of her life and despite all her work, she worried that she'd done almost nothing of significance. "You should write a book," I said to her a year before she died. "I'd have nothing to write," she answered. "All I ever did was teach children with intellectual disabilities to swim." The work was never done for her, and rest never came. She kept the faith. That was enough.

At the end of her life, she was surrounded by her husband, her five children and their spouses, and nineteen grandchildren. She was enveloped by all of us. The brash games she'd played were finished, and she was ready for the heaven she'd always believed was her most important goal. In the bedroom of her house, there were thirty-four different images of Mary of Nazareth.

Two thousand years earlier, Mary had declared, "My soul proclaims the greatness of the Lord . . . He has cast down the mighty from their thrones and has lifted up the lowly" (Luke 1:46, 52). Such was my mother's life. Her great gift was to make it possible for Daniel and Loretta and Donal and Pearl and Ramadhani and millions more like them to have their rightful places of belonging and triumph. But I believe that perhaps her greatest gift was to those of us whom she taught to see them. She taught us to play her Olympic Games, so that each of us might know the unimaginable beauty of every child of God. Her games make no sense without the belief that each of us is precious, never to be left alone. And they make no sense if the beauty of all creation isn't worth trusting all the way to death and beyond.

SEVENTEEN

Storm the Castle

On October 19, 1962, President John F. Kennedy arrived in Cleveland, Ohio, for a campaign appearance at the Public Square. He was there to support his fellow Democrat Ohio governor Michael DiSalle, who was up for reelection against a tough Republican opponent. DiSalle was serving his first term as governor and had triggered widespread controversy with his adamant opposition to the death penalty and his attempt to expand services for the "mentally retarded" at taxpayer expense. With the election only two weeks away, DiSalle was trailing badly in the polls and the president was on hand to lend his support.

He was also there for another reason: to maintain the appearance of a normal schedule in order to protect the secret of the presence of recently discovered Soviet intercontinental ballistic missiles just ninety miles from U.S. shores in San Cristobal, Cuba. That week was, by most accounts, the most intense week of his presidency and among the most dangerous in history. Just two days before the rally in Cleveland, the president had received an intelligence briefing documenting incontrovertible evidence of nuclear missile construction in Cuba. He had immediately begun meetings with top military commanders to prepare for a series of possibilities, including a nuclear attack against the United States and nuclear war with the Soviet Union. Within days, he would order a blockade of Cuba and the readying of the U.S.

nuclear arsenal. When the blockade began, Secretary of State Dean Rusk alerted heads of state worldwide to "as grave a crisis as mankind has been in." Soviet premier Nikita Khrushchev threatened "catastrophic consequences." The fate of the world hung in the balance.

But the threat had not yet been made public, and the president's agenda was a world away from nuclear Armageddon: he was there to advocate for activism in government and in support of DiSalle's agenda for Ohio. Days earlier, the president had received the report of the panel he'd appointed to study the issue of "mental retardation." It argued for a significant increase in federally funded research, training, treatment, care, and community support for the nation's largest population of people with disabilities, those with intellectual disabilities. DiSalle was the rare governor who thought the issue important.

Just a month earlier, a resident of the Columbus State School (formerly the Columbus State Asylum), a twenty-one-year-old man with an intellectual disability named Eugene, had reported that he had been beaten with a pitchfork and baling wire. The sad probability was that beatings like Eugene's in Columbus, Ohio, were probably the norm across the nation, though almost no one knew or cared. When Kennedy spoke in support of DiSalle at the noonday rally, he was acutely aware that no significant attention was being paid to the residents of institutions such as the Columbus State School. But with the report of the presidential panel now completed and the recommendations thoroughly worked out, the president was ready to act.

He invited the crowd in Cleveland to recognize the extent of the challenge facing the nation: "Do you know today that in the United States today three percent of the children grow up mentally retarded?" He cited the reduced levels of incidence in countries such as Sweden, where effective maternal health systems were in place and where more attention was being accorded to early treatment and education. "Can you imagine," he continued, "that two percent of our children live with mental retardation who could be saved if we had the programs and the recognition of the need . . ."

He looked straight at the crowd, and his voice rose a notch: "For those of us who have seen children live in the shadows"—and here he put the full weight of his voice behind the word—"a country as rich as ours can't possibly justify this neglect."

"Can you imagine?" President Kennedy asked. He could imagine a nation that denied rights and privileges to those at the margins, because he'd grown up in that very nation. He knew the wages of neglect. He knew that there was no justification.

But he could also imagine a nation that asked citizens to give themselves to the country so the country could give them back their best selves. He was a politician "tempered," as he said in his inaugural address, "by war," but shaped not just by a fragile global peace but also by the joy of loving a fragile sister. In Cleveland, he echoed, albeit indirectly, the theme of his inaugural: that freedom depends on the power of imagination unleashed to believe in a more just future, on an unvarnished confrontation with the horrors of injustice and the pain and tenderness they elicit, on the self-gift of citizens willing to become agents of healing that injustice with strength and love, on the sure conviction that in giving one's self to another, one receives one's truest and happiest self in return. Freedom for everyone depends on no one's being relegated to the shadows. He could imagine.

Rosemary's story remains an enigma. She was a symbol of the shadow side of life, but she also unlocked the compassion necessary to change it. She was born in an era when people like her were sent to the shadows by the millions. But she was also a part of a family whose bonds were like steel and whose faith was relentless. Just by being herself—fragile and vulnerable—she taught service, empathy, and tenderness. Her parents and her brothers and sisters tried to include her, heal her, fix her, protect her. As strong as they yearned to win in politics and in sports and in life, they knew she was not that kind of winner. They were afraid of Rosemary and afraid for her, too. What is understandable about the era in which she lived does little to lessen the sadness of what happened to her.

But the bonds within Rosemary's family and the faith its members practiced were ultimately stronger than the fear. Her loss to the operation was devastating, but unlike her three brothers and one sister who were also lost in tragedy, Rosemary didn't die. For more than sixty years, my mother brought her back to life—first by revealing her existence and then by challenging others to bring light to the shadows and the dark places to which Rosemary and others like her were relegated. If there is one lesson I've learned from our family's experience and from praying my way to try to make sense of it, it's that the shadow is us. What we hide hides us. What we fear creates fear. What we fail to love in ourselves makes it impossible to love in others. Happiness can come only when the shadow is revealed, welcomed, accepted. There is no other route. Shining a light on the shadows is the only way.

By revealing Rosemary to us, my mother taught us children that by force of will, we should see Rosemary as a winner. But sadly, I don't think that my mother felt that she herself had been successful. What she wanted for people with intellectual disabilities, she never gave herself. The work of shining a light on Rosemary and on millions of people with intellectual disabilities never produced the wattage she wanted. Her life's work brought attention to people who deserved it, and she did it with a relentless focus on proving the world wrong. She was able to follow her faith to the end and she never gave an inch. But in her eyes, the work—the welcome, the healing, the understanding—had barely begun. In her later years, she focused on ensuring that others would follow.

And millions have. The games she created and left behind continue to invite new generations to ever new journeys of discovery. All over the world today, volunteers come to the games to be reminded that fear cannot withstand a direct gaze. Over and over again, they find themselves believing anew in the power of their own imaginations to conjure distinctive visions of what is possible and to see that possibility as theirs to bring to life. In laughter and smiles and tears, the athletes remind us to realize that ideals like "heaven" are not places we go but rather the place where we belong already. They invite us to unlock the greatest source of energy and power known to humankind: the recognition that each person is already everything that he or she desires to be and, in that recognition, to know that we each deserve to live that truth with affirmation and delight.

The athletes of Special Olympics are the unlikely teachers of these secrets. The recurring question that most of us face in our encounters with them is this: Is it possible that those on the edge—those people we consider "different" and those parts of ourselves that we hide—are a pathway to strength and unity? What I've found is a simple answer: there is no other pathway. To live fully alive is to do what so many of these athletes have done: face the fear—whatever fear lies within each of us and within our countries—and in facing it, break its hold and defeat it. And when the fear is defeated, we are free to be ourselves, to pursue our unique gifts and dreams, to find the places and people to whom we belong and with whom we are affirmed, and together with them, to give ourselves unselfishly to life.

I think belief is at the heart of why the Special Olympics adventure still attracts millions of devoted advocates and volunteers and friends every day around the world, and why it inspires them not just to work for a more inclusive future but also to be more fearless in pursuing their own dreams. At some level, playing together awakens us all to the possibility of believing in one another and not being afraid. I think that's why more than ten thousand medical professionals have joined the Special Olympics movement and, under the leadership of pioneers Dr. Steve Perlman and Dr. Paul Berman, created a program all their own, "Healthy Athletes." Together, they work to provide free health care at Special Olympics games all over the world for hundreds of thousands of people who otherwise might never have it. They came to help and found a way to believe.

I think that's why hundreds of thousands of non-disabled school-age young people around the world are participating in Special Olympics Unified Sports, in their schools and neighborhoods. I think that's why a whole team of them, led by my son Tim and his friend Soeren Palumbo and Loretta Claiborne and the actor Eddie Barbanell, found the energy to change hearts all over the world with their appeal to "Spread the Word to End the Word" and end the humiliating use of the word "retard." They work to change attitudes, but what they really do is create believers.

I think that's why there are more than a million athletes in both China and India who participate every year in thousands of volunteer-driven Special Olympics games. I think that's why tens of thousands of law enforcement officers around the world carry the Special Olympics torch to raise money and dignity. I think that's why volunteers continue to join in countries such as Lebanon and Morocco and Rwanda and Malawi and Afghanistan and Myanmar. In the poorest villages of those countries, volunteers are assembling today, preparing fields for games, inviting families to join support networks, following the leadership of people with intellectual disabilities, and promoting the gifts of those same people—thus, the gifts of all of us—to anyone who will listen. Pick a day and offer to volunteer and chances are, the opportunity will be yours. You may come to give your time, but you are likely to leave believing in something that transcends time.

I think what these volunteers have in common is that they have all been cracked open just enough to know that a world of believing is a world in which they want to live. In a moment, in the blink of an eye, in a smile or a cheer or a goal scored in the most pure and beautiful of ways, they are given back their imaginations, not the ones they first used as children but their fully adult imaginations, free to believe, free to be in love, free to follow believing wherever it leads. It is no small irony that many of us stumble into this encounter with believing through the athletes who seem to represent our darkest doubts and fears. It is absolutely miraculous that through them we become suddenly less afraid and suddenly more confident in the unimaginable beauty of life.

Albert Einstein wrote that the mysterious was at the root of all true art and science. Einstein had it right, I think, when he pushed the importance of dwelling in mystery to its extreme: "He who knows it [the mysterious] not and can no longer wonder, no longer feel amazement, is as good as dead, a snuffed-out candle." Even for the great scientist Einstein, "wonder" and "amazement" are not just the provenance of the physical universe but also the delightful reward of the inward journey to being fully alive. Mystery isn't something confusing or imprecise but rather more full of clarity than we can fully grasp. "A knowledge of the existence of something we cannot penetrate," Einstein realized, "of the manifestations of the profoundest reason and the most radiant beauty, which are only accessible to our reason in their most elementary forms—it is knowledge and this emotion [the mysterious] that constitute the truly religious attitude." It also constitutes the center of the true meaning of Special Olympics.

Needless to say, defeating one's fears and coming to believe and finding "awe" and "wonder" at the center of the universe cannot be learned or experienced by reading a book. It's impossible to convince someone else to believe by telling them to do so. I could write a whole additional book with the hope of being more convincing, and I assure you that there are many more heroes and sheroes who have crossed my path who are more than deserving of books themselves. I could write about Mostafa Galal, the Egyptian Special Olympics athlete who greeted me on my first visit to Beirut for the Middle East North Africa regional games, when I was skittish about entering a city known for war. I arrived at the hotel in the middle of town and Mostafa charged up to me and gave me a huge bear hug and a kiss on both cheeks. He somehow knew the kiss would make me squirm just enough to ease out of the tension I was carrying. I could write about Chrissy Rivera, whose three-year-old daughter Amelia was rejected for a transplant in 2011 because she was "mentally retarded." Chrissy fought back and won her the lifesaving treatment. I could write about Sari Altino in the Philippines, who was given a pair of glasses at a Special Olympics Healthy Athletes clinic and for the first time, at the age of twenty-two, could see. She chose her first words upon seeing as wisely as any great poet might have: "Mom!" she shouted. "I see you! Mom! You're beautiful."

Would their stories resonate? I have no doubt. Would these gifted human beings be welcomed as leaders and teachers? I doubt it. Today, estimates suggest that more than 90 percent of children diagnosed prenatally with Down syndrome are aborted, more than 95 percent of children in the developing world with intellectual disabilities don't go to school at all, routine medical care is still denied even in the wealthiest of nations, and loneliness is still the most common fate for these human beings and their families. We have not yet recognized the severity of the discrimination that persists, nor have we mounted the kind of civil rights movement that these citizens and their families deserve. Fear has not lost its power to create suffering. Our work is far from done.

As in ancient times, prophets are most often ignored, not because their words aren't beautiful but because the listeners have never felt the beauty for themselves. Little Amelia Rivera and her amazing mother, who donated her own kidney so that her daughter could live, are not, in our culture, such aspirational figures as television stars or the superstars of big-time sports. They don't go in for hair and makeup before the cameras roll, and they don't look to polling data to know what they believe. They offer a much more fulfilling life, but the cost, as T. S. Eliot wrote in "The Four Quartets," is "not less than everything."

We're all looking for our own "everything," our own "something bigger," and we're as hungry as ever for role models of how to achieve it. It may be scary to take a chance on trusting one another and believing in our dreams, but it's much more scary to live afraid and hopeless. So why not follow those who are living fully alive and try? Some of us long to act on the big stage of political and social change; others want to make a difference in our schools and communities; and still others want to look inward to heal and belong. All around us, there are role models who continue to inspire us if only we have the eyes to see them and the guts to believe in ourselves enough to try to emulate them in our own way.

The secret is believing. Of course, believing isn't easy, but thankfully we have role models such as Han Rongfeng, a mother in China who gave birth more than twenty years ago to a son who, she was told, was "stupid and useless." She cried for days.

"I was so alone as he grew up," she recalls. Other parents directed their children not to play with her son; friends abandoned her. There was "an enduring bitterness" that came from the looks and glares. "If you have a child with a disability in my province, you have done something wrong in your past life." But the stares and rejections didn't change one thing: "Deep in me," Rongfeng said, "I wasn't sure I could go on, but somehow I knew I must try . . . I am a fighter. My son is a life, and he's a person, too. I refused to waste him."

And so she faced the fears and they lost their power to defeat her. And she became like the character in the Maya Angelou poem, chanting, "I rise, still I rise." She visited other mothers of children with intellectual disabilities, asked them to share their ideas, and organized a small group to ask local officials for help. She made no progress. In the course of her organizing, she attended a Special Olympics event. "It was deep and memorable," she said, "to see all these people helping and cheering and happy." The event showed her what was possible for her son, but every day was a reminder of all the things he didn't have. He didn't have friends, he didn't have a school, and he didn't have a chance.

A few months later, she decided to escalate her efforts and confront the government directly. Friends counseled her against provocation, citing the risks. But she had nothing to lose. "I have a special child," she said matter-of-factly; "I wanted to help him. I wanted others to understand him. This was my only purpose in life."

Rongfeng is a full course in living fully alive. "Life is hard, so hard. My mission is nothing big," she said, betraying the strength of her conviction. Her mission wasn't big; it was enormous. Her mission was not only to love her son at all costs but also to change the course of her nation. She had been given the gift of a child—about that she had no choice. But she had chosen to accept the gift of making the world a place worthy of her child, and so off she went. "I just marched right into the government office and had no appointment or anything. I walked up to the first person I met and I told them, 'I want the government to support our children. I want a school and a field and a place to meet and offices.' The woman looked at me and went to get another person."

As she recounted the confrontation, she giggled, then grimaced. "I said it again. Then another person came and I said it again. I didn't know if they were going to take me away forever, but I just kept saying it. I kept saying I have the names of all the parents and we want programs for our children." She felt like there was a force within her that was unleashed and she could do nothing other than let it out. The last official that came into the room and heard her story turned to his subordinates and then looked back at her: "He told me, 'You are a shining light.' I almost cried but I tried so hard not to. He promised to work with me and he did. It made me so happy and proud. My son does matter." Months later, Rongfeng got the approval for a new school for her son and for other children with intellectual disabilities. Official policy began to change because she believed enough to risk herself to make it happen.

She believed and, by believing, changed the arc of history in her nation. China, like every country, has a long way to go to be a place of welcome for people with intellectual differences, but I think they're moving in the right direction thanks largely to the efforts of women such as Rongfeng.

Most of us don't aspire to change nations, like Rongfeng. For most of us, making a difference in our local schools and businesses and communities is more than challenging enough. Take just one example. At Kellis High School in Phoenix, Arizona, a small group of youth leaders, together with their unstoppable special education teacher, Michael Wakeford, launched a Special Olympics Unified Sports program just three years ago. Hoping to attract twenty-five or so students with intellectual differences and the same number of non-disabled peers, they started with practices and training sessions after school. The kids who joined played and bonded and discovered one another in ways they had never understood before. "I just went to the program because Coach Wake told me to try it," Colin Davis said, "but I really didn't understand anything before I went. Then all of a sudden, I meet these kids and I had walked past them in the halls my whole life and they turn out to be the best people I've ever known. I mean Treveon Wimberly is now my friend, not my special needs friend. He's my friend, and to be honest, he's the best friend I've ever had in my whole life. So what if he can't speak? I couldn't care less."

Because these young people knew how much fear and bullying existed in their own school, they decided to take the lessons they were learning and try to teach them to others. But how to get the message out to 1,800 kids? How about a dance? The kids in the Unified program developed a six-step dance and named it for the school mascot, the Cougar. They coined their dance "the Cougarlude" because they wanted to perform it at every game or show at the school instead of an "interlude." Well, pretty soon the Cougarlude went viral and the biggest school events—varsity basketball games, dances, assemblies—were all interrupted by a thousand kids joining the Unified Team in the Cougarlude. It became the symbol of Kellis: everyone dances together.

The kids didn't stop there. The following year, Coach Wake created a credit class, "Unified Sports," with a curriculum of physical activity and study of the social and cultural dimensions of disability and inclusion. The class is an elective that requires a seven-page application and yet, each semester, almost fifty non-disabled students apply. The students created a motto for themselves, "We Are Able," and designed T-shirts for their team with the words blazoned across the chest. What they didn't expect was that the T-shirts associated with the "special ed" kids would become the hottest article of clothing in the school. The first year, they sold almost four hundred to students, and that number is rising every year. To be a Kellis student is to believe in "We Are Able." Kids with Down syndrome hang out with varsity athletes. Kids with autism sit at lunch tables with kids headed to elite colleges. Kids in wheelchairs move through the halls with student council members and yearbook editors.

At graduation in 2013, Colin and Treveon took the message of "We Are Able" to a new and climactic level. For virtually his whole life, Treveon has been in a wheelchair. He's a great communicator, but he doesn't use words. Instead he uses animated facial expressions, gestures with his arms, and barely formulated sounds to communicate what's important. So early in his senior year, he told his Unified partner, Colin, what was most important to him: somehow, he wanted to walk across the stage when he received his diploma at graduation. Colin heard him loud and clear, and together they committed to a daily routine of exercises and therapies that would increase the chances that Treveon could bear his own weight. Medically, it seemed impossible with legs and muscle systems made unworkable by disease. But they decided to try nonetheless, and they worked together every day of the week for the entire year. No exceptions. Raw determination. Every day. Grit magnified on the hope that Treveon could stand.

And wouldn't you know it: graduation day was May 16, 2013, and with Colin standing behind him, Treveon was wheeled onto the stage and then rose out of his wheelchair and into a walker with a brace for his elbows and with the entire school cheering and crying and standing and pulling for him, Treveon walked. He walked—it's on video—about three steps. And the principal, Jeff Wooton, handed

him his diploma as he stood and waved at his classmates and leaned
back toward Colin, who was covering his every move. No one could
mistake the moment for anything other than what it was: a moment
when two people who were fully alive together joined to become the
symbol of a new Kellis High School, tilting it inexorably toward a
culture of unity. Of course, Kellis still has work to do, and of course,
it isn't perfect. But thanks to Coach Wakeford and Colin and Treveon
and dozens of other young leaders, it's a place where it is safe to be
caring and vulnerable; safe to take a chance; safe to believe.

There's a distinctive energy in moments where belief and struggle
create breakthroughs like these, an alertness and crispness that's ar-
resting. The great writer Alice Walker captured the energy of such
moments beautifully:

> There is always a moment in any kind of struggle when one
> feels in full bloom. Vivid. Alive . . . To be such a person or to
> witness anyone at this moment of transcendent presence is to
> know that what is human is linked, by a daring comparison,
> to what is divine. During my years of being close to people
> engaged in changing the world, I have seen fear turn into
> courage. Sorrow into joy. Funerals into celebrations. Because
> whatever the consequences, people, standing side by side,
> have expressed who they really are, and that ultimately they
> believe in the love of the world and each other enough to
> be that.

I love the idea of feeling "in full bloom." And I love even more that
it's possible to be in full bloom just by standing "side by side" with
others in pursuit of the daring connection between the human and
the divine. Walker reminds us of the lessons of the atheletes and their
families. I think she's right: when we join in the "struggle," we find
others and we find ourselves. This is the real "something bigger."

One final story. John Frank Stephens was born with Down syndrome on April 9, 1992, in Arkansas, and moved to Virginia in 1996.
He went to public school there, graduated as a letterman from Chan-
tilly High School, and played basketball, golf, softball, and other

sports in Special Olympics. Today, his business card reads "Actor, Author, Advocate," and he's proved himself in each. He's five feet one-half inch tall. (He likes to mention the half inch.)

A few years ago, he led a delegation of advocates to Capitol Hill for a day of meetings with senators and representatives and leading policy makers. His agenda was simple: to ask for more funding for Special Olympics programs promoting health and inclusive schools and international development. He went from office to office for a full day, stopping to speak to anyone who would listen.

Despite their best efforts, Frank and his colleagues were only partially successful. Trips to Capitol Hill can be frustrating for anyone, and this one was intensely frustrating to Frank and his fellow athletes. Most meetings ended with brush-off pleasantries: "The congressman thanks you for your message and your visit and will consider your request." "The senator wants you to know how much he appreciates your work and only wishes that he could do more." And so on.

At the end of the long day, the team of athletes and volunteers and family members gathered for a reception in one of the function rooms in the House of Representatives' Cannon Building. About fifty of us wandered into a hearing room for refreshments and reflections. Elected representatives whom we'd met or tried to meet were invited to stop by and share a message. A top-ranking Democratic leader of the House of Representatives, Steny Hoyer, stopped by the reception and spoke of his admiration for the athletes. Similarly, Roy Blunt, a supportive Republican from the state of Missouri, came by to say he would be a sponsor of the Special Olympics legislation. The leader of disability issues, Senator Tom Harkin, spoke of his unconditional support. My cousin Patrick Kennedy, a representative from Rhode Island at the time, swept into the room with his typical good cheer. He exhorted the group to fight harder and lobby more. "The Congress of the United States can and must do more," Patrick declared. "We cannot stand by as people with mental illness and intellectual disabilities get treated as second-class citizens in this country, and I'm ready to fight with you." A cheer rose up.

As we began to wrap up, I extended one last offer to the room: "Would any of the athletes who worked today want to add any last thoughts?" I looked around. It was late. Rides home were waiting;

everyone was tired. But one person walked slowly to the microphone: it was Frank Stephens, all five feet and one-half inch of his well-dressed frame.

He began to speak, very slowly and with his characteristic cadence— a few words followed by a pause and then the rest of the sentence. He began, "I want to say that I am . . . ha-ha-ha-happy to be here." Nothing special. A typical greeting. Frank continued without a note. He recognized his father and mother, and then thanked the volunteers of his home state of Virginia. He spoke of the sports he loved and elicited a belly laugh when he bragged about his gold medals. He kept eye contact without a blink, holding the mic high and keeping his head tilted slightly backward so as to keep his line of sight through his glasses onto the people in front of him. Slowly, he gathered our attention in that dark room as we stood with our plastic cups of soda and juice and our tired legs and our frustrated hearts.

Frank Stephens moves slowly. His eyes glide slowly. His body shifts slowly, deliberately. As I watched him speaking, I could feel a slowness come to my mind, as though my thoughts became quieter, my breathing became quieter, and my attention sharper. "Some pe-pe-people think that I'm . . . just disabled, that being like me is bad." His words felt crushing. He went on: "Some pe-pe-people don't even think we should be here . . . on Capitol Hill because we don't co-co-count. Some pe-pe-people don't even think—"

Frank stopped. He looked around the room. The pause was so long I almost thought he needed help. He held the audience with his gaze. Then he drew in his breath. "They don't even think I should li-li-live. That's why I'm he-he-here."

Then his voice rose and he surged ahead. "I'm here to say to all those people that . . . my life is worth living! My life is worth living! My life is worth living!" There was not a sound in the room. Frank brought the mic a little closer to his mouth. "I love my life and my life is worth living."

A few years later, I went to the White House with Frank and a dozen other athletes for a ceremony where President Obama signed a bill removing the words "mental retardation" from U.S. law. It was a triumphant moment for our community. Their voices had been heard and the Congress had acted, and now the president of the United States was signing into law a change that would forever banish the painful taunt—"retarded"—from official language. We were ushered into the East Room and seated while the president took his place. He spoke briefly. "Rosa's Law," as it became known, for Rosa Marcellino, who pushed for legislation, was official.

When the ceremony was over, I rounded up our gang and we headed for the exit as security officials edged us to the door. I hailed two cabs outside the White House and began to load the first group into one when all of a sudden, I realized Frank was missing.

I scrambled back to the White House security desk, only to be told that all the guests had departed. I frantically asked the Secret Service to help me find Frank. "He must be in there," I said. "Frank Stephens is his name and he didn't come out. He doesn't have a cell phone. Maybe he's in the men's room or somewhere, but he must be inside."

"Calm down, sir," the agent said sternly. "We don't believe there's anyone in the house, but we will sweep it again."

Twenty minutes later, I saw Frank walking out the side door of the White House, two security guards on either side. He had a huge smile on his face. So did they. I was relieved beyond description. "Frank, where did you go? What happened?"

He looked at me, with his most mischievous smile and eyes so tender. "Tim. It was so beautiful in there."

For me, Frank Stephens is in the category of the great teachers, a master of the journey to living fully alive. Frank loves the life he's been given and sees beauty all around him. Another such mystic, Saint Catherine of Siena, summed up this way of life: "If you are who you were meant to be, you will set the world ablaze."

That's the final lesson. When you are who you are meant to be, it is so beautiful everywhere. Keep your heart open and you will set the world ablaze.

Years ago, Loretta gave me her own slogan for setting the world ablaze. She was staying at our house for a few days in between speeches and meetings. After breakfast one morning as I headed to the door to take the children to school and go to work, she turned to Kathleen and Caroline and said, "See you later, Kathleen and Caroline. And don't forget to storm the castle!"

I've been barking those words to my children every morning every day since. "Storm the castle!" Every time I say it at school dropoff, Caroline, our youngest and the only one of our children who has been a part of Special Olympics since a few days after her birth, always charges away from my car with a roguish smile on her face. She's a Unified partner with Joelle Packard, a rigorous dancer, and tough enough to take down any castle. I know deep down that she and our other children understand those words. If you are who you are meant to be, if you know deep in your bones that your one precious life is lovely and worth living—then you'll storm the castles of your life and set the world ablaze.

And therein lies the challenge from Loretta to us all. There are castles in each of our lives. Some are global struggles for peace and justice that will require great sacrifice and courage. Others are local struggles that need the creativity and attention of citizens who believe. Others are between us, in families and among friends, where wounds linger and pain is passed on and on and where belief and forgiveness and healing are in desperate need. Still others are within us, shadow castles waiting to be stormed with light.

Loretta reminds us all that healing and welcoming are great adventures and they await each of us. She reminds us to be unafraid of whatever castle stands before us. She reminds us to storm ahead and take on the challenges with belief beyond imagination.

So wherever you are, and whatever you're doing, there's a castle close by that only you can storm. Don't delay another second. Take aim, be brave, and have fun. All it takes is a willingness to enter the game and believe. Just by playing, you'll surely win the medal that matters most.

A Note on Language

LABEL ME ABLE

The words we use to describe one another tell a story all their own. We use labels to convey gender, color, religion, political persuasion, geography, tribe, and more.

In this book, I've tried to share the story of many heroes of living fully alive who also happen to have intellectual disabilities. The issue of how society labels them has become central to their struggle to tell an affirming and hope-filled story of their identities, lives, and dreams.

When I was a child, we often spoke of "the retarded" and thought of the term "mental retardation" as medically and politically accurate and fair. Before my time, "idiot," "imbecile," and "moron" were equally acceptable terms to describe people based on their IQs or "mental age" assessments. "Handicapped," "invalid," "deviant," "educable," "trainable," and "defective" have all been used at one point or another. In the many languages of the world, comparable terms are still common today. There remain institutes of "defectology," teachings that children are "exchanges" for past sins, references to people "suffering" from Down syndrome, and rituals of rape and assault against people with intellectual disabilities for the purposes of healing diseases or purging evil spirits.

In writing this book, I chose multiple words to identify the 250 million or so people in the world who have "intellectual disabilities." When using historical material, I retained the original language even when that language would be offensive by today's standards. The history of the words used to describe people is itself instructive about social, religious, political, and cultural attitudes and practices. In reviewing this history, I frequently found myself wishing I could dodge the words or soften the horror that they convey. But they are what they are and I retained them. They are a part—a painful part—of the world we inherit.

In writing about the present, I chose to use the commonly accepted term "intellectual disabilities." I say "commonly" because it is not universally accepted. Some prefer to broaden the definition to include "developmental disabilities," since that term includes populations who have many of the same challenges as people with intellectual disabilities but do not necessarily have intellectual disabilities. Others prefer more colloquial terms such as "intellectual challenges," which properly emphasizes that we are all less about a diagnosis than about a process of facing our limitations. More than a decade ago, I began using the term "difabilities" to underscore the enormous variation in human abilities and, hopefully, to communicate that differences are universal, broad, and welcome.

Perhaps most important, wherever possible, I have followed a general consensus among disabilities advocates and those who love, care for, follow, and believe in individuals with intellectual disabilities—use "people first" language. "People first" has a simple message: Whenever labeling an individual or a group, place the label after the word "person" or "people." Emphasize that whatever the label might be, it is not an identity but just a part of an identity. In this usage, one writes about "people with intellectual disabilities" in order to underscore that the respective "intellectual disability" is only a part of who those individuals are—that they are "people first." Similarly, one could refer to "people with physical disabilities" or "people who have cancer" to make the same point.

Even "people first," however, has its detractors. Recently some advocates have argued powerfully that they want "disabilities" to be a primary descriptor as a way of claiming it without shame or fear. "I am autistic" or "I am gay" are examples of words that describe identity. The debate will continue, I'm sure, and it's important in countless ways. It has nothing to do with being politically correct and everything to do with respect and dignity. This is but one indication of a movement that is dynamic, changing, and claiming ever new ways of speaking about personhood and society.

When confronting the challenge of words, people with intellectual disabilities have been their own best advocates—as expected. It was people such as Loretta Claiborne and Mark Swiconik and Eddie Barbanell and Rosa Marcellino who moved the U.S. government and people to abandon the term "mentally retarded" and the slur "retard." And it was the Australian Special Olympics athlete Gabrielle Clark who brilliantly addressed the issue more than a decade ago. "If you want to know what to label me," she said in a speech, "label me able!"

Someday, Gabrielle's vision will be a reality. We will look at one another and see ability, gifts, goodness, possibility. Until then, we will struggle to use words that help us both understand our many differences and see beyond them. It is in that spirit that I have chosen the words I use in this book.

Notes

INTRODUCTION: A SCHOOL OF THE HEART

7 *"a love so great"*: Bernard of Clairvaux, *On Loving God: De Diligendo Deo* (Point Roberts, Washington: Eremitical Press, 2010), 43.

7 *"honey sweet teacher"*: The phrase is a translation of the title of Pope Pius XII's 1953 encyclical on Bernard of Clairvaux, *Doctor Mellifluus* (May 24, 1953), available at www .vatican.va/holy_father/pius_xii/encyclicals/documents/hf_p-xii_enc_24051953_doctor -mellifluus_en.html (accessed August 13, 2014).

8 *"nearer to you than yourself"*: Muhyiddin Ibn 'Arabi, "Theophany of Perfection," available at www.beshara.org/principles/selected-reading/ibn-arabi/theophany-of-perfection.html (accessed July 10, 2014).

9 *"The intellect says"*: Rumi, "Thousands of Rose Gardens," in *The Penguin Book of New Age and Holistic Writings*, ed. William Bloom (New York: Penguin, 2001); also available at www .williambloom.com/writings/penguin-new-age-intro-63.htm (accessed August 13, 2014).

10 *"one wild and precious life"*: Mary Oliver, "The Summer Day," in *New and Selected Poems Volume One* (Boston: Beacon Press, 2004), 94.

2. MUCH IS EXPECTED

15 *Joseph P. Kennedy was*: David Nasaw does an excellent job of telling the story in his biography *The Patriarch: The Remarkable Life and Turbulent Times of Joseph P. Kennedy* (New York: Penguin, 2012), 204–37.

15 *"The money changers have fled"*: Franklin Delano Roosevelt, first inaugural address, March 4, 1933, Franklin D. Roosevelt Presidential Library and Museum, Grace Tully Papers, subseries 4, box 5, folder 11, available at www.fdrlibrary.marist.edu/_resources /images/tully/5_11.pdf#search=First%20Inaugural%20Address (accessed January 21, 2014).

23 *"Should anyone be afraid"*: Eunice Kennedy Shriver, "Hope for Retarded Children," *The Saturday Evening Post*, September 22, 1962.

25 *"anyone who has survived"*: Flannery O'Connor, *Mystery and Manners: Occasional Prose* (New York: Farrar, Straus and Giroux, 1970), 84.

3. PITY OR PURGE

27 *Pity or Purge*: I am deeply indebted to the historians David L. Braddock and Susan L. Parish, authors of "An Institutional History of Disability," in *Disability at the Dawn of the 21st Century and the State of the States*, ed. Braddock (Washington, DC: American Association on Mental Retardation, 2002), as well as the theologian Amos Yong, author of *Theology and Down Syndrome: Reimagining Disability in Late Modernity* (Waco, TX: Baylor University Press, 2007), for their sensitive accounts of the sad history of "pity or purge" prior to the twentieth century.

28 *In sections of the Torah*: Rabbi Julia Watts Belser, correspondence with the author, 2014.

29 *The Qur'an, which Muslims believe to be*: I am indebted to Professor Sara Scalenghe for her very helpful insights into disability in the Muslim tradition.

29 *"There is no harm if the blind"*: This and all quotes from the Qur'an are from Ahmed Ali (trans.), *Al-Qur'an: A Contemporary Translation* (Princeton, NJ: Princeton University Press, 2001).

30 *"one should run away from the leper"*: Muhammad al-Bukhari, *The Translation of the Meanings of Sahih al-Bukhari*, vol. VII, trans. M. M. Khan (New Delhi: Kitab Bhavan, 1984), 408–409.

30 *The Hindu tradition has*: Vibha Rupariela, "Marriage and Family Life," in *Caring for Hindu Patients*, ed. Diviash Thakrar, Rasamandala Das, and Aziz Sheikh (Oxford: Radcliffe Medical Press, 2008), 73.

30 *Such capacities were sometimes seen*: Yong argues that nevertheless, "even if some people with intellectual disabilities are unable to cultivate yoga or mindfulness practice, the nondisabled who are able to do so will see the world in a more enlightened way and thereby relate to disabled people apart from the stigma and stereotypes that characterize conventional views of these phenomena" (Yong, *Theology and Down Syndrome*, 148).

30 *There is of course more complexity*: Belser, correspondence with the author.

30 *There are many accounts*: Sir James George Frazer, *The Golden Bough: A Study in Magic and Religion* (New York: Macmillan, 1922), available online in its entirety at www.bartleby.com/196 (accessed July 7, 2014).

30 *Greeks practiced infanticide*: Braddock and Parish, "An Institutional History of Disability," 7–8. They add, however, that "infants with hearing impairments, vision impairments, and mental retardation were not categorized as 'deformed,' and were not put to death, except perhaps for those most profoundly limited intellectually who could have been 'diagnosed' early on . . . M. L. Edwards's (1996, 1997) reviews of the scant documentary records from ancient Greece indicates that deformity was not perceived as absolutely negative by the Greeks, but that this perspective was developed by historians

during the nineteenth century, who applied contemporary contempt for people with disabilities to their assessment of the ancient world" (15).

31 *"This is the kind of medical provision"*: Plato, *Republic* 409e–410a, trans. Sir Henry Desmond Pritchard Lee (New York: Penguin, 1987), 114.

31 *"Let there be a law"*: Aristotle, *Politics* 1335b21, trans. Benjamin Jowett and H.W.C. Davis (New York: Cosimo, 2008), 296–98.

31 *Thus, people with intellectual disabilities*: Yong, *Theology and Down Syndrome*, 37; Braddock and Parish, "An Institutional History of Disability," 15; John Locke, *An Essay Concerning Human Understanding* (Oxford: Oxford University Press, 1975).

31 *"In 1752, with leadership from"*: Braddock and Parish, "An Institutional History of Disability," 16.

32 *Although the hospital's founding*: Ibid., 17.

32 *The first American mental asylum*: Ibid., 21.

32 *A handful of other almshouses*: Ibid.

32 *"in cages, closets, cellars"*: Dorothea Dix, *Memorial to the Legislature of Massachusetts* (Boston: Munroe & Francis, 1843), 2, 5 (emphasis original), cited in Braddock and Parish, "An Institutional History of Disability," 22. A 1904 facsimile of this text can be viewed at www.archive.org/details/memorialtolegisl00dixd (accessed May 27, 2014).

32 *Her pleas would result*: Braddock and Parish, "An Institutional History of Disability," 22.

32 *By 1870 or so*: Ibid., 26. See also Peter L. Tyor and Leland V. Bell, *Caring for the Retarded in America: A History* (Westport, CT: Greenwood Press, 1984), 74.

32 *conditions in the institutions deteriorated*: These conditions persisted for decades. "Patients were beaten, choked, and spat on by attendants. They were put in dark, damp, padded cells and often restrained in straitjackets at night for weeks at a time. *Life* magazine's article 'Bedlam 1946' vividly described the deplorable conditions that existed in most of the 180 state mental institutions. The conditions were said to have degenerated 'into little more than concentration camps on the Belsen pattern.' A photograph taken at Philadelphia's Byberry Hospital showed nude male patients on concrete floors: they were given 'no clothes to wear and live in filth.'" Elliot S. Valenstein, *Great and Desperate Cures: The Rise and Decline of Psychosurgery and Other Radical Treatments for Mental Illness* (New York: Basic Books, 1986), 174–75.

32 *In addition, almost as soon*: Braddock and Parish, "An Institutional History of Disability," 23.

32 *What then happened around the turn*: On the subject of eugenics in the early twentieth century, see Daniel J. Kevles, *In the Name of Eugenics: Genetics and the Uses of Human Heredity* (Berkeley: University of California Press, 1985); J. David Smith and Michael L. Wehmeyer, *Good Blood, Bad Blood: Science, Nature, and the Myth of the Kallikaks* (Washington, DC: American Association on Intellectual and Developmental Disabilities, 2012); and, for a horrifying example of what passed for public discourse in 1913, *The Menace of the Feeble-Minded in Massachusetts: The Need of a Program* (Boston: Massachusetts Society for the Prevention of Cruelty to Children, 1913), available at www.archive.org/details/menaceoffeeblemi00mass (accessed May 27, 2014).

33 *The eugenicists recast*: Kevles, *In the Name of Eugenics*, 86.

33 *"the chief determiner"*: Goddard's famous remark, made during a lecture at Princeton, has been widely quoted, for instance in Stephen Jay Gould, *The Mismeasure of Man*, rev. ed. (New York: W. W. Norton, 1996), 190; Kevles, *In the Name of Eugenics*, 84; Smith and Wehmeyer, *Good Blood, Bad Blood*, 130; and Leila Zenderland, *Measuring Minds: Henry Herbert Goddard and the Origins of American Intelligence Testing* (Cambridge, UK: Cambridge University Press, 1998), 297.

33 *In America (though not in Britain)*: Kevles, *In the Name of Eugenics*, 96–112.

33 *"By legislative reform"*: William Cecil Dampier Whetham and Catherine Durning Whetham, *The Family and the Nation* (London: Longmans, Green, and Co., 1909), 212, available at www.archive.org/details/cu31924013729409 (accessed May 27, 2014). See also Kevles, *In the Name of Eugenics*, 93.

34 *"The idiotic child"*: "Was the Doctor Right? Some Independent Opinions," *The Independent* 85 (January 3, 1916).

34 *"The day of the parasite"*: Ibid.

34 *"Never again will such a story"*: Sharon Snyder, "Infinities of Forms: Disability Figures in Artistic Traditions," in *Disability Studies: Enabling the Humanities*, ed. Sharon Snyder, Brenda Jo Brueggeman, and Rosemarie Garland-Thomson (New York: Modern Language Association, 2002), 181.

34 *The plaintiff in the case*: Paul A. Lombardo, *Three Generations, No Imbeciles: Eugenics, the Supreme Court, and* Buck v. Bell (Baltimore: Johns Hopkins University Press, 2008), 106. See also Stephen Murdoch, *IQ: A Smart History of a Failed Idea* (Hoboken, NJ: John Wiley & Sons, 2007), 99–115.

34 *This foster family*: Lombardo, *Three Generations*, 103–104.

35 *"It is better for all the world"*: Buck v. Bell, 274 U.S. 200 (1927).

35 *Later research showed*: Lombardo, *Three Generations*, 103, 140.

36 *"The very vocabulary"*: Irving Kenneth Zola, *Missing Pieces: A Chronicle of Living with a Disability* (Philadelphia: Temple University Press, 1982), 206.

36 *Not surprisingly, the treatment*: Braddock and Parish, "An Institutional History of Disability," 30.

36 *Remarkably, at the Nuremberg trials*: Edwin Black, "Eugenics and the Nazis: The California Connection," *San Francisco Chronicle*, November 9, 2003, adapted from Black, *War Against the Weak: Eugenics and America's Campaign to Create a Master Race* (New York: Basic Books, 2004).

37 *The philosopher Arne Vetlesen*: Arne Johan Vetlesen, *Evil and Human Agency: Understanding Collective Evildoing* (Cambridge, UK: Cambridge University Press, 2005).

37 *Only by facing the "dis"-abilities*: The distinction between pain and suffering is in much religious and spiritual literature. It was taught to me by the contemplative writer and guide Martin Laird, Order of Saint Augustine.

4. ROSEMARY

38 *"mentally retarded persons"*: Edward Shorter, *The Kennedy Family and the Story of Mental Retardation* (Philadelphia: Temple University Press, 2000), 15.

38 *"She was slow in everything"*: Rose Fitzgerald Kennedy, *Times to Remember* (Garden City, NY: Doubleday, 1974), 151–52.

39 *"They all told me"*: Rose Fitzgerald Kennedy, "Diary Notes," Box 10, John F. Kennedy Presidential Library and Museum; and *Times to Remember*, 152.

40 *Finally, in 1929, when she was*: David Nasaw, *The Patriarch: The Remarkable Life and Turbulent Times of Joseph P. Kennedy* (New York: Penguin, 2012), 152.

40 *The school's founder, Helena Devereux*: "Reaching the Mind, Touching the Spirit: The Helena T. Devereux Biography," Devereux Foundation website, www.devereux.org/site /DocServer/HTDBio.pdf?docID=281 (accessed April 22, 2014), 6. See also Nasaw, *The Patriarch*, 152.

41 *"Dear Mother, I miss you"*: Letter from Rosemary Kennedy to Rose Fitzgerald Kennedy, November 17, 1930, Joseph P. Kennedy Papers, Series 1.1—Family—Family Correspondence, 1930, Box 1, John F. Kennedy Presidential Library and Museum.

41 *"I miss you very much"*: Letter from Rosemary Kennedy to Eunice Kennedy, April 13, 1931, Joseph P. Kennedy Papers, Series 1.1—Family—Family Correspondence, 1931, Box 1, John F. Kennedy Presidential Library and Museum.

41 *"She has developed enough"*: Report from Devereux School, June 23, 1930, Joseph P. Kennedy Papers, Series 1.2.5—Family: Subject File: Rosemary Kennedy—Withdrawn: Education, 1930–1940, Deed Closed Box 3, John F. Kennedy Presidential Library and Museum.

41 *"Due to the fact that her reactions are"*: Report from Devereux School, June 23, 1930, Joseph P. Kennedy Papers, Series 1.2.5—Family: Subject File: Rosemary Kennedy—Withdrawn: Education, 1930–1940, Deed Closed Box 3, John F. Kennedy Presidential Library and Museum.

42 *"Joe and I, knowing we wanted"*: Kennedy, *Times to Remember*, 153.

42 *She even went so far as to begin*: Ibid., 155–56.

42 *"She resented having someone always go"*: Ibid., 155.

42 *"I am hopeful that a systematic treatment"*: Letter from Dr. Frederick Good to Joseph P. Kennedy, October 24, 1934, quoted in Nasaw, *The Patriarch*, 223.

43 *"that she may not know"*: Letter from Amanda Rohde to Rose Fitzgerald Kennedy, October 18, 1936, Joseph P. Kennedy Papers, Series 1.2.5—Family: Subject File: Rosemary Kennedy—Withdrawn: Education, 1930–1940, Deed Closed Box 3, John F. Kennedy Presidential Library and Museum.

43 *"After I have been able to change"*: Ibid.

43 *Rosemary required constant supervision*: Nasaw, *The Patriarch*, 265.

44 *"Dear Mother and Dad"*: Letter from Rosemary Kennedy to her parents, June 11, 1936, Joseph P. Kennedy Papers, Series 1.1—Family—Family Correspondence, May–December 1936, Box 1, John F. Kennedy Presidential Library and Museum.

44 *"Dear Bobby, The Lafayette was"*: Postcard from Rosemary Kennedy to Bobby Kennedy, July 6, 1936, ibid.

44 *"Dear Pat, Jean, and Bobby"*: Letter from Rosemary Kennedy to her siblings, July 19, 1936, ibid.

44 *"The boys over here are"*: Letter from Rosemary Kennedy to Kathleen Kennedy, July 15, 1936, ibid.

45 *She was allowed to make her debut*: Will Swift, *The Kennedys Amidst the Gathering Storm: A Thousand Days in London, 1938–1940* (New York: HarperCollins, 2008), 49–54, 112–13.

45 *"many other occupations of a domestic kind"*: Letter from Mother Isabel to Rose Fitzgerald Kennedy, December 20, 1939, Joseph P. Kennedy Papers, Series 1.2.5—Family: Subject File: Rosemary Kennedy—Withdrawn: Education, 1930–1940, Deed Closed Box 3, John F. Kennedy Presidential Library and Museum (emphasis original).

46 *"It really makes me very happy"*: Letter from Joseph P. Kennedy to Miss Dorothy M. Gibbs, April 23, 1940, Personal Papers of Eunice Kennedy Shriver, box 10, folder 22 (private collection in possession of Shriver family).

46 *With war encroaching*: Poignant excerpts from her letters around this time are published in Swift, *The Kennedys Amidst the Gathering Storm*, 227; and Nasaw, *The Patriarch*, 424–25. She wrote to her father on April 4, 1940: "Mother says I am such a comfort to you. Never. to leave you. Well Daddy. I feel honour because you chose me to stay . . . I am so fond of you. And. Love you very much" (Swift, 227).

46 *The flight itself was harrowing*: Swift, *The Kennedys Amidst the Gathering Storm*, 250.

46 *Even her younger sister Kathleen*: Laurence Leamer, *The Kennedy Women: The Saga of an American Family* (New York: Villard Books, 1994), 289.

46 *She got a job as a summer camp counselor*: "Dear Daddy, I had decided to go to Camp Fernwood to be a junior counselor. (For July. And perhaps August. They thought that I had experinced [*sic*] in Arts, and Crafts in Europe. So. I am teaching it now." Letter from Rosemary Kennedy to Joseph P. Kennedy, July 4, 1940, Personal Papers of Eunice Kennedy Shriver, box 10, folder 22. See also Nasaw, *The Patriarch*, 457.

46 *"I am sorry I did not talk"*: Letter from Rosemary Kennedy to Joseph P. Kennedy, June 4, 1940, Personal Papers of Eunice Kennedy Shriver, box 10, folder 22.

46 *"I appreciate more than I can say"*: Letter from Joseph P. Kennedy to Mother Térèse, June 18, 1940, Personal Papers of Eunice Kennedy Shriver, box 10, folder 22.

47 *The nuns at St. Gertrude's did*: Nasaw, *The Patriarch*, 532–35.

47 *The school normally took students*: Ibid., 526.

47 *She repeatedly ran away*: See Ibid., 533–34; and Doris Kearns Goodwin, *The Fitzgeralds and the Kennedys: An American Saga* (New York: Simon & Schuster, 1987), 640. Nasaw (and many others) cite cousin Ann Gargan's remark to Goodwin: "Many nights, the school would call to say she was missing, only to find her out walking around the streets at 2 a.m." (Goodwin, *The Fitzgeralds and the Kennedys*, 640).

47 *"She was upset easily"*: Kennedy, *Times to Remember*, 286.

47 *Even during its heyday*: Nasaw, *The Patriarch*, 535; Valenstein, *Great and Desperate Cures*, 142–43, 181.

47 *"Manifestly there were other factors"*: Kennedy, *Times to Remember*, 286.

48 *Patients were kept mostly conscious*: Valenstein, *Great and Desperate Cures*, 149–51.

48 *When a patient's responses*: Ibid., 151.

49 *"Rosemary's was the first of the tragedies"*: Kennedy, *Times to Remember*, 287.

49 *"Rosemary," she wrote, could be*: Letter from Sister Margaret Ann to Eunice Kennedy Shriver, January 6, 1988, Personal Papers of Eunice Kennedy Shriver, box 11, folder 130.

49 *"at one point even Rosemary said"*: Letter of Sister Margaret Ann to Eunice Kennedy Shriver, July 1, 1989, Personal Papers of Eunice Kennedy Shriver, box 11, folder 130.

49 *"Rosie is finding walking more difficult"*: Letter from Sister Margaret Ann to Eunice Kennedy Shriver and family, January 9, 1997 (emphasis original), Personal Papers of Eunice Kennedy Shriver, box 11, folder 130.

50 *"What's going on here anyhow?"*: Letter from Sister Margaret Ann to Eunice Kennedy Shriver, June 3, 1999, Personal Papers of Eunice Kennedy Shriver, box 11, folder 130.

5. THE GREATEST EFFORT

60 *"In 1948, my father"*: Eunice Kennedy Shriver, recorded interview by John Stewart, May 7, 1968, page 1, John F. Kennedy Library Oral History Program.

60 *If the foundation was going to help*: David Nasaw, *The Patriarch: The Remarkable Life and Turbulent Times of Joseph P. Kennedy* (New York: Penguin, 2012), 697.

61 *So she and my father visited*: Eunice Kennedy Shriver, recorded interview, 1; see also Nasaw, *The Patriarch*, 697–98.

61 *the cost would be estimated at*: Ronald Conley, *The Economics of Mental Retardation* (Baltimore: The Johns Hopkins University Press, 1973), 97.

61 *"there were literally {only} a handful"*: Eunice Kennedy Shriver, recorded interview, 1. See also David L. Braddock, "Washington Rises: Public Financial Support for Intellectual Disability in the United States, 1955–2004," *Mental Retardation and Developmental Disabilities Research Reviews* 13 (2007), 172: "The federal presence in intellectual disability was previously so modest that a grant of $1.25 million from the Kennedy Foundation in 1952 to establish a private school in Illinois exceeded the entire federal services budget for intellectual disability at that time."

61 *Before 1960, "the federal presence"*: Braddock, "Washington Rises," 172.

61 *"The solution of Rosemary's problem"*: Letter from Joseph P. Kennedy to Sister Anastasia, May 29, 1958, Joseph P. Kennedy Papers, Series 1.2.5 Family: Subject File: Rosemary Kennedy, Withdrawn Correspondence 1931–1958, Deed Closed Box 3, John F. Kennedy Presidential Library and Museum.

62 *A mathematician and chemist*: Boggs Center website, http://rwjms.umdnj.edu/boggscenter /about/about_elizabeth.html.

62 *"I have to say that this was an incident"*: Elizabeth M. Boggs, recorded interview by John F. Stewart, July 17, 1968, pages 5–6, John F. Kennedy Library Oral History Program.

63 *"the validity of the finality"*: The Arc website, www.thearc.org/page.aspx?pid=2339. The site adds: "This article was written for, and copyrighted by, the Encyclopedia Americana, Chicago and New York, 1952 edition. It is reproduced with the permission of the publishers for members of the National Association of Parents and Friends of Mentally Retarded Children."

63 *I can only imagine the anger*: The 1971 short film *Who Should Survive?* by Guggenheim Productions chronicles the death of a baby with Down syndrome by starvation at Johns Hopkins Hospital. The DVD is available from Guggenheim Productions, 3121 South

Street NW, Washington, DC 20007, or online at www.gpifilms.com/orders.html (accessed July 7, 2014).

63 *"I have seen sights"*: Eunice Kennedy Shriver, "The Sun Has Burst Through," *Parade*, February 2, 1964, cited in Edward Shorter, *The Kennedy Family and the Story of Mental Retardation* (Philadelphia: Temple University Press, 2000), 75.

64 *Feldman was assigned to smooth over*: Myer Feldman, recorded interview by John F. Stewart, September 21, 1968, PDF pages 6–7, 14, John F. Kennedy Library Oral History Program. See also Nasaw, *The Patriarch*, 761; and Laurence Leamer, *The Kennedy Women: The Saga of an American Family* (New York: Villard Books, 1994), 528–31.

65 *"There aren't any major problems"*: Shorter, *The Kennedy Family and the Story of Mental Retardation*, 80.

65 *"Call Mike Feldman"*: Edward M. Kennedy, *The Fruitful Bough* (Halliday, 1965), 223, quoted in Shorter, *The Kennedy Family and the Story of Mental Retardation*, 85.

66 *"Anything that is in the power"*: Leonard Mayo, recorded interview by John F. Stewart, April 30, 1968, page 7, John F. Kennedy Library Oral History Program.

66 *"This is a matter which I think"*: Remarks of John F. Kennedy to the President's Panel on Mental Retardation, released by the White House Press Office on October 17, 1961. Papers of John F. Kennedy: Presidential Papers: President's Office Files: Mental Retardation, Digital Identifier JFKPOF-102-008, John F. Kennedy Presidential Library and Museum, available at www.jfklibrary.org/Asset-Viewer/Archives/JFKPOF-102-008.aspx (accessed May 27, 2014).

66 *"It's interesting to"*: Leonard Mayo, recorded interview, 3.

67 *The president himself told Mayo*: Ibid., 14.

67 *"went for it a hundred per cent"*: Ibid., 6.

67 *"Why not invite them"*: Ibid.

67 *"I'm going up and see"*: Ibid.

67 *No one knew for sure*: During economically prosperous periods of American history, such as the 1920s, people with intellectual disabilities had often been "paroled" from institutions and allowed to hold paying jobs in the community. But during economic downturns they had just as often been casualties, warehoused in institutions because there were not enough jobs available even for "normal" citizens—even though it was during those same periods that conditions at the underfunded institutions tended to deteriorate. See Peter L. Tyor and Leland V. Bell, *Caring for the Retarded in America: A History* (Westport, CT: Greenwood Press, 1984), 123, 136; and James W. Trent, *Inventing the Feeble Mind* (Berkeley: University of California Press, 1995), 275.

68 *"The marvelous thing is"*: Sargent Shriver in an interview with Peggy Dillon and John C. Rumm, Special Olympics Office, Washington, DC, November 30, 1999.

68 *Séguin, a nineteenth-century French physician*: See Trent, *Inventing the Feeble Mind*, chapter 2, "Edward Seguin and the Irony of Physiological Education": "To carry out physical exercises, Seguin employed various types of gymnastic equipment, often devising such equipment to meet the needs of a particular pupil. Some children benefited from dumbbells, rope ladders, swings, balancing bars, and the like. Other children, capable but unwilling, required the continual guidance and motivation from a teacher even to

stand on their own. Whether complex or simple, however, Seguin insisted that exercises meet the individual needs of the pupil and be undertaken only after careful planning based on experimentation" (47).

69 *the brain thrives on exercise*: See, for example, the CDC paper "The Association Between School-Based Physical Activity, Including Physical Education, and Academic Performance" (2010), available at www.cdc.gov/healthyyouth/health_and_academics/pdf/pa -pe_paper.pdf (accessed May 28, 2014).

69 *"My camper got off the bus"*: Jim Turner, personal conversation with the author, summer 2013.

69 *"that mentally retarded children* can *be"*: Eunice Kennedy Shriver, "Rebel with a Cause," essay from the Special Olympics files dated to the 1960s.

70 *"As far as I was concerned"*: Leonard Mayo, recorded interview, 25.

70 *Her influence, Mayo recalled*: Ibid., 13.

71 *My mother was adamant*: See D. Spitalnik, *The President's Panel and the Public Policy Contributions of Eunice Kennedy Shriver* (New Brunswick, NJ: The Elizabeth M. Boggs Center on Developmental Disabilities), 10.

71 *"I just read the draft"*: Leonard Mayo, recorded interview, 45.

72 *"You know, I got a lesson"*: Ibid.

72 *"If you can't come now"*: Ibid., 28.

73 *"What have we learned"*: Ibid., 33.

73 *"I don't know any member"*: Ibid., 12.

73 *"You can see what would have happened"*: Ibid., 33.

73 *"The Food and Drug Administration"*: A *Proposed Program for National Action to Combat Mental Retardation*, report of the President's Panel on Mental Retardation, October 16, 1962, Papers of John F. Kennedy: Presidential Papers: President's Office Files: Mental Retardation, Digital Identifier JFKPOF-094-022, John F. Kennedy Presidential Library and Museum, page 81.

74 *in Baltimore, for example*: Ibid., 71–72.

74 *"Many city hospitals now charge"*: Ibid., 73.

75 *"{Rosemary} was a beautiful child"*: Eunice Kennedy Shriver, "Hope for Retarded Children," *The Saturday Evening Post*, September 22, 1962.

75 *A mere half century after the chilling*: Trent, *Inventing the Feeble Mind*, 249–55.

76 *"Dear Jack"*: Letter from Eunice Kennedy Shriver to John F. Kennedy, June 22, 1962, Papers of John F. Kennedy: Presidential Papers: President's Office Files. Series Name: Special Correspondence. Series Number: 02. Digital identifier JFKPOF-032-016, John F. Kennedy Presidential Library and Museum, available at www.jfklibrary.org /Asset-Viewer/Archives/JFKPOF-032-016.aspx (accessed May 27, 2014).

76 *The population of these institutions*: David L. Braddock and Susan L. Parish, "An Institutional History of Disability," in *Disability at the Dawn of the 21st Century and the State of the States*, ed. Braddock (Washington, DC: American Association on Mental Retardation, 2002), 35.

6. DAYBREAK

79 *Anne Burke, however, thought*: The information that follows is taken from a series of personal conversations between Burke and the author, 2013.

81 *Dan Shannon, an accountant*: Monogram Club profile, University of Notre Dame website, www.und.com/sports/monogramclub/mtt/shannon_dan00.html (accessed April 23, 2014).

82 *My mother had pushed research*: The monograph is Robert J. Francis and G. Lawrence Rarick, *Motor Characteristics of the Mentally Retarded, Cooperative Research Monograph No. 1* (Washington, DC: Office of Education, 1960).

83 *Head Start, the nation's first*: Edward Zigler and Susan Muenchow, *Head Start: The Inside Story of America's Most Successful Educational Experiment* (New York: Basic Books, 1992), 25–28.

83 *What Gray found surprised her*: Zigler and Muenchow, *Head Start*, 4–6; Susan W. Gray and Rupert A. Klaus, *The Early Training Project for Disadvantaged Children: A Report After Five Years* (Monographs of the Society for Research in Child Development, vol. 33, no. 4, 1968), 52–53.

83 *"Sarge and I went to visit"*: Unpublished notes of Eunice Kennedy Shriver, Kennedy Foundation archives.

84 *"a new enthusiasm"*: Address of Pope John XXIII, October 11, 1962, in *The Encyclicals and Other Messages of John XXIII* (Washington, DC: TPS Press, 1964), 423–35.

84 *"at last possible to be properly human"*: Remarks of Archbishop of Canterbury Rowan Williams to the Synod of Bishops in Rome regarding the new evangelization at the invitation of Pope Benedict XVI, available at http://rowanwilliams.archbishopofcanterbury .org/articles.php/2645/archbishops-address-to-the-synod-of-bishops-in-rome (accessed May 27, 2014).

84 *"mystical way in everyday life"*: Karl Rahner, *The Mystical Way in Everyday Life: Sermons, Prayers, and Essays*, trans. and ed. Annemarie S. Kidder (Maryknoll, NY: Orbis Books, 2009).

85 *"it is faith itself that shapes"*: Remarks of Archbishop Williams.

85 *"The joys and the hopes"*: Second Vatican Council, *Pastoral Constitution on the Church in the Modern World: Gaudium et Spes*, December 7, 1965, available at www.vatican.va/archive /hist_councils/ii_vatican_council/documents/vat-ii_const_19651207_gaudium-et-spes _en.html (accessed May 27, 2014).

86 *"Almighty God, we thank you"*: Sargent Shriver, address to the Board of Directors of Special Olympics, 1997.

89 *"The need for a special athletic competition"*: Brochure announcing "Chicago Special Olympics." Published by the Chicago Park District and the Joseph P. Kennedy, Jr. Foundation, 1968, Archives of the Kennedy Foundation.

89 *"The value of exercise and games"*: Introduction and welcome letters to the official program, July 20, 1968, Chicago Park District and Joseph P. Kennedy, Jr. Foundation, 1968, Archives of the Kennedy Foundation.

91 *"It wasn't easy"*: Iris Sheets, personal conversation between the author and Dave and Iris Sheets, 2013.

92 *"We were concerned about it"*: Dave Sheets, personal conversation between the author and Dave and Iris Sheets, 2013.

92 *"I was outright scared"*: Frank Starling, personal conversation with the author, summer 2013.

92 *"I went to an all-black school"*: Rafer Johnson, personal conversation with the author, 2013.

98 *"Those at the edge of any system"*: Richard Rohr, "Those at the Edge Hold the Secret," *Radical Grace: Daily Meditations* (Cincinnati, OH: St. Anthony Messenger Press, 1995), 28.

7. AS SIMPLE AS POSSIBLE

101 *"He loved it, not only because"*: Frank Gifford, personal conversation with the author, ca. 2000.

102 *In 1975, the president of the United States*: Special Olympics chronology, available at www .specialolympics.org/history.aspx (accessed July 10, 2014).

114 *"Among the Syrian Jews"*: M. Basil Pennington, *Centering Prayer* (New York: Doubleday, 2001), 98.

115 *"Like Mullernestredon, we often look"*: Ibid., 98–99.

116 *"There is another story"*: Ibid., 99.

8. BEING IN LOVE

122 *"lure of the transcendent"*: Title of an essay collection by the scholar of religion Dwayne Huebner: *The Lure of the Transcendent: Collected Essays by Dwayne E. Huebner*, ed. Vikki Hillis and William F. Pinar (New York: Routledge, 1999).

128 *"One's being becomes being-in-love"*: Bernard Lonergan, *Method in Theology* (Toronto: University of Toronto Press, 2007 [reprint of 1990 edition, original copyright 1971]), 104–105.

129 *"At this point"*: Richard Rohr, *Yes, and . . . : Daily Meditations* (Cincinnati, OH: Franciscan Media, 2013), 117.

9. SOCIAL AND EMOTIONAL LEARNING

140 *"He worked in the stone quarry"*: This and the quotes that follow are from personal conversations between the author and Loretta Claiborne in 2012.

142 *"to ship the mentally retarded"*: NBC News, "Suffer the Little Children," 1968.

10. LORETTA

156 *"Students, faculty, parents, and friends"*: Loretta Claiborne, Quinnipiac University commencement speech, 1995. Transcript supplied by the university.

159 *"Desire. Strength. Heart"*: Denzel Washington, presentation of the 1996 ESPY Arthur Ashe Courage Award to Loretta Claiborne, Radio City Music Hall, New York, February 12, 1996.

11. TOUGH WORLD

167 *and thus, in one small house, began*: L' Arche website, www.larche.org/en/discover/larche _since_its_creation (accessed April 23, 2014).

167 *"My goal was simply to welcome"*: Jean Vanier, words spoken at a retreat, Christmas 2011.

168 *"In the Bible, we hear"*: Ibid.

170 *"When I left {the lepers}"*: St. Francis of Assisi, "The Testament," October 1226, in *Francis and Clare: The Complete Works* (Mahwah, NJ: Paulist Press, 1982), 154.

170 *I was there thanks to the generosity*: The Very Special Christmas series has published dozens of albums, videos, DVDs, and television programs since 1987. For more information, visit specialolympics.org.

12. THE FUN THAT LASTS

190 *"{Man} is only completely a man"*: Friedrich von Schiller, "Letters upon the Æsthetic Education of Man: Letter XV," in *The Harvard Classics*, vol. 32, *Literary and Philosophical Essays: French, German and Italian* (New York: P. F. Collier & Son, 1910), available at www.bartleby.com/32/515.html (accessed May 27, 2014).

13. I AM SO PROUD

195 *"courage, spirit, resolution"*: See freedictionary.com.

195 *"Men the world over possess"*: William James, *The Energies of Men* (New York: Moffat, Yard and Company, 1914), 9, 14.

196 *But Duckworth and her colleagues have found*: Angela L. Duckworth, Christopher Peterson, Michael D. Matthews, and Dennis R. Kelly, "Grit: Perseverance and Passion for Long-Term Goals," *Journal of Personality and Social Psychology* 92, no. 6 (2007): 1087–1101.

198 *more than 75 percent of the population*: United Nations Statistics Division, Millennium Development Goals Database, available at http://data.un.org/Data.aspx?d=MDG& f=seriesRowID%3A580 (accessed May 27, 2014).

14. THE HEART OFF GUARD

206 *"Céad míle fáilte"*: Mary McAleese, remarks, 2003 Special Olympics World Summer Games opening ceremony, transcript available, Special Olympics Library, Washington, DC.

207 *"the president of everywhere"*: Bono, remarks, 2003 Special Olympics World Summer Games opening ceremony, transcript available, Special Olympics Library, Washington, DC.

207 *"The Special Olympics give"*: Special Olympics Ireland YouTube channel, www.youtube .com/watch?v=L301FOdn1-8 (accessed April 23, 2014).

207 *"History says, don't hope"*: Seamus Heaney, *The Cure at Troy: A Version of Sophocles' Philoctetes* (New York: Farrar, Straus and Giroux, 1991), 77.

216 *"Useless to think you'll park"*: Seamus Heaney, "Postscript," *The Spirit Level* (New York: Farrar, Straus and Giroux, 1996), 82.

15. HUMILITY AND SIMPLICITY

217 *He grew up under*: Nelson Mandela, *Long Walk to Freedom* (Boston: Back Bay Books, 1995).

219 *Hundreds of thousands of people with*: A 2001 census estimated that 2,255,982 South Africans had disabilities, of whom about 12.5 percent had intellectual disabilities. "Prevalence of disability in South Africa" (Pretoria: Statistics South Africa, 2005), 12–14, available at www.statssa.gov.za/census01/html/Disability.pdf (accessed April 23, 2014).

223 *"choiceless singularity of human identity"*: Amartya Sen, *Identity and Violence: The Illusion of Destiny* (New York: W. W. Norton, 2007), 16.

223 *"our ability to identify"*: Simon Baron-Cohen, *The Science of Evil: On Empathy and the Origins of Cruelty* (New York: Basic Books, 2012), 18.

223 *"Empathy erosion arises"*: Ibid., 7.

223 *"empathy has been turned off"*: Ibid., 21.

232 *"Hunger, toil, and solitude are"*: Evagrius Ponticus, *The Praktikos and Chapters on Prayer*, 15–40, trans. John Eudes Bamberger, OCSO (Kalamazoo, MI: Cistercian Publications, 1970), reproduced in *The Essential Writings of Christian Mysticism*, ed. Bernard McGinn (New York: Modern Library Classics, 2006), 56–57.

16. FULLY ALIVE

235 *"Our happiness comes from creating"*: Jean Vanier, words spoken at a retreat, July 2012.

236 *"Faith . . . means ultimate trust"*: David Steindl-Rast, *Deeper than Words: Living the Apostles' Creed* (New York: Doubleday, 2010), 60.

249 *"The Chinese government and people"*: Text e-mailed to the author by Mary Gu, Special Olympics East Asia, April 15, 2014.

17. STORM THE CASTLE

256 *"He who knows it"*: Albert Einstein, *The World as I See It* (New York: Citadel Press Books, 1956), 7.

257 *more than 90 percent of children diagnosed prenatally*: Caroline Mansfield, Suellen Hopfer, and Theresa M. Marteau, "Termination Rates After Prenatal Diagnosis of Down Syndrome, Spina Bifida, Anencephaly, and Turner and Klinefelter Syndromes: A Systematic Literature Review," *Prenatal Diagnosis* 19, no. 9 (September 1999): 808–12.

257 *more than 95 percent of children in the developing world*: From Exclusion to Equality: Realizing the Rights of Persons with Disabilities—Handbook for Parliamentarians on the Convention on the Rights of Persons with Disabilities and Its Optional Protocol (New York/Geneva/Le Grand-Saconnex [Switzerland]: United Nations Department of Economic and Social Affairs, Office of the United Nations High Commissioner for Human Rights, and Inter-Parliamentary Union, 2007), 82, available at www.ipu.org/PDF/publications/disabilities-e.pdf (accessed July 3, 2014).

262 *"There is always a moment"*: Alice Walker, reflections on "Working Toward Peace," www.scu.edu/ethics/architects-of-peace/Walker/essay.html (accessed April 23, 2014).

Acknowledgments

In a way, this book is my attempt to say thank you to the amazing human beings who have made me the richest man in the world (okay, not literally, though definitely in the way that matters most). I can't begin to list them all, nor capture their gifts in words, nor count the blessings they have given me. But if there is anything of value in this book, it is because so many people have tried so hard to teach me how to be fully alive.

The earliest inspiration for this book were my parents, Sargent and Eunice Shriver, pioneers, revolutionaries, believers, lovers. The greatest gift my parents gave me is faith; a close second are my brothers, Bobby, Mark, and Anthony, and my sister, Maria—together we were the "Lucky 7." They, along with Alina, Jeanne, and Malissa and all their children, are my links to the past and the best party I could ever hope to find in the present. I love them all from a place I cannot describe and won't try to.

When I set off on my career in New Haven, Connecticut, my understanding of the ways of living fully alive took a turn toward intensity. I met educators who made me laugh, think, cry, and fall in love with school for the first time. Bob Brown, Iris Kinnard, Red and Anne Verderame, John Dow, Rosa Quezada, Burt Glassman, Ben Hunter, Harry Reid, Carl Marottolo, Burt Saxon, Wendy Samberg, Wanda Gibbs, Ernie Roth, Bridget Hardy, Mustafa Abdul-Salaam, Sandi White, Lonnie Garris, Gary Highsmith, Karol DeFalco, Mickey Kavanagh, Miriam Camacho, Dee Speese-Linehan, Willie Elder, and Karen O'Conner all taught me how to teach, how to listen, how to laugh, how to stop fights—and how to start a few as well. They mentored me in just the ways I needed most. The lessons about school in this book were taught to me by them.

I worked with so many young people, too, who were spellbinding: Charles Salters, Stephanie Lockett, Kevin Huckaby, Jeffrey Jones, Rori Myers, Tashena Middleton, Mark Wylie, Nancy Cato, Lorrine Wilson, Tanya Baskin, Darrell Mickey, Lamont Young, Lamont Hamilton, Tom Wilkins, Deidre Bailey, Medria Blue, Cavell Godbolt, James "Tiny" Wilkins, Danielle Kimber, Marlene Cannady, Doug Bethea, Wade Simmons, Marquise Baskin—these are just a few of the thousands of children and teenagers who encouraged me to see the world honestly with all its flaws and to learn how to listen with authenticity and respect and love. I hope this book reflects even a tiny bit of their generosity and truth.

Jamie Price; Rev. Joe Komonchak; Rev. Stephen Happel; Bernard Lonergan, S.J.; Rev. Richard Rohr; Rev. Cynthia Bourgeault; and Rev. Martin Laird are among those who by teaching, writing, and praying tried hardest to teach me how to think and live from a divine center. If this book has even a few moments in which that center appears on the page, it is because these men and women (often without knowing it) didn't give up on me and instead led me to the great mystics and to the mystic within me.

I also asked a lot from my spiritual directors of various types and sorts, and without complaint, they held my questions, my rudderlessness, and my impatience with grace. Over the years, Rev. Richard Russell; Rev. Martin Curtin; Rev. Jose Salazar; Rev. Joe Elko; Rev. Richard Fragomeni; Bertha Corley; Maud Leal; Ella Scantlebury; Sandy Nelson; Rev. Maurice Shepard; Patricia Mason; Vernon Jones; Fred and Anna Smith; Dan Santos; Mark Horak, S.J.; Greg Schenden, S.J.; Leo Murray, S.J.; Rev. John Enzler; Rev. Percival D'Silva; and the good people of Blessed Sacrament and Holy Trinity in Washington, DC, and of St. Martin de Porres Parish in New Haven were my communities in faith. They taught me more about the deep cries and transcendent smiles of the divine than I ever dreamed possible.

The ideas of child development were opened to me by some of the most distinguished scholars in the world who somehow took the time to teach me to understand the dynamic and often misunderstood process of growth and learning. Together with Dr. James Comer and Dr. Donald Cohen, Dr. Al Solnit, Barbara Nordhaus, Etta Burke, Jean Adnopoz, Dr. Elisabeth Dykens, and Dr. Mary Schwab Stone all welcomed me to the Yale Child Study Center and sent me off determined to represent the needs and dreams of children. On the other side of the Yale campus, Dr. Roger Weissberg, my friend and collaborator of almost three decades, and Dr. Ed Zigler were and remain incomparable scholars of psychology and action. At the Yale Divinity School, Dwayne Huebner first explained to me that education was about the "lure of the transcendent." I've never forgotten their generosity in trying to help me see children from the inside out.

The team that created the field of social and emotional learning and then the Collaborative for Academic, Social, and Emotional Learning (CASEL)—believers in school being a place that cracks open the heart—became my friends. At the beginning there were my colleagues in the New Haven Public Schools whom I've already thanked; later I found my way to Linda Lantieri, Mark Greenberg, Dave Sluyter, Eileen Growald, and Dan Goleman. The group quickly grew to include amazing educators, scholars, and change agents such as Mo Elias, David Hawkins, Steve Arnold, Norris Haynes, Janet Patti, Joe Zins, Eric Schaps, Ann Nerad, Cynthia Coleman, Shelley Berman, Linda Darling Hammond, Larry Aber, Carl Cohn, Joan Lombardi, and Jennifer and Peter Buffett. Again, Roger Weissberg was at the center—a collaborator, scholar, and leader without peer. If social and emotional learning sweeps the country as I think it will, I hope that someday the story of the people who created the Social Development department at New Haven Public Schools and of those who created CASEL will become a celebrated tale of innovation and teamwork and love.

At Special Olympics, I have so many people to thank: Lowell Weicker, who bet on me when I didn't deserve it; and Peter Wheeler, Kim Elliott, Drake Turrentine, Adam Bozzuto, Bob Fiondella, and Susan Saint James, all of whom played significant roles during my time in Connecticut and in the 1995 World Games and for many years before and after. I can't thank Senator Chris Dodd enough for being our champion in Washington when we really needed him, nor President and Mrs. Clinton for making history by coming to the 1995 opening ceremonies. I'll never forget Ramesh Mali, who lost his life during those games. Flo Consiglio of Sally's Apizza hosted my family then and so many times before and since. Yes, Sally's has the best pizza in the world. The Knights of Columbus led the creation of the host towns program that Peter Wheeler invented. Tens of thousands of people in New Haven and across the state of Connecticut who volunteered for days and weeks and months only reminded me of why I love Connecticut so much.

Over the past fifteen years, I have been guided, toasted, led, challenged, chased, raced, defeated, hugged, and loved by the most devoted workforce in the world at Special Olympics. The amazing people who built and continue to build Special Olympics include Drake Turrentine, Ayman Wahab, Dennis Brueggeman, Mary Gu, Mary Davis, Bob Gobrecht, John Dow, Steve Corbin, Kim Widdess, Dave Lenox, Angela Ciccolo, Tom Songster, Bob Montague, Donna Maxwell, Andrea Cahn, Helen MacNabb, Lee Todd, Mohammad Nasser, Charles Nyambe, Jon Paul St. Germain, Janet Froetscher, Jeannie Main, Kirsten Seckler, Kate McKenna, Will Schermerhorn, Steve Neill, Garrie Barnes, Terrel Limerick, David Evangelista, Bobby Jones, Charmaine Dittmar, David Gang, Cristian Ispas, Kathy Wilson, Brady Lum, Renee Dease, Ben Collins, and Darcie Mersereau. Gary Siperstein helped create our research capability, making Special Olympics not just a center of action but also a global leader in ideas and accountability. Sue Swensen, George Jesien, Steve Eidelman, and Dr. Robert Cooke have been powerful innovators and advocates from the Kennedy Foundation perch. Our health leaders, Dr. Steve Perlman and Dr. Paul Berman, have changed the world. Thank you all.

In the many states and countries of the world, leaders emerged who embraced the vision and took it higher than we often thought it could go. I think of Shi Derong, Mickey Boutilier, Marc Edenzon, Keith Fishburne, Matt Aaron, Peter Mazunda, Yan Mingfu, Magda Moussa, Air Marshall Denzil Keelor, Hermann Kroll, Joanna Despotopolou, Randy Mascorella, Beau Doherty, and all of you whose profession is or was Special Olympics: there is no group of people more dedicated or more passionate or more effective at changing the world than you are. I am so proud to have you as my inspiration for so much of what is in this book and so much more that I wish I could have included. You each have your own book to write, and I hope you will!

Our local Montgomery County Unified Team has been a classroom of the heart for my wife, Linda, and me, as well as our five children. To Maureen Yap, who got us going, and to Dave and Meredith Ficca, Dean and Darian Packard, Stu Nibley, and our gang of amazing partners and athletes: your opening ceremonies and joy and games are second to none.

The board and global ambassadors of Special Olympics supported me every step of the way in the process of writing this book, while at the same time creating the best leadership of an international nonprofit in the world. I am forever grateful to Mike Feldman, Jay Emmett,

John Manley, Ossie Kilkenny, Bart Conner, Stephen Carter, Nadia Comaneci, William P. Alford, Andrei Pavlov, Angelo Moratti, Yolanda Eleta, Mark Booth, Steve and Jean Case, Tom Golisano, David Braddock, Ray and Stephanie Lane, Florence Nabayinda, Stacey Johnston, Dr. Michael Hardman, Denis O'Brien, Donna De Varona, Muhtar Kent, Eddie Barbanell, Brian Phillips, Joe Hakim, Ephraim Mohlkhane, Yao Ming, Scott Hamilton, Stevie Wonder, and Vanessa Williams. Each of you and all the amazing leaders of our movement have given and then given more. I can only promise that I am going to continue to ask again and again! I know you will keep echoing the motto of our amazing partners from the Lions Clubs International, whom I thank, too. Their motto says it all: "We serve."

Vicki Iovine, Jimmy Iovine, and my brother Bobby: What can I say about $100 million? Only that your genius and generosity has given millions of people what matters most—a place to belong, a chance to shine, a community of love. You and the many artists of A Very Special Christmas are the quiet angels of the dignity revolution. I have been honored to be given the chance to try to fulfill your vision.

There are so many athletes in our movement who have rocked my world that I can't even begin to thank them all. Frank Stephens, Martha Hill, Jia Sirui, Kester Edwards, Rita Lawlor, Cyndy Bentley, David Egan, Mark Swiconik, Billy Quick, Dustin Plunkett, Paul Maretti, Constantinos Triantofoulou, Deion Namiseb, Lior Liebling, Troy Ford King, Danielle Liebl, Daniel Thompson, Eddie Barbanell, Mostafa Galal, Matthew Williams, Ricardo Thornton, Ashley Counts, Peter Fleming, Andy Miyares, Katie Wilson, and dozens more: you each cracked me open and taught me a lesson all your own. I hope I've captured even a fraction of your wisdom. Loretta Claiborne: you are really the cofounder of Special Olympics. I hope readers will begin to appreciate the depth of spirit and wisdom you bring to the world.

Thanks to Jean Vanier, the poet of tenderness and compassion and faith. "Living saint" only approximates his gift for being the hands and words and eyes of God.

About ten years ago, I went to a talk given by Paul Elie about his book The Life You Save May Be Your Own: An American Pilgrimage. I couldn't have known that a few years later, he would look me in the eyes and tell me I could write a book and that he would edit it. Sarah Crichton believed him and so did I—sort of—and thus the long journey began. Paul Orzulak helped me get started and Rafe Sagalyn made it happen and nudged—carefully and helpfully. Christine Neulieb was a life saver over the last two years and a brilliant thought partner. I spent two months in the basement of the L'Arche community in Arlington, Virginia, where Fritz Schloss, Linda Garcia, Eric Arntson, Hazel Pulliam, and Liz Yoder allowed me join their family to try to get my thoughts on paper. After my first day of writing, Linda Garcia asked me, "Is your book finished yet?" That was almost three years ago and I'm proud to finally be able to answer, "Yes, Linda. My book is finished!"

Several people read sections and drafts and made invaluably helpful comments: Jamie Price, Rev. Nancy Lane, Matthew Dowd, David Braddock, Steve Corbin, Martha Beck, John Dow, Anne Burke, Bob Brown, Roger Weissberg, Loretta Claiborne, Sally Quinn, Randy Mascorella, Dr. Sara Scalenghe, Rabbi Julia Watts Belser, Mary Davis, and Mary Gu. In a special way, my sister, Maria, has been willing to listen to me through every confusing manifestation of what I was trying to write and who I'm trying to become. She's not only a brilliant author, editor, leader, and journalist, but she also knows me better than I know myself. I'm lucky to be loved by a sister like Maria.

Thank goodness that my closest friend, Dan Melrod, hasn't and won't read the book. Everyone needs a friend like Dan, but few are as lucky as me to have one.

Martha Beck wrote a book ten years ago and I fell in love with her before I'd seen her or heard her voice. She is the perfect coach—writing coach, speaking coach, grieving coach, laughing coach, playing coach, exploring coach, reckless coach, life coach. Thanks, Martha. I'm finally letting go.

Rose, Tim, Sam, Kathleen, and Caroline: It's done! You don't have to read it anymore, hear about it anymore, help me out of my book funk anymore, watch me close the door to write weekend after weekend and month after month and year after year anymore. You know this book is for you. You know I couldn't have written this book without you. You know that when we're together, I'm most fully alive.

Linda: I know you've lost track of the versions, the changes, the deletions, the stories. You never stopped reading, never stopped helping me find my voice, never stopped telling me to get out of my head and into my heart. Thanks for allowing me to tell a version of our love story and, more, for being the author of it. Love at first sight and love forever. I'm still the luckiest man in the world.

I own the shortcomings of this book. Its gifts, whatever they may be, I owe to all of you.